PYRRHURA PARROTS

AVICULTURE, NATURAL HISTORY, CONSERVATION

REVISED EDITION 2022

Rosemary Low

INSIGNIS PUBLICATIONS

DEDICATION

I dedicate this book to Fabio Nunes and his team at AQUASIS in northern Brazil, who have worked with extraordinary knowledge and enthusiasm to ensure the survival of the Grey-breasted Parakeet (*Pyrrhura griseipectus*). They are setting examples in parrot conservation that need to be emulated throughout the tropics. I would also like to thank those organisations who generously donated to their field work. This had increased the population from about 10 breeding pairs in 2007, to between 200 and 300 pairs by 2020.

ISBN 978-1-7399130-2-1

Cover design: Rosemary Low
Photograph: Grey-breasted Parakeets by Fabio Nunes/Aquasis

Designed by Bradley Davis

Printed by New Energy Printing

Published in the UK by
INSiGNIS PUBLICATIONS, Mansfield, Notts NG20 9PR, UK.

www.rosemarylow.co.uk

CONTENTS

2. Species with lighter coloured beaks, less pronounced breast markings and red or reddish ear coverts:

3. Blue-throated or Ochre-marked *P. cruentata*...........................235

FROM READERS AND REVIEWERS

WHAT READERS SAY:

Ruben van de Worp, *Pyrrhura* breeder
A week ago I got your *Pyrrhura* book and I must say it is a collector's item. It is full of nice tips and beautiful pictures. The manner you care for your birds is priceless and has my compliments. Thank you for writing this book.

Dr Stacey Gelis, avian veterinarian, Australia
I have really enjoyed reading it, not only for how thoroughly you cover the various species but also for reinforcing the basics of good avian husbandry (a subject that is rarely dealt with seriously these days).

Gareth Orr, *Pyrrhura* breeder
May I congratulate you on what is another excellent read. I haven't put the book down since I received it! Many thanks for writing a book about *Pyrrhuras* – it has given me a much better understanding of these incredible little birds and their habitat.

Sandra Olsen, Florida, USA
I received the book today! I have been reading it for 45 minutes and I love it!

Michael McKaig, Oklahoma, USA
For many years I have wished for a way to tell you how much I enjoy your books and value your contributions to aviculture. Today I discovered your web page and email address, so I am very pleased to be able to communicate with you. Starting with your "Aviary Birds," I gradually bought all your books. *Pyrrhura Parakeets* is a beautifully-written and much-needed reference on those amazing birds.

REVIEWS

***Cage & Aviary Birds*, January 15 2014**
A must-read for conure lovers
Some 32 species of these little jewels are now recognised and there's no finer guide to them than Rosemary Low. A devotee of the genus since the 1960s, Rosemary has

vast experience of *Pyrrhura* in captivity. She has also travelled over Latin America to study them in the wild.

Rosemary's superb new book, *Pyrrhura Parakeets (Conures): Aviculture, Natural History, Conservation*, is in two parts. The first tells us what a *Pyrrhura* is and summarises the history of the genus in captivity. This is largely recent: major imports to Europe commenced in the 1970s and the next two decades saw demand and supply peak, as breeders savoured the variety of species available. Recently the focus has changed to smaller collections and the breeding of colour mutations of the green-cheeked conure (*P. molinae*).

Rosemary goes on to offer a masterclass in practical husbandry. This is grounded in first-hand experience and is pure gold for the beginner who wants to know the basics of housing and feeding, and also needs expert advice concerning health issues and breeding problems. She then proceeds to the lifestyle of wild *Pyrrhura* and connects this with conservation issues. Part two of the book offers a pen portrait of every *Pyrrhura* species, with unique detail on its behaviour, history and status. In fact "unique" is the best word for this book. I doubt anyone else could have written it. If you love conures, snap it up.

— **ROB INNES, Editor,** ***Cage & Aviary Birds.***

Talking Birds **(Australia), January 2014,**
Pyrrhura **volume covers all the bases**
Rosemary Low is probably the most prolific author of avicultural books the world has ever known. With 30 books to her name, she is a household name to most aviculturists and the breadth of her knowledge is astounding.

Her latest volume *Pyrrhura Parakeets (Conures)* is easily up to the standard set by her previous works and is a must-have book for anyone with an interest in conures. The book's 261 pages contains a wealth of information, all of it set out in an orderly, organised fashion... This author clearly loves conures – and keeping the maroon-bellied and pearly species in the 1960s ignited her passion for *Pyrrhuras*.

— **LLOYD MARSHALL, Editor,** *Talking Birds*

INTRODUCTION

I WAS very young when I was first captivated by the *Pyrrhura* Conures. I kept and bred two species: Maroon-bellied and Pearly. At that time (the 1960s) the species available to aviculturists were limited to these two plus the Black-tailed and White-eared with, more rarely, the Painted. They were definitely a minority interest. I loved the members of this genus because they were so lively and inquisitive and they nested readily. Their plumage colours were subtle and attractive. With the exception of the Black-tailed, which seemed aloof, they were also very friendly and confiding. To me, that is extremely important. I don't want to keep birds that fly away from me when I approach their aviary! They made ideal aviary birds because they were not too loud and they were fun to watch. They ignited my passion for Neotropical parrots. This had a big influence on my life and resulted in me travelling to South and Central America on many occasions. My joy in seeing these birds in the wild never fades.

Today, more than five decades later, the *Pyrrhuras*, especially the Green-cheeked, are among the most popular birds in aviculture. Their enchanting personalities, as aviary birds and as companions, are now fully appreciated. Back in the 1960s and almost until the end of the century, very little was known about their status in the wild. Now we know that, sadly, this genus of beautiful parakeets contains some of the most endangered parrots in the whole of South America. Habitat protection combined with local education programmes is the key to saving them. Significant progress has been made with some species but much more will need to be done to save others from extinction in the next few decades. I hope this book will raise the profile of this fascinating group of small parakeets, that it will alert aviculturists to the threatened status of a significant proportion of them and stimulate interest in their conservation.

Rosemary Low,
April 2022

ACKNOWLEDGEMENTS

I THANK the photographers and artists whose images of these wonderful birds have brought the book to life:

Thomas Arndt, Nick Athanus, Simon Boner, Esteban Botero (SELVA), Steve Brookes (Wild Parrots Up Close), Agnes Coenen, Mery Juiña (Jocotoco), Karl Heinz Lambert, Horst Mayer, Ron and Val Moat, Fabio Nunes (Aquasis), Claus Nielsen, Alonso Quevedo, Paul Salaman (ProAves), Mark Scrivener, Barbara Tomotani, Marcia Weinzettl, Jason Wright and René Wüst. Artists' illustrations: Thomas Arndt, Eduardo Brettas (*Pyrrhura lucianii*), Barbara Tomotani. Maps of Brazil generously drawn by Raphael Sabongi Lúcio Marcelino and *Pyrrhura frontalis* map by Alex Bovo.

My grateful thanks to those who generously provided information. All the above listed people, also Jörg Asmus, Steve Beaver, Ray Berman, Donald Brightsmith, John Caldwell, Robert Dietrich, Edson Endrigo, Sandra Escudero, Hein van Grouw, Cecilia Herrera, Jeff Hornsby, Carlos Keller, Doug Kelson, Alan T.K.Lee, Stuart Marsden, Ian Price, Robin Restall, Nathan H.Rice, Matthias Reinschmidt, Robert Ridgely, Paul Salaman, Martin Schaefer, Gerhard Schmidt, Marina Somenzari, Luís Fabio Silveira, Howard Voren and Les Waring.

1. WHAT ARE *Pyrrhura* CONURES?

A CONURE is a parakeet of the neotropics. The name is normally used for the genera *Aratinga* and *Pyrrhura*, also for Nanday *(Nandayus)* and Patagonian Conures *(Cyanoliseus)*. In the ornithological literature the word parakeet is invariably used but this is not precise as it also refers to several other neotropical genera (such as the small *Brotogeris* parakeets). Within the text, I have often used the word parakeet, rather than conure, for species which are unknown in aviculture.

Pyrrhuras are a group of very lively and sociable parakeets. The name originates from the Greek for fire *(pyrrhos)* and tail *(oura)*. This is a little misleading as the tail in most species is maroon, not fiery.

They are distinguished by

- their size; they vary from about 22cm up to 28cm. Only the Blue-throated *(cruentata)* exceeds 25cm in length. Incidentally, some of the lengths given in field guides are too large, probably because they were derived from measuring skins.

- Their plumage: typically they have barred or scalloped plumage from the throat, extending to or over the upper breast. These markings result from the amount of melanin deposited between the centre and the edge of the feather. Six species lack these markings.

- The bare area surrounding the eye (periophthalmic ring) which is prominent and white in most species. In several it is grey.

- The upper side or the underside of the long tail which is maroon. (Tail not pointed but bluntly rounded.)

- Their voices, which are much less strident and not as loud as those of *Aratinga* conures.

Also the flight feathers are partly bluish and there is a maroon patch or hint of maroon on the abdomen of most species. Note that these constant factors are not mentioned in species' descriptions. Relevant features for identification are in bold text.

Appearance and possibly related species

Pyrrhuras are long-tailed birds; their tail feathers are nearly uniform in width, rather than tapered to a narrow point. Their proportions are very pleasing. Their beautiful plumage is gaudy or subtle or even gaudy and subtle in the same species. For example, the Crimson-bellied has that stunning feature which gives it its name – but look further and you will see exquisite combinations of green and blue. Included in various members of the genus is every colour of the rainbow and more – from the obvious green, blue and red to rich brown, white and yellow.

Most species have the ear coverts of a fainter or contrasting colour and they have scalloped breast markings; these vary in prominence, colour and design. This scalloping is quite unusual in parrots and distinguishes most members of the genus from other parrots. One other neotropical species possesses this

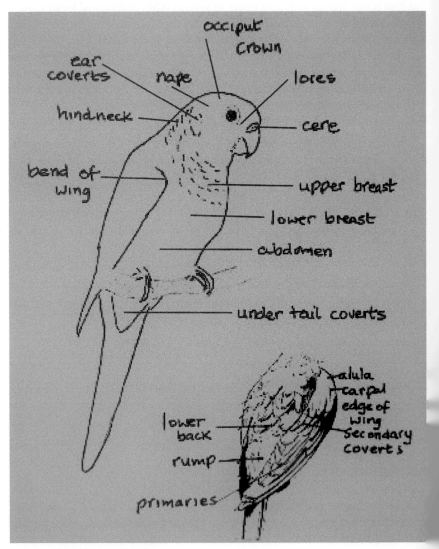

Features of a *Pyrrhura* conure.

feature but to an even more marked degree: the Hawk-headed Parrot *(Deroptyus accipitrinus)*. When I kept simultaneously this parrot and the Blue-throated Conure I could observe some behavioural similarities between the two especially in their aggressive posturing and the streaked feathers on the head. Perhaps they share a distant ancestor.

The only other genus that seems close to *Pyrrhura* in appearance is *Enicognathus* – the Austral *(E. ferrugineus)* and the Slender-billed *(E. leptorhynchus)*. Because the Austral Conure is the short-billed form, it is easier to see the resemblance. Indeed, one could almost say that these are the two cool-climate forms of the genus – although I would not go as far as to include them!

Jessie Zgurski wrote: "I often call *Pyrrhura* conures 'Macaws compressed into a little bird', since they are small with big personalities" (Zgurski, 2013). I can see her point! Most of them are very confident, assertive birds. Especially when in threatening mode, they sway and swagger and hold their ground, as do macaws.

Bare eye skin and eye

The colour of the bare skin surrounding the eye (periophthalmic ring) is grey or white. However, this can vary in the same species in captive birds and might depend on the conditions under which the birds are kept. Some parrots kept without access to sunlight have paler or white skin. Skin colour can differ in adult and immature birds. Most *Pyrrhuras* have a prominent area of bare white skin surrounding the eye which adds to their appeal, giving them a soft and gentle look. The White-eared/Painted complex of species and sub-species have grey skin around the eye and the iris is yellowish or orange, not dark brown. The Blue-throated Conure looks quite different and less gentle with very dark grey skin around the eye and a yellow iris. It is the least typical in every aspect – behaviour, as well. However, it is recognisable as a member of the genus. There is one species, however, which is not and could be mistaken for a *Psittacara* conure. This is the Rose-crowned or Rose-headed Conure *(P. rhodocephala)* whose appearance – plain green plumage with red head and pale beak – is reminiscent of that of a *Psittacara*. To a lesser degree, this also applies to the El Oro Conure *(P. orcesi)*.

Three groups

The members of the genus *Pyrrhura* can be divided into three groups.

. The typical members with black beak, intricate breast markings and green, buff or white ear coverts:
molinae
frontalis/devillei
coerulescens/perlata
leucotis complex

picta complex
melanura and *pacifica*
rupicola
albipectus

2. Species with lighter coloured beaks, less pronounced breast markings and red or reddish ear coverts:
calliptera
egregia
hoematotis
hoffmanni
orcesi
rhodocephala
viridicata

3. A larger species with a different plumage pattern:
cruentata.

These three groups are covered in that order in the Species section.

Species or sub-species?

As mentioned in various parts of the text, there is as yet (and perhaps never will be) a clear picture of which members of the genus are species and which are sub-species. This is a matter of opinion, also of science (DNA sequencing). There is another reason for considering some forms as species. Many *Pyrrhuras* have small ranges in the wild and are threatened with extinction. As sub-species receive no attention for conservation action, it is prudent to consider them as species.

Why are there so many forms? We have only to look at the small pockets of different habitat types throughout the range of these birds and the fact that they are not nomadic to understand the answer. The British vet, the late George Smith (probably the first original thinker on the subject of neotropical parrots) wrote: "Being of small size and disinclined to fly long distances, they find it difficult or nearly impossible to cross vegetative or geographical boundaries. The ones that under very rare circumstances, have surmounted these barriers immediately become genetically isolated and over the many years since, have formed geographical races (or subspecies). Very likely this break-up into geographical forms was helped by being largely residential – not prone to great movements of territory – and by the inherent 'instability' of parrot coloration" (Smith, 1982).

Sexual dimorphism

A male usually has a broader head and beak and is slightly larger than a female. The only species in which dimorphism in the plumage is described in the literature

(Forshaw, 2006) is the El Oro Conure. However, DNA research has shown that this species is NOT sexually dimorphic. Some breeders state that in the Rose-fronted Conure *(roseifrons)* the red extends further beyond the eye in the female. In other words, DNA sexing is the only reliable method of sexing. However, in a group it is usually quite easy for experienced breeders to select males and females: males have bigger, rounder heads and larger beaks. Note that in the species with a maroon patch on the abdomen, the extent of this colour bears no relation to the sex of the bird. The maroon patch is often smaller and duller in young birds.

Abnormal coloration

Abnormally coloured birds showing such colours as brownish upper breast, dark red cheeks, wings, lower breast and abdomen, are sometimes recorded. This is acquired coloration – not a mutation – and is usually caused by a metabolic disorder (perhaps liver malfunction).

In the December 1981 issue of the magazine of the Parrot Society (UK), Margaret Street wrote that over the years her White-eared Conure's plumage had changed from green to red to maroon. The conure was at least twelve years old and had started to change colour ten years previously. By about 1973 it was completely red but occasionally produced a red feather with a green stripe. Having lived for at least ten years in good health, it seems unlikely that liver disease was the cause.

Abnormally coloured plumage in Blue-throated Conures, probably caused by a metabolic disorder.

Photographs © Rosemary Low

Acquired pied markings are not uncommon in *Pyrrhuras* and are sometimes lost after one or two moults. The plumage might be marked with red or yellow. Prospective buyers beware. This is not a wonderful new mutation!

Identification

Even the best artists have problems illustrating the often complex plumage patterns and subtle markings of these birds, thus the illustrations in some books are not useful for identification purposes. Until recent years photographs of captive birds were the only reliable means of identification but now excellent photographs exist of birds in the wild. This is partly due to the many birders and their 'digiscoping' techniques (digital photography through the lens of the telescope) and because several rare species are being studied intensively in the wild. These days many photographs of parrots in the wild, with the precise locality, can be found on the internet. They can be very useful in showing breeders of *Pyrrhuras* what a certain species or sub-species looks like. However, in species with a very extensive range, such as the Black-tailed Conure *(melanura)* and the Black-capped Conure *(rupicola)* considerable variation can be seen in the plumage. Either more sub-species have yet to be described or there is local plumage variation.

It should be noted that photographs mislead. The plumage of one individual bird, especially the head coloration, can look different, depending on whether or not flash was used. Without this knowledge, one should hesitate to identify sub-species from photographs.

Behaviour

Pyrrhura conures are extremely active, sociable and inquisitive little parakeets whose flight is very swift and agile. In captivity their inquisitive nature is endearing but calls for extreme vigilance on the part of the keeper because they will find the smallest hole and escape. Their voices are pleasant in comparison with the *Aratinga* conures, and seldom harsh or repetitive unless the birds are alarmed. A friend who had previously kept only the larger, short-tailed parrots found, to his surprise, that the conures were more entertaining because they are so active.

They have many interesting behaviour traits. I feel sure that if *Pyrrhura* behaviour and vocalisations were studied closely, it would be found that they communicate much information to each other. They are exceptionally watchful, observant birds and have lightning-fast reflexes to react to danger or any other stimuli.

When feeling threatened (in captive birds when the nest is inspected), they ruffle the head feathers, stretch the neck and sway from side to side. Even young birds close to fledging behave like this. When excited they make a rapid clicking sound with the mandibles. Similar behaviour is seen when the male displays to the female. However, both sexes display when excited and prance up and down the perch, sometimes stretching outwards, with nape and throat feathers ruffled.

Gerhard Schmidt from Germany informed me that "with *Pyrrhura perlata* and *P. egregia* the breeding females are protected by the males. The males are always looking out of the nest box, and when someone enters the bird house they make a special noise with their beak or they even knock with their beaks on the wood."

Their desire for physical contact with their own species is very great. Pairs or several birds sit together, preening each other – not only the head but also around the vent and the tail, sometimes sitting head to tail to do so.

More so than any parrots I know except the Hawk-head, they have an almost obsessive desire to roost in cavities.

Vocalisations

Their conversational notes are pleasant. They can chatter quietly and almost warble! Only the alarm call is harsh but under normal circumstances is not heard often. To my ear, the vocalisations of the different species do not sound very different, with the exception of Hoffmann's Conure which are more plaintive: a thinner sound. *Pyrrhura* calls are quieter (at a lower volume) than the macaw-like calls of the larger *Aratinga* conures and are not found to be unpleasant by most breeders (or their neighbours!). *Pyrrhuras* can also make sounds so quiet, presumably only to communicate with the bird next to them, that they might never be heard by the keeper unless the environment is very tranquil. The sound is something like a buzz.

They are highly communicative vocally, constantly making sounds that keep them in contact with the flock or their mate. The Crimson-bellied, for example, has a contact call that is a short whistle, repeated twice. In my breeding pair and in the two hand-reared young, they will make this call to attract my attention and when I mimic it back, they repeat the call, and I mimic it again – and so it goes on. The two that I hand-reared will also use my language to get my attention, using one of the only two phrases they know.

Common names

The use of scientific names is preferable for two reasons. Some species have two or more frequently used common names and often one is not at all appropriate. For example, the Black-tailed Conure *(melanura)*, is also known as the Maroon-tailed Conure: most members of the genus have the underside of the tail maroon. The scientific name of one species, the Blaze-winged Conure, *Pyrrhura devillei*, is the common name of another species, Deville's Conure, *Pyrrhura lucianii*. The White-eared Conure has less strikingly white ear coverts than the Grey-breasted Conure. And the Black-capped *(rupicola)*, formerly called Rock Conure, is one of several species that might have been called the Green-cheeked instead of *molinae*. And so on!

Some aviculturists confuse the Rose-fronted Conure *(roseifrons)* with the Rose-crowned or Rose-headed *(rhodocephala)* – and as the two species can have extensive rose colouring on the crown and forehead, this is not surprising. So aviculturists are advised to learn the scientific names, especially if they are buying birds unseen. The scientific names are not always appropriate, either – but that is another story.

When the species were originally named, not all the members of the genus had been described. Probably only a few were known to those who named them which accounts for some of the anomalies in the common names. When Count Salvadori catalogued the birds in the British Museum in 1891, the following species were represented in the collection:

Species	Year originally named
picta	1648
frontalis (then called *vittata*)	1801
cruentata	1820
perlata (now called *coerulescens*)	1820
melanura	1824
leucotis	1832
rupicola	1844
lucianii	1851
calliptera	1854
molinae	1854
devillei	1854
hoematotis	1857
souancei	1858
roseifrons	1859
hoffmanni	1861
rhodogaster (now called *perlata*)	1864
emma	1868
rhodocephala	1870
berlepschi	1873
egregia	1881

Since Salvadori catalogued the *Pyrrhuras*, the following have been described:

griseipectus	1900
amazonum	1906
anerythra and *coerulescens*	1927
snethlageae	2002
parvifrons	2008

Increasing knowledge

Since the 1990s, when mutations of the Green-cheeked Conure became available, the popularity of members of this genus in aviculture has soared. Previously, few *Pyrrhuras* were kept as pets in the home; now hand-reared Green-cheeked Conures are perhaps within the top ten of all pet parrots. And the proliferation of mutations has seen their popularity with breeders equal that of Ring-necked Parakeets and Peach-faced Lovebirds.

During the past 20 years or so it is not only avicultural knowledge that has increased. The taxonomy of the genus has been almost completely revised and in this book I treat the genus as consisting of 33 species. Information relating to their habits and status in the wild has increased enormously – possibly more than any other genus of neotropical parrots except the little known *Hapalopsittaca*.

Taxonomy

When Joseph Forshaw published his epic *Parrots of the World* in 1973 he recognised 18 species and 28 sub-species, a total of 46 forms. In 2006 his *Parrots of the World: an Identification Guide* recognised 27 species and 20 sub-species (47 forms). The El Oro Conure *(Pyrrhura orcesi)* had not been discovered in 1973 and the species called the Yellow-sided Conure *(P. hypoxantha)* is now known to be but a mutation of the Green-cheeked Conure. Furthermore, the former sub-species of the Painted Conure are now recognised as distinct species.

Origin

The *Pyrrhura* conures are widely distributed over South America but they are missing from Chile and from the Caribbean islands. They occur in most types of forested habitat except treeless areas of grasslands. Most species occur in lowland forests and in sub-tropical forests from 300m to 1,800m. A few species range higher, in cloud forests between 1,800m to 3,000m and even in the cold páramo/puna zones above 3,000m.

Two similar-looking Brazilian species inhabit areas in excess of one thousand kilometres apart, with the intervening area devoid of any *Pyrrhura* despite the presence of Atlantic forest. The White-eared Conure inhabits the eastern lowland Atlantic forest from southern Bahia to Rio de Janeiro whereas the Grey-breasted Conure *(P. griseipectus)* is restricted to montane forest areas that have strong Amazonian affinities in otherwise semi-arid Ceará and Pernambuco. Their similarities must be due to the fact that they possessed a common ancestor.

In addition to South America, two species occur in Central America where their ranges are small: Azuero Conure *(P. eisenmanni)* in central Panama; and Sulphur-winged Conure *(P. hoffmanni)* in southern Costa Rica and western Panama.

2. CAPTIVE HISTORY

ONLY two species of *Pyrrhura* were well-known prior to the 1960s. The White-eared Conure *(P. leucotis)* was regularly imported into Europe between the 1880s (and probably previously) until the mid-1950s. This was the only member of the genus that W. T. Greene mentioned in his three volumes of *Parrots in Captivity*. In the second volume, published in 1884, he wrote of this species "...a little larger than the Australian Undulated Parakeet [Budgerigar], it was very rare until a year or two ago, but latterly the birds are frequently offered for sale. I believe that no other Conure will afford his owner so much pleasure as this one. A pair I kept for a long time proved very intelligent, lively, and hardy, and were quite free from the destructive mania of other Conures, and never indulged in screaming. Their price was £2, and even upwards a piece."

In 1903, David Seth-Smith wrote in his book *Parrakeets, A Handbook to the Imported Species*: "...but five species have been imported as cage birds, at any rate within the last thirty or forty years."

For decades the Red-bellied, now more often called Maroon-bellied Conure, was well known. The first recorded breeding in Britain was by W. Shore-Bailey whose pair reared one youngster *(chiripepe)* in 1923. Two years later his pair of the nominate race reared four young. In Australia the first reported breeding of a member of the genus was that by Sir Edward Hallstrom in 1953.

Way back in the 1960s the *Pyrrhuras* seemed like a fascinating group to me because, unlike the *Aratinga* species, most of which were well-known in aviculture, many of them were just pictures in a book. When Joseph Forshaw published his epic *Parrots of the World* in 1973 he recognized 18 species and 28 sub-species, a total of 46 forms. Of these eighteen species, eight had never been kept in captivity outside their native area. Knowledge keeps moving forward and in this book I treat the genus as consisting of 32 species.

In the 1960s there was little interest in *Pyrrhuras*. Imported birds were inexpensive, with prices much lower than the more sought-after Australian parakeets which were the most popular of all parrots as aviary birds. Imported birds advertised by dealers were seldom correctly identified with the exception of the Maroon-bellied. Rosemary Cooper recalled buying, in 1970, a pair of "Scaly-breasted Conures" – as dealers would label *Pyrrhuras*. She wrote: "I could not identify them as there was so little about the *Pyrrhura* conures in print at that time" (Cooper, 1979). This echoed my comments of 1968: "The difficulty of identifying the rarer species is great, partly due to the fact that such descriptions as do exist are not full enough to be helpful or are even contradictory and partly because many members of this genus are very similar" (Low, 1968). I bought my first Pearly

Conures, unseen, as "White-eared" – and I was not alone in this. In the autumn of 1967 a dealer was advertising "Flame-winged Conures". They were *souancei*.

(Today's bird keepers do not realise how fortunate they are to have such a wealth of published literature available! Conversely though, when searching the internet, many people are not able to distinguish reliable information from that which is incorrect or misleading.)

Newly imported birds were often in poor feather and in even worse health. The first Black-tailed Conure *(souancei)* I bought, in 1967, was unidentified, with bad plumage, fat and very nervous. It cost me £6 (not cheap) and was for sale because its mate had died. It looked as though it would soon be following it. By sheer chance, six months later, a friend asked me if I wanted a conure in poor condition. I said "yes" and was delighted to find it was the same species, although its plumage included nasty black areas and it had no tail. He offered it free but I was happy to give him £1 for it! The two birds co-existed happily. One year later I noted that they were in wonderful condition: "the white scaling is particularly bright and attractive." Their sexes were unknown and they showed no interest in breeding.

Illustrations of the White-eared Conure from (left) Greene's *Parrots in Captivity* (1884) and (right) White-eared and Pearly Conures from Seth-Smith's *Parakeets* (1903).

Large-scale exports begin

In the late 1970s export of parrots from Bolivia and Argentina started on a large scale, thus the Green-cheeked Conure was introduced to aviculture. Because so many were exported, it soon became common. In 1967 Brazil had banned the legal export of parrots, followed by Paraguay in 1975, thus Argentina was left as the only exporting country within the range of the Maroon-bellied Conure. Many reached Europe yet by the late 1980s the Green-cheeked had become the more common of the two.

In the early 1960s Pearly Conures, endemic to Brazil, became available in Europe. There was no legal export after 1967. In Britain the first breeder, probably of the sub-species *lepida*, was B.M.Killick of Wellingborough in 1963. In Denmark the first breeder (sub-species unknown) was Albrecht Moller in 1960 or 1961. Mrs Spenkelink van Schaik, who specialised in small neotropical parrots when few were interested, bred *coerulescens* in 1982.

The Crimson-bellied Conure, at the time known as *Pyrrhura rhodogaster*, was very rare and sought after when it was bred at Chester Zoo in the UK in 1976. The first recorded importation into the UK had occurred in 1927. London Zoo acquired a pair but there is no record of breeding success. It was not until the early 1980s that aviculturists had an opportunity to keep this species. The Spenkelink family in the Netherlands acquired some captive-bred birds from Brazil.

For a period of a decade or less, starting in 1967, the Black-tailed Conure, nominate race and *souancei*, were imported into Europe. This situation was short-lived as most countries within its range banned parrot exports – Brazil in 1967, Venezuela 1970, Peru about 1973 and Ecuador in 1981. By the late 1980s *melanura* was (and remains) uncommon in aviculture.

The Painted Conure (probably *lucianii* from northern Brazil) was known in Europe as long ago as 1866 when it was bred in France. This was in an era when many birds were imported from Brazil, often with sailors. In the first two decades of the 20th century it was bred in at least two collections in France so the conures might have come from French Guiana.

In the 1960s, when my interest in the genus commenced, the only other species known to aviculturists was the Blue-throated (*P. cruentata*) – but it was rare and expensive. First bred in the UK by Herbert Whitley in 1937, from the late 1970s it was bred in Germany, Denmark, the Netherlands and the UK, and gradually became available across Europe. In June 1981 all species of parrots were listed on CITES (Convention on Trade in Endangered Species) appendices. It was then possible to assess how many parrots were in trade and imported into a particular country. At this time it was believed that approximately 10% of all parrots imported into the UK were captive-bred. These would have been mainly prolific species such as lovebirds and Budgerigars. For the period 1981 to 1984 only three *Pyrrhura* species were imported into the UK: 500 Maroon-bellied from Argentina, 160 Painted Conures from Guyana and 73 Black-tailed Conures from Ecuador (Broad, 1987). The total parrot imports for these years were believed to number about 20,000 per annum, thus *Pyrrhuras* made up less than 1% of imports. The same was almost certainly true of other European countries.

The 1980s saw an increase in the number of species in aviculture. This occurred despite the fact that by 1985 nearly all the countries of South America, except the Guianas and Argentina, had banned the export of parrots. However, thousands were smuggled across borders to countries where export was permitted. In addition, the illegal trade continued by sea – from Brazil to Portugal, for example.

Small importations of rare species

In 1980 breeders in the USA and in Switzerland acquired Black-capped Conures, then often known as Rock Conures. In the same year, Hoffmann's (Sulphur-winged) Conures from Panama were exported for the first time (through Dr Nathan Gale who was working there). The first breeding occurred in the following year.

The Fiery-shouldered Conure *(P. egregia)* was next on the scene, imported in small numbers into Europe from Venezuela in 1988. It seems likely that this species was established in aviculture from rather few specimens.

When the third edition of my book *Parrots their care and breeding* went to press in 1991 the Rose-headed or Rose-crowned Conure *(P. rhodocephala)*, also from Venezuela, had not yet (or had only just) been introduced to aviculture outside its native country. This occurred before the end of the decade. The same was true of the Red-eared Conure *(P. hoematotis).*

The remaining members of the genus, sub-species of *leucotis* and *picta* not then promoted to full species, the Santa Marta Conure *(P. viridicata)*, White-necked *(P. albipectus)*, Flame-winged *(P. calliptera)* and El Oro *(P. orcesi)* were endangered species about which little was then known in the wild. They are all subjects of ongoing conservation programmes and it is unlikely that legal export will ever occur.

The peak of *Pyrrhura* interest

The 1980s and the 1990s were an extraordinary time for those interested in this genus – a time that will never be repeated. This is true of parrot keeping in general, in Western Europe. More species and sub-species of *Pyrrhuras* became available than ever before. People were discovering what delightful aviary birds they are and how responsive to attention they can become, clinging on the wire mesh when spoken to and chattering away excitedly when you bring a favourite item of food.

Many breeders kept one or two pairs but there were only a few specialist breeders. One of these was Jeff Hornsby in the UK. All his birds were legally imported, most of them from European countries such as the Netherlands, Germany, Switzerland and Spain. With the rarer species he could acquire only single birds – often from different countries because they were so hard to find. In this way he built up what was probably the finest private collection of *Pyrrhuras* ever seen.

He produced large numbers of birds, most of which went to a dealer who exported them worldwide, to countries including Canada, Israel, South Africa and Saudi Arabia. Sadly, by the end of the 1990s, the interest in *Pyrrhuras* had peaked and he could not sell so many young. This is a pattern that repeated itself with other kinds of parrots at that time, with breeders failing to realise how lucky they were to be able to keep these birds – and that the opportunity to establish them would never again occur. There has been a shift from larger breeding centres being established mainly in Europe and the USA to Asian countries such as India, Myanmar (Burma) and Indonesia. Today, most *Pyrrhura* breeders maintain a small number of pairs, probably mainly of different species, or concentrate on mutations of the Green-cheeked.

In the UK the Parrot Society invites its members to contribute their results to a Breeding Register, published in most years. This indicates trends but not numbers reared. The figures below of reported breedings by Parrot Society members show trends of *Pyrrhura* popularity which are not very different in other countries worldwide, except in Australia where fewer species are available. The decline of interest in the Maroon-bellied can be attributed to the many mutations of the similar Green-cheeked that became available. The Painted Conure has become rare as females are hard to acquire. Figures for the Painted (not *roseifrons*) are shown as a comparison. This also indicates the avicultural decline of the latter, with breeders commenting on how difficult they are to breed.

Year	Maroon-bellied		Painted	
1977	34 bred by	10 members	0	
1980	45	10	0	
1984	51	11	20 bred by	3 members
1991	164	29	18	4
1998	195	37	92	22
2008	52	5	4	1
2010	37	5	17	5
2021	3	1	4	1

In the 21st century

The *Pyrrhura* conures are popular with breeders in the USA, South Africa and Europe, especially in the Netherlands, Belgium, Germany and the UK. The US was the first country to hand-rear them for the pet trade in significant numbers. Elsewhere they – or more correctly, mainly the Green-cheeked – have become increasingly fashionable as companion birds. In Brazil there are fewer breeders, compared with the 1980s and 1990s, because only the few large parrot centres have the authorisation to rear the native species and others have seldom been available.

Currently, although there are probably more individual birds of the genus in aviculture than ever before, the majority of these are Green-cheeked Conures and their mutations. A different attitude will be required by breeders if the other species are to survive in aviculture over the long term. This especially applies to the rarer species that some are fortunate to keep, in particular *griseipectus* and *pfrimeri*. More about this in the section on *Conservation and Aviculture*.

Availability in Australia

Due to Australia's strict import restrictions and severe penalties for illegal importation, few *Pyrrhura* species were available there and numbers were limited. However, in the early years of the 21st century availability and interest increased enormously. As often happens in aviculture, popularity of a genus peaks and wanes. In 2020 Jade Welch wrote: "*Pyrrhura* Conures have largely fallen out of popularity with many Australian keepers in recent times. This is surprising considering their relatively low noise output, ease of care and the number of species available. While a few species have always remained low in number, even those whose numbers were built up are in some cases going backwards. It is true to say that we risk losing some species if we don't take action now" (Welch, 2020).

Aviculture in Brazil

Although more species of *Pyrrhuras* occur there than in any other country, Ringneck Parakeets and Rosellas and their mutations are more popular. One reason is that breeders need to register with IBAMA (the Brazilian Institute of the Environment and Renewable Natural Resources) in order to sell native species. This deters small breeders. During the 1990s, before this applied, numerous wild-caught birds were available: *picta, amazonum, egregia, rupicola, perlata, roseifrons, griseipectus, pfrimeri, leucotis,* and *cruentata*. By 2020 only *perlata* was popular and only a few breeders kept other species, mainly *leucotis, griseipectus, pfrimeri, roseifrons* and *cruentata. P. molinae* was never popular.

3. HOUSING

THE MOST important factors to consider when planning outdoor accommodation for birds are:

- The basics: adequate space, light and protection from the elements.
- Double wiring: protection from birds in adjoining aviaries and from hawks and other predators.
- Eliminating the chance of escape.
- Security: position aviaries as close to the house as possible, or use security cameras.
- Aviaries that can be maintained in a hygienic condition (earth floors and wooden frameworks are not acceptable).
- Rodent-proof structures, although eliminating mice might be impossible (earth floors not acceptable).

These are the obvious requirements. For *Pyrrhura* conures there is another consideration which affects the relationship between birds and keeper and can affect breeding results. Site the aviaries as close to the house or in an area where family members pass frequently. The more interaction there is between them and people, the more cheeky, responsive and communicative they become and therefore the more enjoyable to keep. Steady birds who are well adjusted to their surroundings, are likely to breed better. One needs to get to know these delightful birds as individuals. Not only is this more rewarding, but problems will be noticed more readily.

Escape artists

This fact is important: the curiosity and fearlessness of these conures can lead to rapid escape. It is absolutely essential to ensure that the aviary is carefully maintained and regularly checked for holes in the wire. No birds are quicker to leave their aviary if the opportunity occurs but, equally, if not frightened out of the vicinity, they can be quick to find their way back. However, due to their fast and agile flight and the difficulty of recapture, except perhaps of a very tame bird, a great effort needs to be made to prevent escapes.

A safety porch (double door) is absolutely essential for a single aviary that is not part of a block with a service corridor. It is also essential in a birdroom which houses these birds or any building to which they have access from an outdoor aviary.

Even when conures are kept in a structure that contains many cages, where there can be no escape into the outside world, precautions must be taken to prevent escape, such as small, closely-fitting cage doors. In the breeding centre at Palmitos Park, Gran Canaria, in one large enclosed building there were twenty or more parrot species, including *Pyrrhuras*. One day a pair of Blue-throated Conures escaped when the keeper failed to secure the cage door properly. I found them sitting on the same perch as a male Eclectus! The Eclectus cages were made of larger mesh and the conures had decided to investigate the interior! The conures looked quite at home but the big green parrot looked rather surprised!

There were a number of "escapes" by *Pyrrhuras* because if the door was not closed properly they would be out in seconds. I gave instructions that they should not be chased with a net. I would clip the door open and place a delicacy inside, such as a piece of fresh corn or a guava, and they would usually be back inside within five to ten minutes. In this respect they differ from most parrots which are unlikely to return voluntarily.

Some young Yellow-sided Conures belonging to a friend had an unusual method of escaping. They removed the screws on the hinges of the door! All cages and aviaries should have close-fitting doors which are secured with a lock. Cage doors that open inwards help to prevent birds escaping. Plastic cable-ties are useful for giving extra security to doors that are not regularly used. The keeper should develop the habit of checking carefully all doors in cages or aviaries. These conures have lightning fast reactions and can spot escape opportunities before you do! This cannot be over-emphasised.

Cage breeding

Cage-breeding of *Pyrrhuras* is common; my concern is always for the quality of life of these most active and most agile in flight of any parrot. They are inquisitive and need stimulation. The bare breeding cages which many breeders make no attempt to improve leave me angry. The breeder has not considered what it is like to be an active bird that needs to be always nibbling and exploring, swinging and flying. Keeping these birds permanently in 90cm cages can be compared to keeping battery hens – except that *Pyrrhuras*, given space, are always on the verge of flight.

Cage breeding is acceptable only if the conures can fly in a large aviary after the breeding season. Nest-boxes should not be available for roosting, or breeding would take place, amid many fights and fatalities. Perhaps the best solution is to house males in one flight and females in another. The fitness of the birds will improve, along with their desire to breed when placed in cages.

Only good quality welded mesh should be used for cage construction; a sample should be obtained before ordering. Some products have flakes of zinc attached to the mesh. This is poisonous and will kill birds that ingest it.

Suspended cages

In warm climates and in protected areas, sheltered from wind, suspended cages can be used. They are not suitable in northern Europe unless inside an enclosed building or with access to one. The word "suspended" is usually a misnomer since most such cages are supported, not suspended. There are two methods of construction: separate cages placed on metal staging or several cages made as one unit. In the latter instance there must be either a solid partition or double welded mesh between the cages, to prevent injuries to toes and beaks. Solid partitions are preferable to prevent aggressive posturing and attempted fighting, usually between males of *Pyrrhuras* in adjoining cages which can become very territorial. This kind of stress can even result in eggs being broken or chicks killed. Indeed, it might be preferable to separate pairs of *Pyrrhuras* by small parrots of a different genus. Larger, noisy parrots next door can also cause problems.

Some breeders construct outdoor suspended cages with completely solid roofs, thus compromising the quality of life of the inmates even further. I think the word inmate came to my mind because these cages look like cells. The birds cannot even take a bath in the rain. At least half the top should be constructed of welded mesh – double to deter hawks.

Most suspended cages are not long enough to provide sufficient flying exercise. One of the reasons is the difficulty of catching birds in lengthy cages. This problem can be overcome by making a hinged panel that opens in the centre of the floor. The person catching can then stand up in the centre of the cage, giving reach at both ends.

In South Africa, Terry Irwin used cages mounted on two rows of round piping, at the rear and in front. This allowed him to slide the cages along and to move them closer or further apart. His pairs of Blue-throated Conures were housed in such cages: 3m long, 90cm wide and 90cm high, about 1m above the ground. The welded mesh on the floor was 25mm x 25mm. This was easier to keep clean than smaller mesh because debris did not accumulate on the cage floor. Note that mesh size must be smaller for suspended cages outdoors. In this case, vermin were deterred because the cages were in outdoor enclosures. These were covered by shade cloth – necessary to counteract the very high summer temperatures. The nest-boxes were protected from the heat by a roof that ran the length of the row of cages (Irwin, 2008).

Catching birds

Because *Pyrrhuras* are so fast in flight, it can be difficult to catch them in a large aviary. It is important to use a net made from strong cloth, not from mesh. I should have a padded rim, if it has a metal frame. If a bird is accidentally hit or the head with such a net, it could suffer a fatal injury. A net should be kept in every building and service passage.

Moving pairs or families to a new location is easy if one gets up early enough and it is still dark! Simply put a cloth in the nest-hole and you have them captured! Some breeders have nest-boxes of identical design in all their cages in order to facilitate moving birds.

Aviary sizes

Do not make the mistake of believing that small aviaries will suffice. *Pyrrhura* conures are very active so the larger the aviary the better. For one pair I would suggest an aviary at least 3m to 4.2m long, 91cm wide and 1.8m high. Where space and finances permit, the flights should be 4.5m (15ft) long or even more – every part will be used in fast and skilful flight.

Recommended size for the indoor quarters is 1.8m long and 91cm wide. Half depth cages, that is, 91cm off the floor and the same height, are adequate. The area below can be tiled for ease of cleaning or, inside, a Vinyl floor can be laid above the concrete.

The use of lightweight aluminium or aluminium angle is recommended for aviary construction. This remains in good condition for many years and is easily cleaned with a pressure washer. Equally importantly, conures cannot find their way out of aluminium aviaries, if they are correctly constructed. They will escape from wooden ones, when the wood rots. Wooden aviaries cannot be maintained in a good and attractive condition for any length of time. They become unsightly, due to being gnawed, by the conures and even by mice, and discoloured by wear and even mould.

An important factor that relates to *Pyrrhura* conures concerns their territoriality. They will kill other birds that enter the aviary by accident or which are misguidedly placed there by the owner. This means that most species cannot normally be kept safely in a colony, although this has been done with Maroon-bellied Conures.

When designing the aviaries, **every pair must have their own enclosure, separated from the next by double welded mesh.** Aviaries must never be designed so that it is entered through a door in the side of an aviary with a common boundary; sooner or later a door will not be closed or it will become out of shape, leaving a gap through which a bird enters the next aviary – almost certainly to be killed. **Aviaries must always be built with a service passage running their length, with a separate entry door to each one.** Aviary doors that lead directly to the great outdoors will soon result in escaped birds.

The same could be true of earth floors. Not only are they impossible to maintain in a hygienic condition, they are unsafe. A hole made by rats or mice will be investigated by inquisitive *Pyrrhuras* and could become an exit route. Because these

The author's aviaries for *Pyrrhuras* and lories. Note the contacts on the doors for the alarm system.

birds sleep in their nest-boxes, they are especially vulnerable to attack by rats and other vermin that enter aviaries that are carelessly constructed. Concrete floors, or gravel laid over concrete for a less stark appearance, with welded mesh sunk into the ground to deter vermin burrowing inside, are recommended.

The aviary roof should have a covered section to provide shade and shelter from heavy rain. Shrubs climbing over the roof provide protection against hawks, cats and other predators. Plant the shrubs at the side of the aviary and place plastic mesh on the sides and roof for the shrubs to climb over as this gives them some protection from destructive beaks!

A shelter or indoor flight must be available in a cold climate. Although these birds are very hardy, they should not be allowed to roost in outdoor aviaries without protection from the weather and from night predators. Panels of PVC on a wooden frame will protect them from wind – which they detest.

Preventing fatalities at night

Unless they are breeding and the nest-box is outside, it is advisable to shut birds into the enclosed part of their aviary at night. *Pyrrhura* conures seek out a hole in which to roost so a box should always be available. When they are not breeding a nest-box will encourage laying at a time when this is not desirable. A solution is to place a small open-topped box, with a perch and no floor, in their inside accommodation.

Mortality is much higher in aviary birds that are allowed to roost outside. Dangers include attacks from or night frights caused by owls, cats and rats. In some locations, disturbance by car headlights or neighbours' security lights can be a problem. Fireworks also cause fatalities. This is why conures are so much safer inside at night. In addition, they are not exposed to severe weather conditions.

I believe that breeders should take pride in their aviaries. This is difficult when their condition deteriorates quickly. With this deterioration sometimes comes a careless attitude towards the welfare of the birds. Every person who takes up keeping birds in aviaries must be prepared for the time-consuming work of keeping them clean and maintained in a sound and secure condition. Disease proliferates in dirty enclosures. One *Pyrrhura* breeder said he did not keep aviaries and swing feeders too clean because birds have no resistance to disease in clean conditions. This might be true of clinically clean aviaries but such a scenario is not practical or necessary. However, the breeder mentioned often picking up dead birds so perhaps disease was present. *Pyrrhuras* are normally strong and healthy and should live for at least twenty years, if cared for correctly.

Perches and wood for gnawing

Natural wood perches are recommended. In cages that come complete with plastic perches, at least one of these should be removed and replaced with a wooden one. This can be a dowel or a length of tree branch. Willow wood is soft and, if used for

Pyrrhura aviaries built by Simon Boner in Switzerland. Photograph © Rosemary Low

Neat inside quarters of Simon Boner's aviaries depicted on page 21. Note that it is safer to use a feeding hatch or swing feeders than opening a door to remove food containers. Photograph © Rosemary Low

perching, will need to be replaced regularly. Given a choice, many parrots opt for surprisingly thin perches. They greatly enjoy thin, springy branches, especially willow. They should be given a choice of perch size, because always gripping a perch of the same circumference is not good for their feet. Perches should be replaced before they become shiny and uncomfortable. Those in cages must be washed frequently; they soon become sticky from fruits.

It is a lot of work to keep *Pyrrhura* cages supplied with suitable branches for gnawing (apple, willow and hazel *(Corylus)* in Europe and eucalyptus and *Casuarina* elsewhere) – but well worth the effort. These little birds would be nibbling and gnawing all day long if provided with enough branches or, in the autumn, berry-laden branches such as hawthorn.

Finding a supply can be a major problem for some urban dwellers. Those with gardens can plant a quick-growing eucalypt, such as *Eucalyptus gunni* (although the wood is rather hard), hawthorn or hazel. Apple or pear trees take longer to mature but the branches are ideal and the trees a good source of fruit if a sweet variety is chosen.

Watering systems

In some large collections automatic watering systems are used in order to save time. However, the most time-consuming part of looking after water containers is cleaning them, not filling them. Using automatic systems can lead to neglect of this important task and the possible spread of disease.

Pyrrhuras are enthusiastic bathers. They need large, shallow water containers for bathing, preferably of stainless steel, as these are the easiest to keep clean and cannot develop cracks, unlike earthenware dishes. Bathing is a social activity. When one bird starts, those nearby are likely to join in. Sunlight reaching the cage or aviary is a certain stimulus to bathing!

Plants and *Pyrrhuras*

Plants enhance the quality of the lives of our conures. It cannot be predicted whether or not a pair will destroy them. Much depends on how dense the planting is and whether fresh branches are available to gnaw. A fig tree *(Ficus)* grows in a crack in the concrete beneath the outdoor cage of my Crimson-bellied Conures which is raised 50cm off the ground. The branches have grown through the bottom

of the cage. During the first year, by the time the leaves fell in October/ November, most of the branches had been gnawed right down to the cage floor – but how the occupants enjoyed them! In following years they allowed the fig leaves to grow, and to drop in autumn.

Most *Pyrrhuras* are destructive to growing plants – but they love to be among leaves. A possible solution is to cultivate fast-growing non-poisonous shrubs such as elder *(Sambucus nigra)*, hawthorn and fig in a tub and when they are a good size, to place the tub in the aviary, just to give them the pleasure and activity involved in nibbling the leaves.

Hoffmann's Conure and hibiscus coexisting in the breeding centre of Loro Parque Fundación. Most *Pyrrhuras* are destructive to growing vegetation. Photograph © Rosemary Low

Birdroom lighting

Good lighting in the birdroom or indoor quarters is important. In these times of high electricity prices, it is worth knowing that halogen lamps are brighter than others and save 30% on electricity. They reputedly have a life of 2,000 hours compared with 1,000 hours of normal lamps and are fully dimmable. If nest-boxes are placed inside a building, the use of a dimmer switch prevents the birds being plunged suddenly into darkness – most important when they have eggs or chicks in the nest. Conures will enter the nest-box as soon as the lights start to dim down.

Ultra-violet (UV) fluorescent tubes are the most beneficial and need to be placed no more than one metre from the birds to be effective. Fluorescent tubes should not be used with a diffuser as this prevents ultraviolet light passing through. Tubes made for reptiles are also unsuitable as they are too strong for birds. Note that those advertised as "sunshine or daylight" tubes are not UV lamps.

Contrary to some reports, the rapid flickering of fluorescent tubes (unless faulty) is not likely to be harmful. Those with electronic ballast, register 40,000 cycles per second so flickering is not seen. Initially they are more expensive but running costs are about 60% lower compared with the switch start type. Switch start fittings can be distinguished by a starter at the side.

Improving quality of life

The quality of life of conures kept in suspended cages is often very poor because no thought is given to keeping them busy and active. Every cage should be fitted with a length of PVC pipe in which a branch can be placed frequently, preferably every week. Shrubs planted beneath the cages and allowed to grow up inside them are, in theory, a good idea. The problem is that the soil provides hiding places for mice, it is impossible to keep clean and fruit which drops onto it will soon grow mould. Thought should be given to the surface below suspended cages. Concrete and tiles are the easiest to keep clean as they can be hosed down and pressure-washed.

Another consideration inside the birdroom is painting the walls. Which colour is best? White is too stark and unnatural. I favour pale green, which is restful and calming, or pale green with small areas of pale blue, to mimic trees and sky.

Finally, bear in mind that aviaries and inside accommodation should be attractive, spacious and clean homes for much-loved birds – not the equivalent of battery housing for parakeets. Why do some breeders assume that parrots have no sense of the aesthetic and actually like living in dingy, dirty and bland enclosures? Please put yourself in the birds' place and ask yourself what you can do to improve their quality of life...

4. NEW STOCK

CAREFULLY consider the purchase of new stock because a mistake can affect your existing birds and jeopardise your future breeding results. If you are wise you will purchase youngsters directly from the breeder. This is because the immune system is not fully functional in immature birds. On the premises of a shop or a dealer birds arrive from various sources, increasing the risk of disease transmission.

This important point is often overlooked, resulting in deaths which cause extreme disappointment and often bewilderment to the purchaser, who has no idea why the bird died. It might look well, but the stress of moving it triggers perhaps a low-grade infection or a virus, resulting in a fatality. Furthermore, a new bird could pass on a virus to existing stock, resulting in devastating losses.

Handling: strength of bill

As in all neotropical parrots, the orbits (eye sockets) of *Pyrrhuras* are completely surrounded by bone, which results in a forceful bite. The correct method of handling these birds is essential if this is not to be experienced! The bird should be held in one hand with the thumb and forefinger firmly gripping either side of the mandibles, to immobilise the beak. My preferred method of removing a bird caught in a net, if it must be handled, is to place the net flat on the ground, watch the movement inside so that you can locate the head, place a towel over the head from outside the net, gripping the head as described, then quickly manoeuvre the other end of the towel inside the net over the conure's head. If the bird will then be released into another area, keep it grasped within the towel for extra security.

Type of accommodation

It is important to find out the type and size of the accommodation in which a young conure has been kept. If the eventual intention is to keep it in a larger flight, and it has been bred in a cage, it is advisable to place it in a cage at first until it has gained confidence in its new location. Conures that have been bred in a small space can be very nervous and bewildered and might fail to find the food in more spacious accommodation.

Some breeders do not give *Pyrrhuras* access to a nest-box until they are old enough to breed. In the wild these birds seek cavities in which to roost, with ten or more birds crowding into the same cavity. This must provide them with a sense of security. For this reason, I believe that young conures should be provided with a roosting platform or roosting box (with a perch but no floor or top).

Here are a few suggestions to smooth the transition period.

Don't place new bird in an aviary if there are less than about five hours of daylight remaining, unless in an enclosed shelter. It needs to feed and to find a safe perching place for the night. Keep it in a cage, perhaps for a couple of days, if it has experienced a long journey. You can observe it closely for signs of ill health and observe what it is eating and the condition of its faeces.

Don't assume that it a young bird is eating hard foods just because the seller told you this. Many breeders take young birds off soft foods much too early, resulting in loss of weight or death. They fail to give them easily digested foods such as soaked and sprouted foods, cooked peas, soft fruit and oats in the green stage. I believe that hard seed should form no more than 40% of the diet of young birds which can include plenty of sunflower and hemp if they are underweight.

Don't keep an aviary-bred conure out of sight of its own species. A young one has never been away from its family before and needs the comfort of its own kind close by.

Don't EVER immediately place a newcomer in the cage or aviary of an intended mate: it is at a psychological disadvantage, making it vulnerable to attack. Place it in adjoining accommodation. After a few days of close observation unite the two birds in an aviary that is neutral territory. If this is not possible, place your original bird with the new one, assuming you are satisfied that it is healthy. The correct procedure is to quarantine the new conure for five weeks or so in an isolated place. However, if you are confident that it is healthy and have been careful in your choice of seller, isolating a young bird could cause it to become depressed. If there is more than one newcomer, this is not a problem.

Do ask the seller

- before purchase, about the origins of his stock, to reduce the risk of pairing related birds together.
- on what it has been fed, where the food containers were placed and what sort were used (possible refusal to feed out of unfamiliar containers).
- for a sample of food and make a gradual transition to your diet. Try to learn from the seller about dietary items of which you are unaware.
- for the ring or microchip number to help you to retrieve the conure if lost or stolen.

Making up new pairs

Would-be breeders might believe that buying two adult birds to make up a pair is a short-cut to success. However, adult birds, which might previously have had a mate, are usually not as easy to pair as are young birds introduced as soon as they are removed from their parents. Young birds are less territorial and less aggressive. Being more playful, another young bird is looked on as a playmate, not with the sometimes suspicious eyes of an adult. I refer to parent-reared birds – not young birds that have been hand-reared as pets. If the latter have not been socialised with their own species, another young one might invoke jealousy and dislike.

An advantage of acquiring immature birds is that they more easily adapt to new management. They more readily sample new foods, unlike adults that have been on a limited diet. Finally, you know for certain the year in which the purchased young birds hatched. This is a very important piece of information, especially if the bird is not ringed.

Some breeders expect to save time by buying older pairs. Only if they are lucky will this be the case. There can be genuine reasons for sale, but there are also sellers who do not tell the truth or withhold facts such as: the pair break their eggs or kill their chicks, the pair are carriers of a serious disease, the pair is incompatible and most likely of all, the "pair" consists of two males. Females of most species are in shorter supply.

To this list I can add: the pair are too old to breed, they have been bred as intensively as bitches in a puppy farm and although they are not so old, the female is incapable of laying any more eggs. This happens because some breeders remove eggs as laid, for artificial incubation, resulting in multiple clutches in one year. Then there are the proved breeding pairs who pluck the young in the nest, mutilate chicks' feet and wings or simply refuse to feed newly-hatched chicks.

Pyrrhuras are sexually mature by the age of two years (and some breed before then). Putting them together and watching the bond between them strengthen is very rewarding. If the breeder buys two adult birds that have not previously lived together, their introduction is often fraught with difficulty.

Selling young birds

Carefully consider the best way of finding purchasers for your young birds. If you take them to a selling show and they are not sold, they could pose a threat to your existing birds when you bring them back. Harmful virus particles are likely to be circulating in such conditions. If your birds come back to your aviaries, they could be bringing with them potentially lethal diseases. It is best to find a buyer in advance by advertising, and even better to hand over birds in their boxes in the car park, so that they do not even breathe the air of the sale hall.

5. COMPANIONS IN THE HOME

THINK carefully before you buy your first parrot. You might be tempted by a Grey Parrot with its super talking ability, or a macaw that will stun your friends with its beauty (in other words, a status symbol) or an apparently cuddly young cockatoo with big loving eyes that can grow into the biggest problem your household has ever known. The larger parrots present many difficulties in the home. If you are unaware of this, go to your nearest parrot rescue centre or obtain information about such places on-line. You won't find many *Pyrrhuras* there – perhaps one or two Green-cheeks whose owners' died or their circumstances changed.

One of the aspects of these birds that is so attractive is that they have the strength of character and personality of a much larger parrot. This gives them a charm of their own. Anyone who dismisses them as "just a small bird" is in for a surprise! These conures are exceptionally intelligent, inquisitive and spacially aware. These qualities make them so enjoyable to keep!

The small conures have many advantages in the average home compared with the larger parrots.

- They are less expensive to feed and to house.
- They have much quieter voices.
- They can have periods of freedom without fear of the furniture being reduced to wood shavings.
- They are easy to take with you if your holiday does not involve flying, or if it does, they are easily removed to a friend's home.
- *Pyrrhuras* are much easier to re-home, if necessary.
- A *Pyrrhura* will not send you to the A&E Department of your local hospital if it bites you!
- It will be unlikely to try to dominate you, as would a Grey or a macaw, therefore behavioural problems are less common.
- *Pyrrhuras* in a large cage are usually less demanding and very willing to spend long periods playing or entertaining themselves.
- They will not imitate the ringing of the telephone so realistically that you do not know the difference!
- *Pyrrhuras* eat various foods that are free for the picking, including weeds and berries.

What makes *Pyrrhuras* special? They have extremely appealing personalities, and they are full of energy and curiosity and activity. Their small size and skilful, buoyant flight make them a joy to watch in home or aviary. They have beautiful and often intricately marked plumage.

Preventing escape

If you are considering keeping one of these conures in the home, there are very important facts to consider. Its heightened degree of curiosity means it will never miss an opportunity to exit an open door (cage or house) or window. It will also investigate any small hole or crack, including in or in between items of furniture. Examine your house with this is mind and block any holes or cracks! If you have children, it is wise to keep a locked padlock on the cage door. A child should not be able to let the bird out unattended.

Temperament of different species

Just as in Amazon parrots, for example, in which only a few species are popular as pets, so it is with these conures. Those with the nicest temperament are the Rose-crowned (*rhodocephala*) and Hoffmann's. The latter was described as "docile and gentle. They do not "mark their territories" like *perlata* and *cruentata*" (Reinschmidt and Zamora Padrón, 2007). The latter two species are quite excitable and confrontational. They posture and threaten, swaggering with raised nape feathers, often leaning forward repeatedly. However, a single Crimson-bellied female that I hand-reared has been my companion for five years at the time of writing, and is a very gentle and sweet-natured bird – until you touch her cage!

Of course, individuals of any species might make good companions or poor ones. So much depends on the behaviour and sympathy of the human companion. All hand-reared parrots need a lot of attention, without which their pet potential will never be fully realised. They need to be handled daily and taught the important lesson of stepping onto the hand when requested. It is imperative that they can be moved back to the cage when necessary, not only for their own safety but because if basic discipline is not applied they may show no respect for their carer and become quite nippy.

As with all parrots, they might show a marked preference for one person. Robin Restall told me about an Emma's Conure. "It was very tame and adored me, but would fly at the children, land on their heads and pull their hair. They hated the bird – and, of course, it caused great stress within the family. I remember it was free-flying within the house when I lived alone for six weeks, spending every spare minute writing *Finches and other Seedeating Birds*. It would work its way down my arm to bite the pencil I was writing with. When it reached my wrist I would switch the pencil to the other hand and it would turn and start up the arm to get to the other hand. This would take it five minutes so I would switch the pencil back to my right hand and carry on writing. An adorable bird!"

Hand-reared or parent-reared?

Many *Pyrrhura* conures are hand-reared by breeders on the assumption that they will make better pets. I do not believe that this is true. Most parent-reared birds, if acquired three weeks after leaving the nest, are likely to be more independent and less nippy. As we all know, hand-reared parrots often become so demanding, and perhaps even aggressive towards certain members of the household, that the pleasure in keeping them diminishes.

I acquired two young Crimson-bellied Conures on the same day from different breeders. The male was parent-reared, the female hand-reared. The male was not at all tame but he was curious about the spoon-feeding. Sometimes he would sidle up to the female and take some of the warm food from her beak. Eventually, after about five weeks, he plucked up the courage to take food from the spoon. In so doing, he became less fearful and more inclined to approach me closely. By the time she was five months old, the female was starting to nip me when I placed the food dishes in their holders or removed them. She learned very quickly not to do this when I presented the palm of my hand to her and said "No!". The male, on the other hand, is respectful and never nips. He will approach me closely and display if I talk to him, running rapidly up and down the perch and making the rapid beak clicking sounds so typical of excited *Pyrrhuras*.

This pair are an absolute joy to keep – so cheeky, colourful and communicative. It would be difficult to think of more enchanting birds.

They might be described as falling between the definitions of pet birds and aviary birds. They are not kept in the home but in the birdroom which is close to the kitchen, with an outdoor cage which I pass many times each day. In the summer months I seldom pass by without pushing some oats or wheat in the green stage through the wire so they are constantly watching for me. If I pass them without a glance, they make a single, high-pitched note to attract my attention. They always want to come to "talk" to me – and this surely is the greatest pleasure of bird keeping – when birds have enough space to fly and fly towards you.

Training from an early age, that is, reinforcing commands to step up or fly to the owner on a daily basis, will help to maintain a good relationship between conure and carer. On the other hand, a parent-reared *Pyrrhura* will take longer to become friendly but if it is acquired soon after it becomes independent, it will become tame if it receives much attention. However, my view is that a young bird which has known conure family life (in contrast to hand-reared birds) should not be deprived of the company of its own kind. It deserves a companion. This does not mean that it will never become tame.

Obtain a young bird

A companion bird must be acquired when young. These sociable conures should not be alone unless hand-reared and removed from their own kind at an early age. An adult bird will be most unhappy when confined in a cage away from its own species. I received a telephone call from someone who had naively bought an adult Green-cheeked Conure as a pet. It was so noisy his wife relegated it to the garden shed. An adult bird separated from its species will call endlessly. In this case the husband built an aviary and placed the conure inside with a lovebird. These strange companions were compatible and the lovebird even fed the conure! It is typical of such small, sociable parrots that in the absence of their own kind, they will befriend another species.

Reading body language – and nipping

One of the most common reasons for nipping or biting in a parrot is because the owner is asking it to do something which is not appropriate at that time. It might want to rest or to eat – not to step up and come out. If a *Pyrrhura* is standing upright, with nape feathers erect, and quickly moving the head backwards and forwards, as though preparing to lunge, it will almost certainly nip if approached. When it struts backwards and forwards on the perch, with an exaggerated gait, this is part of a display which could be sexual or aggressive but certainly denotes a state of excitement. Leave it alone! Wait until it is calm and responsive.

Nipping also occurs because of territorial behaviour regarding the cage. Many adult parrots will nip if you put your hand inside. That is their territory and you do not enter uninvited! You wait for the bird to come out if you need to do something to the interior. This behaviour might abate with time but it should always be respected. Forcing your wishes on your conure is not advisable! It is small but it has a mind of its own!

A single hand-reared bird should remain tame and friendly. It will be fearless – but will it go through a nippy stage? Nipping can be difficult to eliminate in a small parrot. Many young hand-reared parrots go through a period when they nip people. Perhaps like wayward teenagers they are just testing – to see how much they can get away with.

In June 2012 I reluctantly removed from the nest the two three-week old young of my Crimson-bellied Conures due to inadequate feeding by the parents of these, their first chicks. Reared in my kitchen, they were allowed to fly there to increase their flight skills. Two or three days after learning to fly they were performing aerial manoeuvres that would put most parrots to shame.

Young pair of Crimson-bellied Conures always looking for mischief in the home.
Photograph © Rosemary Low

At the time of writing they are ten months old and their nippy behaviour is not pleasant! They fly to me a lot but that is their choice as I never handle them except to return them to the cage.

In the evenings they fly free in the kitchen while I wash the dishes. They delight in games that demonstrate their flight skills, swooping and diving, sometimes at me or around me (mischievously just skimming my head).

Sometimes they fly after each other with such speed, making sudden turns, that it amazes me that they do not collide. They always land high up – on the pelmet, the top of the kitchen units or the window handle. After some energetic flying, or sometimes before, they turn their attention to me, landing on my head, shoulders or hands, or climbing on my sweatshirt. This leads to them ending up on my shoulders, biting my ears or the back of my neck – not hard enough to draw blood but still unpleasant.

Why did they develop this biting habit? It was not, as suggested to me, because they did not want to be handled. I never initiated contact with them or handled them when they flew to me. Perhaps nipping is a natural extension of the curiosity they show about everything in their environment. There is no surface in the kitchen, except the floor and the cooker, that has not been explored. I did not realise how often they bit me until both started to say: "Stop it!"

My two explore and nibble almost everything – porcelain parrots, cooking dishes, cupboard doors (care!), the tops of bottles, fruit left on the counter (but not human food), dishes that I am drying, tea towels and hand towels. They particularly enjoy swinging and clinging to curtains and the beaded pull of the window blind, the latter being treated like a sort of liana. Anything that can be tested with the beak is bitten. This includes each other; they play rough, with the female more often being on the receiving end. So why should I be exempt from the activity of their busy beaks?

Biting is often said to stem from attention-seeking – but my two have my full attention, especially when they land on my hand. Perhaps they nip just to get a reaction from me. After all, they seem to enjoy hearing me say "Stop it!", judging by the number of times they repeat this when they are chattering away contentedly. I have tried not to react to their nips but that can be hard! I believe this nipping is just youthful exuberance and curiosity. However, the assertive personality of the Crimson-bellied might also influence this behaviour.

To deter a parrot from nipping a behaviourist would advise a distraction technique such as wobbling the hand just before it bites. This clearly does not work at the back of the neck. Again, the usual advice is not to allow a bird to perch on your shoulder (or neck) but it would damage the relationship to repeatedly prevent this when the conure is so insistent!

Mimicry

The ability to mimic is of no interest to people who love birds for the wonderful creatures they are. I for one do not wish to make them more like humans! However, "Will it talk?" is a much-asked question. Some conures will mimic human language in a small gravelly voice. Terry Quinn wrote: "I consider all my Green-cheeks to be pets. I talk to them all the time and both males in each pairing speak entire sentences. I don't know exactly what they are saying for sure, but they repeat whatever they are saying over and over again – it is very comical" (*Parrots* magazine, November 2009).

One Rose-fronted started to imitate kisses at the age of three months. By ten months he could repeat his name, "Whatcha doin?", "Good boy" and "Bye-bye". Generally, in small parrots, including Budgerigars and Cockatiels, males are far superior mimics to females.

The first words of my male Crimson-bellied, before the age of five months, were: "What are you doing?" One month later the female started to repeat these words. Sometimes, when inside the cage and wanting my attention, they know they can get it by repeating these words in a very appealing little voice.

Wing-clipping

Parrots have their quality of life immensely curtailed by wing-clipping. And their health may be compromised. This is especially true of *Pyrrhuras*: they delight in flight, especially in a large space, and are wonderfully skilful on the wing. I am strongly against wing-clipping under normal circumstances. To deprive a bird of the joy of flight is cruel, in my opinion. If a family cannot cope with a winged pet, obtaining a rabbit or a guinea pig would be more sensible. If parrots are to remain in good health over their full life-span (20-30 years in most small parrots), they need to fly for their muscles and heart to remain in good condition. Many wing-clipped birds become overweight. Some become nervous or nippy due to the fear of falling.

The most usual argument in favour of wing-clipping is that it prevents a bird escaping. This is not true. Some have escaped and been run over in the street. Owners of a wing-clipped bird have a false sense of security. Many forget to check the state of the moult and do not notice when some flight feathers have grown back. An open door or window then leads to the bird's escape. A screen at exterior doors can save your bird's life.

Close supervision is essential when it is outside the cage. There are so many hazards. A play stand, with toys, ropes and swings, might be the focus of the bird's attention, but because *Pyrrhuras* delight in flying, a stand does not interest them as much as it does a larger parrot. To test if a stand will be used, drill a hole in the centre of an old coffee table, search for a suitable branch with branches going out at right angles, and insert this into the centre of the table.

This is a place to fly to when it is let out. It might amuse itself without demanding human attention. A tame bird will spend time out of its cage with a human. However, if it does not receive constant attention it can become demanding or nippy. This is where a play stand would be useful to divert its attention – if only it would use it! Without a focus, it will fly to a high place, such as a pelmet, and can be difficult to retrieve.

Harnesses

One owner of a Green-cheeked Conure complained that her bird would not allow her to put a harness on him and bit her. I believe it is unreasonable to expect a small parrot to tolerate a harness. Some do – but I doubt that it is comfortable for them.

Cages

The small size of *Pyrrhura* conures can lead to the assumption that they do not need a large cage. Not true! They are highly active and forever moving about so a small cage does not suit them. A Cockatiel cage is too small but cages made for larger parrots, such as Amazons, are too tall and the bars too wide. They need a cage with more length than height. The solution is to make a cage from welded mesh. If 12g mesh is used, it will be substantial enough to last for years but not too heavy to move about. Suggested measurements are 1.3m to 2m long, 44cm wide and 58cm high. The base should be high enough to bring the top of the cage to eye-level height. A company that manufactures aluminium products could make a tray to fit, also a base with castors, to move the cage to another location.

Cage contents

A piece of plastic pipe can be attached to one end of the cage to take a branch that can be changed every week. In the autumn, branches with berries will provide nutritious food as well as essential gnawing material. However, beware the type of hawthorn with long thorns. Either cut off the spines or seek out the kind with less vicious spikes, for fear a conure could be trapped by a thorn between leg and ring.

Swings are enjoyed. It is easy to make a simple swing using a short length of branch from an apple tree, for example, and two short lengths of chain from a hardware store secured by a staple. Or a small hole can be drilled in each end of the branch or dowel, and a length of strong 10g wire bent into a triangular shape, each end being inserted into the drilled hole. Conures also like vertical "swings" – easily created by putting a forked twig through the top of the cage.

Toys

Toys made from natural materials, such as wood and pine cones, are recommended. According to veterinarian Dr Ross Perry, plastic toys are a potential source of petrochemicals including those that mimic female hormones. They can interfere with hormone balance. When you provide a new toy, never do so just before you leave the house. You need to see the reaction – fear, delight or exposure of a hazard.

Before purchasing a toy think carefully about its possible hazards. Can the conure get its head or toes trapped in any part of it? Clips and links used to hang the toy are often plated or dipped in zinc. Wash metal parts in vinegar to remove excess zinc residues. (And do the same with new welded mesh if you are making a cage.) Stainless steel links, clips and D-clips are safer, not cheap ones containing poisonous zinc.

A possibly deadly component of toys is polished cotton. Fine threads from this can become wrapped around toes or legs, cutting off the circulation, or can get wrapped around the neck, strangling the unfortunate bird. Carefully examine all toys for fine threads before purchase. A friend's conure nearly died from a toy with a straw hat made from cotton. This thread unravelled and the conure became terribly entangled. It would have died had not the owner been there to release the very shocked bird.

It is often safer to make your own toys – and so easy, using a drill, some small blocks of untreated wood (offcuts), strips of leather and perhaps some old cotton reels. Rope toys that have free ends are quickly unravelled by some parrots, leaving a mass of individual threads. These are a hazard as they could become entwined in the feet or around the neck. Cut them short at the first sign that they are coming loose. The rope used on some toys is not hard or tight enough. It is easily unravelled by some birds, with the possibility of strangulation. Free-hanging ropes must be knotted at intervals to prevent this terrible accident. Rope toys become very dirty so put them in the washing machine every now and then.

Music from the radio

Birds that are left alone for part of the day can derive great enjoyment from the radio. Individual tastes vary. My Crimson-bellied prefers loud pop music to the classics and often responds excitedly to rock 'n roll. On one occasion I watched a concert on the television with her. A famous Romanian man, a virtuoso with the pan pipes, started to play. She was mesmerised. She sat quite still, looking at the screen and listening intently. The instrument was very high-pitched. When he stopped playing her behaviour returned to normal.

Aviary birds that need to be shut inside during bad weather and for long periods during the northern winter, also benefit from music.

Plumage care

Access to water for bathing is essential. The small water container that comes with the cage is not adequate for bathing purposes. An owner might see their bird dipping his head inside and trying, unsuccessfully, to flick the water over its plumage. A bird bath, such as one made for Canaries to hang on the side of the cage, might suffice. Many owners let their birds enjoy a bath in the sink under a running tap (not hot water). Some like going in the shower. Others will bathe in a dish. Alternatively, a plant mister can be used to give them a fine spray. Care should be taken not to spray young birds too heavily and to ensure that the room is warm.

One or two birds?

Whether or not they are tame, *Pyrrhuras* will appreciate a companion of their own kind – preferably acquired at the same time or soon after. Only the purchaser of a hand-reared bird, who can spend much time with it daily, should consider buying a single pet. The behaviour of these highly social birds is always more interesting to observe when they can interact with others. I had never had two young birds as companions until I hand-reared two young Crimson-bellied. I would whole heartedly recommend it. They are never alone and they always have a playmate For me the benefit lies in being able to observe them interacting together in a natural way. It is more satisfying than a single, clinging hand-reared bird which is totally dependent on a human companion for amusement and affection and lacking in many opportunities to practice normal behaviour.

A behavioural problem

It is not the case that there will never be a problem with a companion *Pyrrhura*, only that problems are rarer than with most parrots. One owner was very distressed about the behaviour of her Maroon-bellied Conure of whom she was very fond. It was 21 years old and had been with her for twenty years. She rescued it from a family whose children had mistreated it and it was so wild it would not go near her for three months. After such a long problem-free period, it became extremely noisy and aggressive and was inflicting serious bites. Previously it was tame and affectionate, and would sit with her for one hour at a time, when let out morning and evening.

It had become so noisy she had to cover the cage to get some peace. Living in council accommodation, she was afraid neighbours would complain. This was a very sad case. She was a pensioner, due to go into hospital and lived on her own and could not tolerate much more. Because the conure was so aggressive she could not give it away to a private individual. What was the alternative, she asked? Euthanasia? All I could suggest was finding it a home in an aviary.

What triggered this behaviour after two decades without problems? Without knowing more, one can only guess the reason. Twenty plus years is a fair age for a *Pyrrhura* conure. Perhaps the answer was that the bird had an underlying health problem and it was in pain. Consulting an avian vet who could carry out a blood test might have thrown some light on this difficult case.

Sometimes owners perceive some aspect of behaviour as problematical. One man wrote to me about his mother's male Green-cheeked Conure which was trying to mate with the perch and even with its own tail. Such behaviour is often seen in single birds when in breeding condition. It can last a few weeks. The bird was very tame and was his mother's constant companion. Buying a mate for it was not the answer. If we keep birds on their own, depriving them of a mate, we should not be surprised if they show sexual behaviour!

Sufficient sleep

An adult *Pyrrhura* needs at least nine hours of sleep each night. A young bird needs about twelve hours. For this reason the cage should not be in a room at night where a television is turned on or there are other lights and disturbances. A small cardboard box will be appreciated for sleeping. Cloth tents made for parrots can be hazardous if there are loose fibres.

6. HEALTH CONCERNS

GOOD nutrition, plenty of flight exercise and a safe environment are the principal requirements for keeping *Pyrrhuras* healthy for two decades or more. They are tough little birds that will give no cause for concern if common sense is exercised in their care.

Infections

Infections of any kind are rare where conures are kept in a clean, vermin-proof environment. Mice, rats and parasites carry disease and could contaminate food and water containers. Dirty perches are likely to result in an eye infection. These symptoms of bad management must be avoided. Cleanliness is so important.

Fungal infections can result from badly stored or contaminated seed. Contamination by aflatoxin is common in cereal grains and nuts and is produced by the fungus *Aspergillus flavus*. Exposure to it can cause cancer of the liver, destruction of the immune system and eventually death. Peanuts are a likely source – but conures should not be given peanuts, especially those in the shell that might hide mouldy nuts.

Be aware that infections, bacterial or viral, can be contracted by birds in places where a large number are present, such as sale days or pet stores. If you are buying or selling at a sale day, it is wiser to make the transaction inside a vehicle, rather than take a bird into the sale venue. Also be aware that birds that have been removed from their usual environment, and perhaps kept in a box for many hours, are susceptible to stress. *(See Chapter 4, New Stock.)*

Signs of disease are:

- Ruffled feathers and lethargic appearance.
- Frequent closing of eyes and/or sleeping on two feet.
- Difficulty in or rapid breathing.
- Weight loss. (A sick bird can lose 25% of its weight in 24 hours).
- Excessive thirst or food intake.
- Diarrhoea and/or blood in the droppings.
- Sudden loss of use of legs.

If any of these signs are noted, the bird should be isolated and placed under a heat lamp (see page 42), with a temperature of at least 27 °C (80°F). A sick bird loses heat rapidly. If you have to go to a vet surgery, keep the bird's cage covered with a blanket and make sure the car is heated. A sick bird might rapidly become dehydrated. Try to encourage it to drink and put some glucose or honey in a small amount of water. If it is tame, it might readily take liquid or food from a spoon.

It is no good guessing at the cause or asking other birdkeepers. It is important to consult a vet. Even although many vets have no specialist knowledge of birds, they can carry out basic tests. The starting point might be to take a faecal sample so that tests for bacterial infections and intestinal parasites can be carried out. If a bird has to stay at a vet's premises, take your own food and give instructions the bird should not be offered anything else. This applies especially to pellets; if it has never seen them before, it would probably starve.

In the home

Companion birds live in very close association with humans, thus any change in their behaviour, appetite, faeces, hours of sleep and alertness should be quickly apparent. If the change cannot be explained and suggests ill health, do not delay in consulting a vet. This can be expensive. The person with only one or two birds should consider veterinary insurance. Every bird keeper should also know the location of the nearest avian vet as most vets in general practice have little experience with companion birds. Note that some avicultural magazines list vets who are used to dealing with parrots. If a specialist is not available, consult a vet who is prepared to be advised by an avian referral service.

Conures in the home should never be left unattended when outside the cage. They are so fearless and inquisitive that they can easily get into serious trouble that leads to death or escape. Care must be taken to protect them from fumes such as those from glue, hairspray, cleaning products, curling irons (PTFE fumes) and air fresheners. Conures should not be allowed in the kitchen – not only because open doors and windows lead to escape but because cooking hobs and pots are dangerous. However, the biggest dangers are Teflon pans. When heated they give off lethal fumes that kill small birds in seconds and also kill larger parrots.

Another possible danger is inhaling gas fumes from a faulty gas appliance. If your bird seems sleepy the cause might be gas fumes. They can kill – birds and human. A carbon monoxide alarm is a sensible and inexpensive investment.

Most owners know that regular exposure to cigarette smoke can cause respiratory disease that will eventually kill parrots. It can also cause eye and skin diseases. Smoking in the home is not compatible with parrot keeping.

Access to sunlight

Conures in a breeding situation should not be permanently deprived access to outdoor flights, that is, to direct sunlight or to rain on their plumage. It can have a highly detrimental effect on their health and on their plumage. See *Birdroom Lighting* in Chapter 3 for information on the importance of good lighting.

Wing and tail feathers of two Crimson-bellied Conures, moulted by the age of nine months. The worn tail feathers are the result of daily bouts of wrestling!

Photograph © Rosemary Low

The moult

Pyrrhuras moult once annually over a period of several weeks. At no time should the fact that they are moulting be apparent – except in a single bird that has no one to preen its head, which will show a number of pin feathers. The moult will not affect the health of a bird in good condition, but all moulting birds will benefit from extra protein during the moult.

Young birds start to moult at the age of about four and a half months. The first feathers to be shed are those of the head and breast, and other small contour feathers. The wing and tail feathers are shed over a period of several weeks, between the ages of six and nine months. At nine months, my Crimson-bellied were still shedding primary feathers, about one every one or two weeks. At ten months, the first new tail feather was fully grown.

Heavy metal poisoning

Few birds are more inquisitive and adventurous than *Pyrrhura* conures. They boldly go where other parrots fear to tread! And they nibble at everything in their path. This means that they are susceptible to heavy metal poisoning. Ingestion of lead and zinc will kill unless the bird is treated by a vet as a matter of emergency. Items containing chromium, copper and mercury are also risky. The following are dangerous: galvanised metal (it contains zinc), silver paper and fruit juice cartons lined with it, lead pencils, mirror backing (it contains mercury), metal key rings and keys, curtain weights, galvanised items, mobile phones and some items of jewellery. Do not assume that parrot toys are safe: some are not! Artificial colouring, usually food colouring, is used to make most toys – but some dyes have heavy metal components. Bells and metal rings are usually chrome-plated. If they become rusty they are potentially a source of heavy metal poisoning. These products can interfere with a bird's metabolism, possibly causing infections or cancer.

The symptoms of heavy metal poisoning include abnormal thirst, gastro-enteritis, loss of weight, anaemia, feather plucking and, in some cases, seizures. The condition can be diagnosed by a blood test.

Blood sugar level

In the USA a Green-cheeked Conure became covered in ash after landing in a fireplace. It was bathed to remove the dirt but this caused it stress and the conure went limp in the hand. It recovered in less than a minute. This state was probably caused by lowered blood pressure resulting in a sudden drop in blood sugar level. In such rare cases veterinary advice should be sought and a health check carried out. Incidentally, bathing a bird with soiled plumage is usually only necessary if it has been contaminated with oil. Otherwise it is safer to spray it with warm water.

Toxic human foods

Tame birds often want to sample what the family is eating and drinking – but there are some items that should be avoided due to their toxicity. These include alcohol, avocado, asparagus, chocolate (especially the 70% and higher solids dark chocolate) and caffeinated drinks such as coffee and cola.

Aviary birds in winter

If a conure is feeling the cold, this could indicate an underlying disease problem or that the bird is older than you think. If possible, shut it into the indoor quarters and place a heat lamp above the cage; otherwise bring it into the house or birdroom. This is not always convenient and could mean it will be some weeks before it can be returned outside – but the alternative might be its death. Its welfare must take priority – and anyone not prepared to take a little trouble to prevent this, should not be keeping birds. Their lives are in our hands.

During the winter careful observation of every bird, morning and evening, is essential because when a bird becomes sick it can deteriorate very quickly.

Unfortunately, many beginners do not realise the importance of extra heat for birds that are unwell.

Every birdroom should contain a small open-fronted cage (enclosed sides to retain heat) set up where an infra-red lamp can be plugged in. Buy a lamp, holder and reflector. Ceramic holders for ceramic infra-red lamps have a ring on the top. Attach a length of chain to this and screw a cup-hook to the roof above this small cage so that the lamp can be lowered to the desired height, and moved higher as the bird recovers and needs less heat. It is important to have this ready because a motive for not bringing in a bird that looks unwell is lack of time. Be prepared and it takes only a few seconds to catch the bird and place it in the cage.

A ceramic infra-red lamp is vitally important for sick birds. It emits only heat – no light.

Photograph © Rosemary Low

Note that inexpensive infra-red lamps that look like large red light bulbs, are not suitable and break easily. They give out light whereas ceramic infra-red bulbs do not and, if treated with care, they last for years.

Adequate feeding

Birds maintain their body temperature better in cold weather when they have a suitable diet. Seed-eating parrots in aviaries will benefit from a slightly higher oilseed intake. Hemp is a favourite and highly nutritious and often withheld during the summer months – but limit the amount available when it is added to the winter diet as many parrots would eat little else if given the opportunity.

Note that birds that are plucked on the body and head cannot retain heat efficiently. Bare-headed birds will lose most heat. They are best housed inside for the duration of the colder months, as are old birds.

Longevity

The potential life-span of a *Pyrrhura* is in the region of 23 years. Please look after your birds carefully to ensure that they do not die prematurely.

7. DIET AND NUTRITION

WHAT DOES any parrot in cage or aviary look forward to most? As with many humans, it is feeding times. Note the word *times*. I believe that all parrots should be fed more than once daily; this increases the interaction between birds and carers, and provides diversion for these intelligent birds. They soon become bored and varying what they receive on a daily basis, adds greatly to their contentment and anticipation. Conures and other parrots have more taste buds than most birds and are therefore more discerning about what they eat. They really enjoy their food. So much so, that some males with chauvinistic tendencies have no hesitation in stealing food from the foot or the beak of the female!

When you give them something they really relish, such as a green ear of wheat, they make little chittering sounds of contentment. It always makes me happy to hear this!

Pyrrhuras hold everything larger than a small seed in the foot and consume it with apparent relish! The way food is presented can be important. If I give a piece of orange on a fruit hanger, it might only be nibbled around the edges. But if I cut orange into tiny pieces it will be eaten down to the rind because it is easily held in the foot.

One of the satisfying aspects of keeping them is that they readily sample almost any food, in contrast to cautious birds, like Grey Parrots. *Pyrrhuras* are very food-orientated birds and greatly look forward to feeding times. This is why I give different food items during the day: seed and fruit in the morning, sweetcorn kernels and wholegrain bread at midday and a soaked fig and berries, as available, late afternoon.

One breeder told me that he feeds only seed and apple, except during the breeding season. "I get good results", he said. "So why should I change anything?" Why? Because this philosophy does not take into account the quality of life of his birds. Quality of life means a safe and suitable environment, the company of their own species, enough space to fly strongly and a diet that is VARIED, not monotonous. That diet must be suited to the species' requirements. In the case of *Pyrrhuras* the defining words should be: Think green! During the warmer months I grow and pick foods such as green oats and green wheat and push them through the wire as I pass the aviaries at various times. Lack of time is no excuse; if this is not possible, there are too many birds in the collection.

Some breeders base their diet on convenience: what is quick and easy to feed. They also standardise the diet if there are other parrots of different genera in the collection, even though these have varying dietary needs. This is regrettable, as it invariably results in dietary monotony and even deficiencies.

Seeding grasses and dandelion flowers provide food and entertainment. Note the hanging bath which is the best way of providing water to aviary birds.

Photograph © Rosemary Low

Pyrrhuras, even more than most parrots, seem to have a need to be constantly nibbling, preferably food or fresh-cut branches, but in reality anything in their vicinity, and preferably something green that was growing a few minutes before.

Nature's foods

The finest foods our birds can eat are natural ones. I firmly believe that nature provides the very best. *Pyrrhuras* seem to know this. They will always eat something green in preference to dry seed – and in this respect they differ from many other parrots.

Despite the warnings regarding collecting weeds from public places, this is generally safe. Obviously, the foods should be clean, not frosted and from an uncontaminated source – that is, not in areas where herbicides or pesticides are used. I regularly collect wild foods from verges and hedgerows (even along main roads) without problems. However, look at the location through a dog's eyes and avoid those near lampposts! Also, some local councils spray verges and even pavements with weed killers during the summer months – so it is wise to check with the council office.

The items I collect include:

Dandelion *(Taraxacum officinale)*: a common and highly beneficial weed with long leaves, usually jagged when mature, that rise upwards in a tight cluster or rosette. The root is thick and dark brown, white and milky inside and the flowers have a dense golden crown. You can feed a whole young plant with some soil attached which makes it more attractive to some birds as they search for minerals. The young tender leaves will be eaten, not the larger, older leaves. The whole plant can be hung in cage or aviary or tender leaves can be added to a mixture of fruit and vegetables or just pushed through the wire. It is a good source of calcium and potassium.

Smooth sowthistle (*Sonchus oleraceus*) has glossy pointed leaves and flowers that resemble those of a small dandelion. I believe that it is equally beneficial. Pull the whole plant or remove leaves when the plant is young and succulent. Prickly sowthistle (*Sonchus asper*) will not be eaten.

Chickweed (*Stellaria media*), with its tender juicy stems and tiny white flowers, is especially good for pairs rearing young. Found on waste ground, and in vegetable gardens and planters, it grows rapidly after rain. It can be cultivated and, with regular watering, available for many months.

Dock (*Rumex crispus*). The seeds (available late summer to autumn) are greatly relished, green or ripe. They can be dried and stored for winter use.

Grasses and cereals

Many parakeets consume seeding grasses with great relish when feeding chicks. You can also plant oats and give them in the green seeding stage – one of the favourite foods of my conures, eagerly consumed. One can also feed in the green stage wheat (another great favourite), corn, buckwheat and oil seed rape. It is worth attempting to grow spray millet but, in the UK, it might not ripen. It is easy to grow canary seed – and the small round heads are relished before they are ripe. When one sees the great enjoyment and benefits from these green growing items, it is well worth the extra effort to provide them. They can be grown and presented in small containers, or picked and pushed through the wire.

Berries

In the wild *Pyrrhuras* feed mainly on soft items such as figs and other fruits, berries, flowers and catkins. The dextrous and rapid way in which they manipulate a berry indicates that this is a natural item of food. Small berries such as *Cotoneaster dammeri* (with its bright red berries), mountain ash or rowan (*Sorbus aucuparia*) and elder (*Sambucus nigra*) are favourites with *Pyrrhura* conures. Berries are preferred when they are plump and ripe. Hawthorn (*Crataegus*) berries are especially relished. The fleshy part of the berry is usually discarded and the small hard kernel in the centre is manipulated between both mandibles until the kernel is extracted.

Along with blackberries, which grow at higher altitudes in South America, this is the nearest we can get to feeding natural foods. The Brown-breasted (Flame-winged) Conure eats blackberries in its Andean habitat, perhaps due to a poverty of food resources. Most captive birds do not take them, perhaps because more attractive foods are available.

Cultivated greenfoods and vegetables

In my experience, spinach beet is the most popular of the green leaves so it is worth setting aside an area to grow it. It is easy to cultivate and will last throughout the winter, even surviving under several inches of snow. The fleshy stalks are especially relished. Broccoli and broccoli leaves will be eaten by many *Pyrrhuras* but cabbage is ignored. Vegetables that are likely to be accepted are carrot (preferably par-boiled), celery, and corn on the cob cut into small pieces. Beetroot and its leaves can also be offered. Peas will be eaten and mange tout, with their soft pods and tiny peas, are enjoyed.

The beta-carotene content of tomatoes, broccoli, sweet red pepper and carrot are converted to Vitamin A which is essential for the health of all parrots. Celery, when crisp and still crunchy, is another favourite, with some Vitamin A benefits.

Photograph © Rosemary Low

Cultivated fruits provide roughage and usually small amounts of vitamins A and C. In minute quantities they contain some important amino acids, such as lysine and methionine, minerals and traces of fat. While captive conures usually like fruits that are sweet, such as grapes, apples and satsumas, in the wild they eat small fruits that are unbearably bitter to the human taste. However, often they are taking the seeds from these fruits, rather than consuming the flesh. In the wild most parrots eat mangoes before they are ripe. Those imported into Europe are not readily eaten, perhaps because they have been in storage for a long time.

The degree of ripeness is important. Strawberries and raspberries bought ready to eat, are over-ripe for conures – but offered while they are still slightly hard they might be enjoyed. Why should we make an effort to feed these red berries? Research on women has shown that strawberries and blueberries have enormous health benefits. Eating just three handfuls per week results in a 32% decrease in heart attacks compared with those who eat them only once a month. This is because they contain flavonoid plant compounds called anthocyanins that help to unblock arteries. As many parrots suffer from atherosclerosis (hardening of the arteries) due to a diet containing an excess of high fat foods such as sunflower, feeding strawberries could have great health benefits.

Pear needs to be fed at exactly the right stage of ripeness – too hard or too soft and it will be ignored. Passionfruit is enjoyed by many conures and they all like apple. For one of my Rose-headed Conures, the best part is the pip. He goes straight for it! No, it is not true that pips are poisonous!

One of the best fruits we can feed to our parrots is **papaya**. It contains enzymes that aid digestion, such as papain, and break down proteins to make the amino acids available. Papaya is especially valuable when added to the food of parrot chicks being hand-reared. Studies at the University of Nigeria revealed that extracts of ripe and unripe papaya and of seeds are active against gram negative bacteria. Fresh crushed seeds yield bactericidal and fungicidal agents.

Figs A soaked dried Turkish fig hung on a fruit hanger is perhaps the most favoured food item of my conures. They usually have one per pair daily. Some of these figs can be fed dry if they are slightly moist. The figs we can buy may bear little resemblance to the types they eat in the wild which are such an important part of the diet of many *Pyrrhuras*.

Cherries are not always accepted but Rosemary Cooper wrote about her Black-tailed Conures: "The sight of a couple of birds with cherries was hilarious; they could hardly eat their way to the stone fast enough; as soon as one had reached it the other would drop his cherry and dash over for a tug of war with the stone, usually won by one bird putting a foot in the other one's face and pushing! They spent hours trying to crack the stones, but eventually gave up and finished the edible part of the cherries" (Cooper, 1979).

In the UK Les Waring's conures enjoyed the wild cherries that fell on to the aviary roof. They would lick them "for hours" until the stone was totally clean of flesh. They also ate any flowers they could reach in the hanging baskets. It is worth noting that parrots readily take items thrown on to the roof of aviary or cage.

Try lots of different fruits!

Breeders have different experiences regarding the types of fruits and vegetables that will be accepted. For this reason, different fruits, presented in different ways, should be offered. However, mine will not eat kiwi or banana. Gerhard Schmidt told me: "Fruits and vegetables are offered daily (apple, grape, mandarin and pear). They eat nearly everything but do not like banana and kiwi very much. They particularly like to eat red items such as strawberries, tomato, rowan berries, *pyracantha* berries and redcurrants. We regularly give fresh branches and foliage."

Vitamin A

This vitamin is of great importance because it promotes healthy skin and healthy cells that line many parts of the body such as nostrils, throat, lungs, stomach and respiratory tract. Respiratory diseases are especially common in parrots and usually the result of a poor diet. Foods that are high in Vitamin A include sweet red peppers, carrot (raw or par-boiled), broccoli and cooked sweet potato (orange-fleshed varieties), and especially mango and papaya. The leaves and roots of dandelion are also valuable sources. Fortunately, *Pyrrhuras* readily take these items so unless seed is fed to excess, they are less likely than most parrots to suffer from a Vitamin A deficiency.

The best source of Vitamin A is fresh foods – not a multi-vitamin preparation, even although these products contain far more of this vitamin than any others, because you can overdose it. Birds convert beta-carotene to Vitamin A as they need it so in the more natural forms it cannot be overdosed.

Pulses

Pulses (peas, beans and lentils) are valuable (especially for pairs rearing young) for their high protein content and for some of the B vitamins when sprouted. Bird food companies sell pulse mixtures for sprouting or cooking but certain beans are not popular with parrots and might be ignored. It is advisable to soak pulses overnight, then rinse well. Tinned products can be used as canning does not affect the protein content, eliminates the need for soaking and reduces the cooking time.

Lentils, mung beans and chickpeas are good for sprouting. Chickpeas and lentils are suitable for cooking. Red kidney beans are toxic unless cooked. Pulses should not be fed to excess because they contain too much phosphorous. A calcium/phosphorous imbalance can cause bone deformities in young birds and inhibit calcium absorption in adults. A teaspoonful per bird a couple of times a week makes an excellent addition to the diet of pet birds when they are moulting but unless they have been offered these from an early age they might be ignored.

Pulses should be sprouted or cooked to destroy the trypsin inhibitors that impair protein digestion. First, soak them for a day, drain, wash and leave in a

The first solid foods eaten by these young Crimson-bellied Conures were sprouted lentils and beans. Photograph © Rosemary Low

warm place until they have just started to sprout. The food value is not so high if they are cooked but in this form they might be more palatable. Sprinkle a favourite food item over them or even the juice of a freshly squeezed orange. Pulses toughen on storage and will take longer to cook. Most dried pulses need soaking for several hours before cooking; exceptions are lentils, green and yellow split peas, blackeye and mung beans. Cook in fresh water without any salt, which toughens the skins and increases the cooking time.

Growing greenfoods indoors

You can grow your own greenfood indoors. All you need is a tall 450g yoghurt container or something similar with a 10cm diameter top, some organic compost and a few seeds. Plant the seeds, water lightly and place in a warm place – perhaps on a sill above a radiator. In a few days you will have a pot packed with fresh green leaves. I use the hanger for a 9cm stainless steel cup, hook it onto the cage and place the pot in the hanger. This prevents it spilling and keeps it securely anchored.

Suitable seeds for producing "baby greens" include milk thistle (*Silybum marianum*) – used for 2,000 years to treat liver disease and to protect the liver against toxins. There are cheaper alternatives, such as mustard and cress. Whichever you use, the fresh green leaves will be a nutritious source of food and occupation.

Bread

Greatly relished by my birds (*Pyrrhuras* and lories) is bread – not the bland white variety but a seeded batch loaf from a well-known company. It contains five seeds: sesame, sunflower, linseed, millet and maw (poppy seed). It has a very pleasant taste and texture. Similar products of a different brand are rejected by most of my birds! The protein content is 12.3% and the fat content is 8.9%. It also contains calcium propionate to inhibit mould growth. My conures will take it dry, removing the small pieces from the food container before anything else. I also feed it moistened with lory nectar and in this form it is *ideal* for young birds and easy to add a calcium supplement. Nectar, as made up for captive lories, is a very good food for conures. We should not forget that flowers and nectar form an important part of the diet for many species in the wild.

Calcium supplementation

Parakeets fed mainly on seed will be deficient in calcium because the calcium content of seeds in parakeet/parrot mixtures is less than 0.1%. Seeds also contain high levels of phosphate in the form of phytic acid, which can form complexes with calcium in the intestine, thereby preventing adequate calcium absorption (Stanford in Low, 2006). What is seldom realised is that conures and other parrots fed on pellets can also lack this vital dietary component. In the USA in the late 1990s the diet of 135 pet parrots was examined. It was found that 96% of those fed pellets were not receiving adequate calcium. Apparently, unless a bird was fed 100% of this food, the calcium intake would not be adequate. A deficiency can have very serious consequences, affecting the health and the behaviour of the bird.

Calcium supplements for birds (combined with Vitamin D3) are readily available. Supplements should be added to food, by putting the powder or syrup inside a grape or in a spoonful of rearing food or other favoured food. It is not advisable to add supplements to water because conures and other parrots drink only small amounts. Adding a calcium supplement daily to the rearing food for birds rearing young and for females one month before the first egg is expected is advised.

Vitamin D3 is essential for calcium absorption and exposure to ultraviolet wavelengths is essential for the synthesis of Vitamin D3. There are two methods of supplying this: direct unfiltered sunlight acquired in outside aviaries, or the use of ultraviolet lights. These can be bought in the form of fluorescent lighting tubes and should be used by breeders who keep their conures permanently inside buildings. The companion bird owner can buy a UV bulb which fits into an anglepoise lamp. Two hours per day exposure to the lamp, especially in winter, will be highly beneficial.

Although some conures eat a lot of cuttlefish bone, especially females prior to breeding, it is inadequate as the sole source of calcium, and is poorly absorbed. Some males also consume a lot of cuttlefish bone. This might be because it contains sodium chloride and magnesium salts. We know that conures seek out minerals from clay licks so cuttlefish bone might help to supply these to captive birds.

A practical way to provide this is to make a hole through the centre of a piece of cuttlefish bone using a screwdriver. Then attach it to the welded mesh using a white cable tie.

Minerals

Dry seed is deficient in minerals and trace elements such as iodine and manganese. Digestive enzymes cannot function properly without them. Minerals needed are phosphorous, manganese, magnesium, zinc, copper, iron, iodine, selenium, potassium, chlorine and sodium. Magnesium is essential for bone formation and for the activation of many enzymes. (Its metabolism is closely associated with that of calcium and phosphorus.) Problems with chicks, such as poor growth,

When offered this branch of red-flowering currant (*Ribes sanguineum*), the Crimson-bellied Conures ate the flowers, the leaves and the bark. The yellow-flowering currant (*Ribes odoratum*) is equally relished. These flowers are much more suitable than fragile blossom such as apple. Photograph © Rosemary Low

convulsions and death can be due to a deficiency of magnesium, as can dead-in-shell. It is advisable to add a small amount of a mineral supplement to the food about once a week. Mineral grit is needed in the crop to grind hard items like dry seed. Grit containers should be emptied and refilled on a regular basis, as not all the different particles will be consumed.

Flowers, nectar, pollen and leaves

In the wild flowers form part of the diet of many, probably most, conures. Unlike lories which remove the pollen and drink the nectar, *Pyrrhuras* actually eat the flowers and take the nectar. In one study in Brazil it was found that flowers formed 10% of the diet of the Green-cheeked Conure, especially the nectar from the *Tabebuia impetiginosa*. During the dry season flowers (mainly large ones with abundant nectar) made up 53% of feeding bouts of Pfrimer's Conure in June.

Some of the flowers we grow in our gardens are not only edible, they are also beneficial (said to contain protein). A well known example is nasturtium. Hibiscus, rose petals and marigolds *(Tagetes)* are also good and, above all, they are readily eaten, but the flowers that are most readily available over a period of some months are those of dandelions. In addition to flowers, captive birds relish young, tender, newly opened leaves. A branch such as elder or hawthorn, containing these, will be instantly investigated.

They enjoy an occasional sweet liquid food and it is an excellent way of ensuring they are not short of calcium by adding this in liquid form. One can buy powdered nectar foods for lories (it will keep in its dry form for months) or make up a mixture using honey, rose hip syrup and water, or other sweet nutritious foods, plus a calcium and/or mineral supplement and perhaps baby cereal.

Pyrrhura conures feed on the pollen of catkins of *Cecropia* trees. In Europe these birds would appreciate being given willow catkins. In Australia they could be offered flowering branches of eucalypts. Pollen is a very nutritious food containing many different vitamins, minerals and enzymes and up to 18 different amino acids.

Dry seeds and grains

Seed is part of the diet of all or most captive *Pyrrhuras* but ideally it would form, at most, 60% and preferably only 40-50%. This would be hard to achieve during the colder months when there are no wild foods and sprouting items is difficult without the right equipment.

Seed diets are deficient in important elements, notably Vitamin A and calcium. A Budgerigar, for example, can live for many years on a mainly seed diet because it inhabits arid areas where rain to produce green shoots is irregular or rare. Its diet consists mainly of small, dry seeds. In contrast, nearly all *Pyrrhuras* are found in humid forested habitats which produce a wide variety of fruits and seeds.

Seeds and pulses:

1. white sunflower;
2. safflower;
3. canary;
4. oats;
5. white millet;
6. hemp;
7. niger;
8. brown perilla;
9. buckwheat;
10 mung beans;
11. pulse mixture for sprouting or cooking.

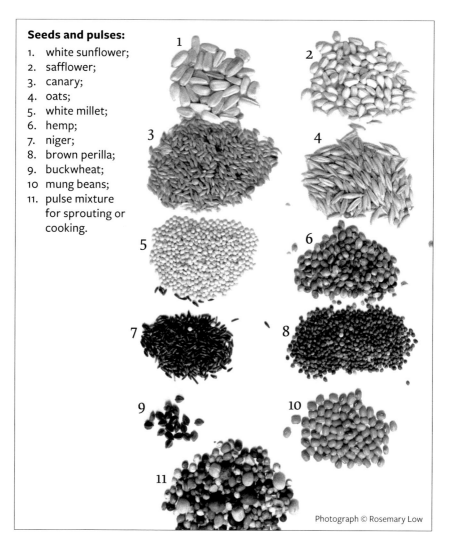

Photograph © Rosemary Low

Pyrrhuras need a mixture that contains mainly small seeds and grains. A mixture (except for underweight birds) should not contain more than about 10% sunflower, small white or small striped – never black sunflower which is grown for oil production (or for wild bird food). Harmful only if fed to excess, sunflower has some health benefits, including the essential fatty acid linoleic acid, B Vitamins, Vitamin E and various minerals.

It can be difficult to find an economical parakeet mixture as many contain inexpensive items that appear to be used to add variety to the *appearance* – such

PYRRHURA PARAKEETS

as flaked peas, mung beans, hard yellow maize and cracked wheat – but are seldom eaten. These items, except flaked peas, would probably be eaten if they were soaked, as would mung beans (tiny green beans) if they were sprouted. Some parrot mixtures contain items so hard, including small round brown beans, hard green peas and maize grains, that only a macaw would be capable of grinding them up .

One company in the UK formulated a conure mixture after research on an extensive collection of conure species. It contained nineteen items: white sunflower, small striped sunflower, safflower, white millet, red millet, canary seed, cut maize, clipped oats, groats, hemp, linseed, buckwheat, niger, perilla, paddy rice, micronised barley, peanuts, tiger nuts (tiny tubers of nut grass) and chillies.

Another conure mixture contained small white sunflower, small striped sunflower, safflower, oats, groats, buckwheat, cracked wheat, white millet, red millet and very small quantities of hemp, canary seed and peanuts. The red millet is seldom eaten by parakeets. Oats and groats are more acceptable if soaked. Peanuts are not suitable for conures, partly because of the high fat content and because of the danger of aflatoxin poisoning.

Some mixtures for small parrots contain items such as very small pieces of dried carrot, tiny pellets, melon seed and sultanas. Some seed mixtures contain dried fruits. There is usually no benefit in giving fruit in this form as the sugar content is very high and conures don't like it anyway.

Look in the seed dishes when you remove them to see which items are always ignored. It is wasteful to feed them and better to formulate your own mixture based on what will be eaten. As an example one could use small white sunflower, safflower, buckwheat, white millet, canary seed, perilla, hemp and hawthorn berries that have been collected and frozen during the autumn. During the winter a little extra hemp could be added for birds in outdoor aviaries in a cold climate, also rape seed, and dock seed. In Europe dock can be collected in dry summer weather when the seed is ripe. If placed in a sack, the seeds will fall out of the stems after a couple of weeks and can be stored for winter use. This seed has a high oil content and is much loved by conures.

In the UK Ray Berman kept eleven species of *Pyrrhura* with three or four pairs of each. He made up a mixture using one part each of small striped sunflower, safflower, buckwheat and groats and half a part of hemp. Frozen mixed vegetables (sweetcorn, cubes of carrot and peas,) were given every day, also apple and grapes. On this diet all his *Pyrrhuras* bred very successfully, except the *roseifrons*, which were not so prolific.

Spray millet is an excellent food for conures, especially for recently fledged young and hand-reared birds being weaned. I have heard people say they will not pay the higher price when there is millet in the seed mixture – but they are missing the point. Conures – indeed, most parrots – enjoy removing the seeds from the sprays. Millet is an excellent form of carbohydrate because it is highly digestible; unlike many grains, it does not acidify in the stomach. It contains Vitamins B1, B2, B3, B6, folic acid, Vitamin K and valuable minerals. In a warm climate, breeders can grow their own and feed them in the green stage. These will be relished. For two months of the year I feed sprays of seeding dock instead of millet sprays.

Protein and fat contents of the various seeds		
Typical analyses of kernels	Approximate %	
Seed	Protein	Fat/oil
Canary	14-17	5-8
Millet	12	4
Rape	19	46
Hemp	20	32
Sunflower	23	30-49
Safflower	16	38

Approximate values only. Content will vary according to the region in which the seed was produced and the seed variety.

How to soak and sprout seed

The nutritional value of dry seeds is limited. Soaking and sprouting them greatly enhances their protein and vitamin contents. Parrot mixtures especially for soaking are available but some contain items like dried coconut and dried fruits which are unsuited to this purpose. One could make up a mixture from safflower, white sunflower, oats (not groats from which the growing part has been removed) and canary seed. If millet is used it is best to soak it separately as it takes longer to germinate. If seeds fail to germinate they are old or not of good quality.

Place the seeds in a container and half fill with water. If larger quantities are required, tiered plastic sprouters and electric seed sprouters are available. Add one or two drops of grapefruit seed extract (effective against hundreds of different moulds, fungi and viruses) or apple cider vinegar to each cup of seed or beans, to prevent mould forming. Leave this in a warm place for 12 hours, then rinse

Rose-crowned Parakeet eating seeds in a head of sunflower.
Photograph © Rosemary Low

thoroughly a couple of times. Repeat the process 12 hours later then leave the contents in the container without water to sprout. Rinse again when germination is evident, then place in a sieve to remove excess water and feed to your birds.

The germinated seeds are best fed when the growth is no more than 50mm to 1cm. To stop growth, the container can be refrigerated. Mung beans and lentils can be sprouted in a colander after being soaked in hot water for about eight hours. They will need to be rinsed twice daily.

Soaked and sprouted seed and beans must be fed in a separate container to dry foods. They should be removed on the same day because they soon become sour or unpleasant.

Proteins

Proteins are comprised of various amino acids. Those termed essential are: lysine, arginine, histidine, methionine, tryptophan, threonine, leucine, valine, and phenylalanine. This means that they cannot be produced in the body. If a protein has a low proportion of one essential amino acid, when this is used up, it restricts the use of all the other amino acids, and protein synthesis ceases. Just looking on the label of a food product and reading the protein percentage can therefore be misleading. Two of the most important amino acids are lysine and methionine which are found in most seeds, especially oil seeds, also in peas and meat.

Feathers consist of 82% protein: if the diet is deficient in essential amino acids abnormal feathers will be produced. It is not unusual to see a green parrot with some yellow feathers. This is probably caused by a deficiency of lysine. Stress marks on the feathers (dark lines that represent a period of stress or malnutrition when the feathers are developing) is often due to decreased amino acid availability, particularly methionine. We can therefore understand the importance of good quality protein, ie, that containing essential amino acids.

In addition to seed, the most usual sources of protein in a breeding conure's diet is eggfood and pulses. Some pairs will take mealworms (and probably also waxmoth larvae) when rearing young.

Eggfood

Eggfood is important for pairs with young, unless they receive pulses daily. The quality of ready-made eggfoods from suppliers varies. You can make your own from hard-boiled eggs, grated carrot and wholemeal or wholegrain breadcrumbs. To this should be added a calcium supplement, perhaps also a very small amount of Spirulina. This can be mixed in a food processor or blender. If the quantity of carrot is not limited, the mixture will be damp and unappetising. It should be crumbly. Ready-made eggfood is dry and best slightly dampened, to make it crumbly moist. Adding sucrose (fruit sugar, obtainable from health food stores) makes this food much more attractive.

Livefood

Some *Pyrrhuras* readily consume mealworms. Others regard them with fear! Live mealworms contain 48% protein and 40% fat and are therefore a good source of protein, especially for pairs rearing young. It is unlikely that dried mealworms would be eaten: they would be unpalatable.

Human foods

There is no harm in offering sensible items (without salt and fat) from the table to companion birds. I recall what happened when I lived in a house at the breeding centre of Palmitos Park. At one time seventeen young White-eared Conures were housed in two cages right outside my kitchen door. They received many leftovers from my table and would eat almost anything offered, instantly investigating whatever I placed in the food dishes. When they were moved to a larger aviary, I missed their inquisitive little faces peering in through the window!

Feeding young birds

The importance of a greater proportion of soft foods in the diet of young birds cannot be over-emphasised. At five and a half months old my two young Crimson-bellied Conures had a wide choice of items but paid little attention to hard seed. It makes up (their choice) less than 10% of the diet. Their favourite foods were pomegranate (Spanish), apple, baby plum or cherry tomatoes, grapes, soaked dried figs, spray millet and seeded batch bread moistened with lory nectar. All these they receive daily, except the tomatoes. In one dish they have a parakeet mixture which was seldom touched until they were about seven months old, and in the other a mixture of soaked and/or sprouted seeds, sweetcorn kernel and green lentils, with cooked pulses every second day. This was mainly replaced by seed by the time they were seven months old. When available they preferred sprays of dock seed (fresh or dried), seeding grasses and anything green, especially green oats in the ear.

Pellets and extruded foods

Except in the USA, pellets and extruded foods are rarely fed to conures. It is claimed that they contain all the necessary nutrients. This may be true but such foods were originally formulated for short-lived birds such as chickens. The long-term effect of feeding pellets is not yet understood. However, it can be difficult to persuade *Pyrrhuras* to eat them. The small kibble found in some parakeet mixtures is usually also ignored. Extruded foods (made through extrusion cooking, that is, by forcing semi-soft material through a specially shaped nozzle) are said by manufacturers to be more palatable to parrots in general and more readily accepted.

The high pressure and high temperature used to produce these foods separates the starches and proteins, making digestion easier. It also effectively sterilises the ingredients, killing all bacteria and harmful organisms. Probiotics (beneficial bacteria) are therefore added. Some pellets are made by less expensive methods, such as steam pressing (as in poultry feeds) or cold pressing.

I see the point of feeding pellets to parrots that are not easily persuaded to eat items other than seed. As all *Pyrrhuras* are likely to choose fresh fruits, vegetables and green, growing foods over seed, I can see no benefit for the birds in feeding these processed foods. If they are fed, plenty of clean water must always be available.

Water

Clean, fresh water for drinking and bathing is very important. Fresh rain water from a clean container can be used, also of course, tap water. Containers should not be placed too close to food dishes, in order to discourage the conures from dropping food inside. The containers should be cleaned or replaced daily, to prevent the accumulation of bacteria. Conures are enthusiastic bathers so the container should be at least as wide as the bird's body is long.

Les Waring asked: "Have you every seen them eat ice? In winter some of my *Pyrrhuras* sit there with pieces of ice from the water dish which they have chiselled with their beak!"

Warning! Safe feeding

Because of the lightning fast reflexes of the conures, special attention needs to be paid to containing the food dishes. It is not desirable to open a main door to change them. Food shelves in which the dishes are set, with a wire mesh covering, leaving only holes above the food dishes, or swing feeders, are recommended. Swing feeders are safe only if one has at hand a piece of wood to cover the gap that is left for a few seconds when the dishes are swung in or out. My assumption is that the birds are tame and cheeky! If they fly away from people there is no problem.

8. BREEDING IN AVICULTURE

BREEDERS fall into two categories: the person who keeps them for the joy of their company (breeding is not important), and he or she who keeps them mainly to produce and sell the young. I would urge the latter to think carefully about the quality of life of these intelligent and sentient little birds that need so much more than a breeding cage.

Compared with most parrots, *Pyrrhuras* are ready breeders, very suitable for keepers "graduating" from Budgerigars, Cockatiels and lovebirds. Possessors of such charm, they will please any bird lover. They can be recommended for keepers who dislike totally enclosed buildings but enjoy seeing their birds in outdoor flights. Unlike *Aratinga* conures, their voices are not too loud.

Some species are easier to breed than others, partly due to their more tolerant and less nervous temperament. Beginners would be advised to start with Green-cheeked, Maroon-bellied and Rose-crowned Conures. However, there are so many factors that affect results that one can only generalise regarding the easiest species.

Pyrrhuras are usually prolific, some species laying eight or more eggs in a clutch. In a suitable climate or if kept in a building, they will be double-brooded. Some pairs have been known to have three consecutive broods. This is not recommended. The number of chicks reared in consecutive clutches, if more than four hatch, is likely to decrease – and with it the quality of the young. To stop a pair breeding remove the nest-box or separate male and female.

Barry Butcher told me about one of his pairs of Crimson-bellied Conures. The male had bred before. In their first clutch the female laid six eggs. She laid again before the young fledged, rearing ten in these two clutches. The whole family was then moved to a new aviary. The female laid six eggs in October and the young fledged in December, to give a total of 15 young in one year.

The main problem connected with breeding used to be distinguishing males from females. Now breeders use certain laboratories for DNA sexing. This non-invasive method is safer and more accurate than surgical sexing. Experienced breeders can often deduce their birds' sex by their behaviour. Males are usually more assertive; however, as hand-reared birds tend to be bolder than those which are parent-reared, the difference might not be clear.

The great popularity of the genus *Pyrrhura* since the 1990s has been fuelled by the prolificacy of the Green-cheeked Conure and its wealth of mutations. But all species make enchanting aviary birds.

Age at start of breeding

Young birds can indulge in courtship feeding and even copulation many months before they start to breed. Some females lay when only one year old but success should not be expected until one year later. One breeder reported obtaining fertile eggs from nine month old Green-cheeked and even Blue-throated Conures. At nine months a female *Pyrrhura* is not usually physiologically mature enough to reproduce. I would not encourage this. Also, young birds are more likely to break eggs and fail to feed chicks – not a good way to start their breeding life. Perhaps ideally immature birds should be kept in same sex groups until they are eighteen months old. The sudden introduction of the opposite sex is a great stimulant to breeding.

Pyrrhura breeders have been known to habitually sell pairs consisting of a young female and an older male. This practice should be strongly discouraged. An older male will persuade a young female to nest before she is fully mature, or he might be aggressive towards her, or just bully her. This can also happen with two young birds of the same age. An older female will be more assertive, less likely to tolerate bullying and, above all, mature enough to breed when the male is ready.

Success is more likely with fully mature pairs. At Palmitos Park, Gran Canaria, three pairs of White-eared Conures produced 54 eggs; 52 hatched, producing 44 fledged young. In a period of 29 months the original eight adult birds had increased to 51. The only failure was an accidental nesting attempt in a cage of six young birds. The single chick died at six days old.

Courtship

As with other members of the parrot family, the male *Pyrrhura* feeds the female by placing his mandibles at right angles to hers, then making a head pumping movement to regurgitate food from his crop.

As in many neotropical parrots (but unlike parrots from other continents), the method of copulation is as follows: the male positions himself at the female's side, he keeps the foot furthest from her on the perch and places the other on her back. Then his tail is placed below hers so that the cloacas meet.

Breeding season

The main triggers to egg-laying for *Pyrrhuras* are a nest site and a regular supply of good food. Hours of daylight seem to be irrelevant. The breeding season is not always well defined and depends on the accommodation (indoors or outside) and the climate. In Europe, birds in outdoor aviaries start to nest about April and are likely to be single-brooded. Those in enclosed buildings could breed at any time. It is usual for breeders to provide artificial lighting to give at least 15 hours of light.

In the UK, Ian Price pairs up his *Pyrrhuras* at Christmas, after males and females have been in separate flights for some months. They are then eager to breed and nest simultaneously, condensing the breeding season and increasing the availability of pairs for fostering. In Australia, Craig and Joanne Aquilina's Green-cheeked Conures in outside suspended aviaries started to nest in June and continued until the year end or even until the following February.

Breeding cages

Unfortunately, some poor specimens are being produced by breeders who use small cages. It might seem like a cliché, but breeders should aim for quality, not quantity. Concentrating on producing excellent birds should be the aim, especially of the less common species.

Breeding *Pyrrhuras* in cages is acceptable if they are allowed to fly in larger flights when the season ceases. It is not desirable to keep these active birds permanently caged; their quality of life will suffer. It is usually counter-productive to try to fit as many cages as possible in the available space because ultimately breeders have too many birds to care for well. To increase the number of cages, they use stackable ones. Seeing birds at floor level suggests to me little concern for their quality of life and no imagination of what their lives are like. It smacks of battery hens and puppy farms.

A transition period is suggested for cage-bred young that are destined for life in an aviary, keeping them in 2m (minimum) flight cages first. Those bred in small cages might seem bewildered and stressed when placed in a sizeable aviary.

Nest-box designs

Unlike many parrots, *Pyrrhuras* do not like to roost on a perch, preferring a nest-box. Its permanent presence might mean that pairs breed at an unsuitable time of year or when they have already reared young and need a rest. In this case they can be given a small box with a perch and no floor.

These conures are known for their readiness to enter holes so they usually do not hesitate to explore any nest-box, whatever the shape. Most breeders use upright boxes measuring up to 36cm (14in) high x 20cm (8in) or 25cm (10in) square. However, egg-breaking is more likely to occur in vertical boxes. Also, for species that lay large clutches, the floor area might be too small. L-shaped boxes are more practical; the female will normally incubate furthest from the entrance hole and the male can keep guard there without disturbing the female.

An excellent design is a horizontal box 28cm long, 15cm wide and 18cm high. Inside, a small wooden shelf, 10cm long, is fitted under the entrance hole and 8cm above the floor. There is a drop of 10cm from shelf to floor which the bird can negotiate with the aid of large staples in the side of the nest-box. This usually prevents it from dropping down on the eggs, and possibly damaging them. This design gives a measure of privacy to females who prefer to incubate underneath the shelf; it enables the young ones to sit on the shelf and look out before fledging. The nest is inspected by a hinged flap at the opposite end to the entrance. Another door can be placed in the centre of the box to make it easier to remove chicks for ringing if the female nests under the shelf. The entrance hole should measure 5cm (2in) to 6cm (2 1/2in) wide, depending on the species.

An alternative is an L-shaped box with a base up to 25cm long and 15cm wide. Depth might be considered important because the deeper the box, the darker the interior and conures probably feel more secure in a dark box. A shallow nest could result in the young fledging too early.

A ladder leading from the entrance hole to the base will be necessary unless large staples are used. Most breeders put welded mesh immediately below the entrance hole; it is easier for the birds to use if it is attached to the side, not the front of the box. However, birds have died inside nest-boxes when the leg ring became trapped in the mesh. Welded mesh used for this purpose should have the

Two entrance holes were made because the male often refused to let the incubating female Rose-crowned exit the nest-box. Photograph © Rosemary Low

loose ends clipped right back to the vertical strands. It should be stapled flat to the wood to prevent a bird getting its foot stuck behind the welded mesh.

The inspection door should be just above the level of the nest litter. Never make the inspection door in the lid (roof) because birds become very nervous when the roof is lifted off.

In extreme climates some breeders make a lid which can be removed during very hot weather, leaving welded mesh covering the top. As most *Pyrrhuras* are sub-tropical rather than tropical species, they tolerate cool or cold weather better than high temperatures. Breeders who use buildings can plan so that chicks do not hatch during the hottest time of the year.

If chicks hatch in very cold weather they could die, because the female ceases to brood them between the ages of two and three weeks. However, the best policy is not to allow birds to breed during cold months unless the nest-box is inside heated accommodation.

Nesting material

As nesting material, wood chips are widely used, or shavings (sieved to remove the finest particles) from untreated wood, slightly dampened to prevent dispersal of dust. A depth of 5cm or more is suitable.

Gnawing stimulates parrots to nest. The birds can create extra nesting material if pieces of wood are screwed to the side. Nails should not be used; they might be hazardous when the wood is destroyed. The interior should be checked regularly. In South Africa, Terry Irwin used a layer of clean river sand covered with pine shavings. The sand prevented the conures from trying to excavate deeper into the base of the box. Previously Blue-throated Conures had gnawed through the base. For this reason the boxes were clad in welded mesh.

Nest-box location

If conures have access to outside and inside flights, where should the nest-box be placed? This will depend on climate, location and circumstances. The presence of night predators such as cats and owls should be considered because even although *Pyrrhuras* inevitably roost in their boxes, if disturbed they could be vulnerable. I would recommend that the nest-box is inside and that the conures are always shut inside at night.

Artificial incubation

If eggs must be removed it is advisable to place them with another pair – any parrot species of similar size – and to use an incubator only if absolutely necessary. If possible, an artificially incubated egg should be returned to a nest of another *Pyrrhura* just before hatching, if the nest contains recently hatched chicks. Then the oldest chick can be fostered or removed for hand-rearing. This is because of the degree of work and difficulty involved in trying to hand-rear newly hatched *Pyrrhuras*.

If an incubator must be used, it should be set at about 37°C. It is usually recommended that eggs should be turned until pipping occurs. But just how important is this in the later stages of incubation? I can recall the case of an egg of a White-eared Conure which I placed in a forced-air incubator. For a reason that I cannot boast about, the egg was not turned after about nine days of incubation. Yet it hatched – and the chick thrived!

Laying and hatching

Clutch sizes vary from four to eight eggs, or even up to thirteen. Females who lay large clutches are extremely vulnerable to egg-binding, and to the production of soft-shelled eggs if they do not receive a calcium supplement (*see Chapter 7, Diet and Nutrition*). While they are laying, females need plenty of soft, easily digestible foods, which will be eaten directly and regurgitated by the male. A calcium supplement should be added and cuttlefish bone and grit should also be available, so that the female has a choice of calcium sources.

During incubation, carried out only by the female, her quiet food soliciting calls can often be heard coming from the nest-box. Depending on ambient temperature

Chicks of *Pyrrhura roseifrons*. Photograph © Claus Nielsen

and number of eggs, the incubation period is usually 22 to 24 days. It could be as short as 21 days, or longer than 24 days in a large clutch where some eggs are not always right under the female. Incubation starts with the laying of the first or second egg. One breeder recorded of her *melanura*: "... from a nest of eight eggs the first two or three young almost hatch at the same time and the others with a shortened incubation time every second day. All the young fledge within a maximum five days" (Spenkelink-van-Schaik, 1980).

I looked at my records of twenty nests produced by four pairs of White-eared Conures at Palmitos Park, Gran Canaria. Nearly all chicks hatched between March and June, with the exception of two nests in February and one in July. Most females commenced incubation when the first egg was laid as in all but four nests it hatched one or two days before the other eggs. In four cases, two chicks hatched on the same day.

It is advisable to foster the last laid egg in a clutch of seven or more to another pair. After about six chicks have hatched, the remaining eggs might have to rely on the heat generated by the chicks, because most females stop brooding chicks after two or three weeks. Later laid eggs therefore take longer to hatch, widening the age gap between the earlier-hatched chicks. With the White-eared Conures, if there was no more than a two-day interval between each chick, all would be fed adequately. If one egg failed to hatch, giving a four-day interval, the youngest chick might not receive its fair share of food if there were already four or five chicks and was more likely to die.

In a second clutch, eggs might be laid before the young had fledged. This would be unusual in most other parrots. On the other hand, the female could wait several weeks to lay again.

Chick development

The beak is whitish, with white pressure pads at the side of the upper mandible that trigger the feeding response in chicks. One first-time breeder wrote to me: "I am worried about the chicks' beaks. They look a bit unusual ... almost puffy at the sides." I reassured her that this was normal.

The first down is white, longish on the back, but most is lost by the age of about one week. The erupting second down appears as dark lines under the skin with a small blob of white where the down has erupted, at about two weeks. The second down is light or medium grey and quite thick on the nape and over the body. The eyes open at about 14 days and the ears soon after.

Weights of parent-reared chicks

During my time as curator at Loro Parque and at Palmitos Park I weighed chicks in the nest fairly frequently, to establish that they were growing well and to

The white down of the 23-day old Rose-headed Conure (*P. rhodocephala*) contrasts with the grey down of the Crimson-bellied chicks aged 20, 27 and 29 days old.
Photograph © Rosemary Low

obtain information on the species. I noted how full the crops were; even in a small parrot like a *Pyrrhura*, the difference between a full crop and an empty one can be about 5g.

The only records I know regarding weights of parent-reared chicks in the wild relate to the Flame-winged Conure (*P. calliptera*) and were published as a graph, thus are not precise (Arenas-Mosquera, 2011). The body weight is approximately the same as that of a Maroon-bellied Conure. A comparison is interesting even although the circumstances are so different, with up to six adults feeding a *calliptera* chick. I never weighed *Pyrrhura* chicks after 37 days because they were too active to stay on the scales and I did not want to stress them by placing them in closed containers.

I recorded weights for three chicks (from one nest) of *frontalis*; only two of which weighed after 24 days. When weighed, all had some food in the crop. How many *calliptera* chicks were weighed is unknown.

| Chicks | Weight in grams | | | |
| | *frontalis* | | | *calliptera* |
	A	B	C	
Hatch	4	–	–	
1	7	5	5	
2		6	8	
3	12	–	7	
4	15	12	–	
5	–	–	14	
6	22	18	16	
7	–	22	19	
8	29	25	22	
9	35	28	27	
10	37	–	30	20
11	41	38	–	
12	–	39	–	30
14	52	49	45	50
16	61	–	–	55
18	–	–	60	65
20			78	70
22	80	80	74	75
24	82	–	80	80
26			92	82
28			92	85
30			84	95
32				96
34				100
38				105
42				97
50				85

The results surprised me as I had expected the wild *calliptera* to grow more quickly in the first two weeks. It might be that food is not as abundant as it is in captivity.

Sometimes early growth can be slow but good weight gains are made later.

Fledging

Young spend seven to eight weeks in the nest. Even when there is a big discrepancy in the chicks' ages, they generally fledge within about five days. It is advisable not to handle chicks in the previous week as it could cause them to leave the nest prematurely. The young should be left with their parents for at least three weeks – unless the parents show any aggression towards them. Breeders tend to be in a hurry to remove young but the very best breeding birds are those which have remained with their parents long enough to help rear the next nest of chicks!

Ringing

I would urge all breeders to fit closed rings with the year of hatching on their chicks. Identifying the individual bird – and the breeder where the ring carries the breeder's code or initials – is important as it reduces the likelihood of related birds being paired together after they are sold. Ringing is especially important for rarer species in aviculture, and for mutations.

Some breeders say that the risk of rejection, injury or killing by the parents is too great to ring their chicks. This risk might be higher if breeders seldom inspect boxes or spend little time with their birds. Rejection can happen – but I believe it is a risk that a breeder should take for the future of the species in aviculture. UK breeder Barry Butcher's pair of Rose-headed Conures (*rhodocephala*) killed three chicks in one nest after they were ringed. These were their first chicks.

The ring size for most species is 5.5mm (nearest UK size N=5.35mm). Exceptions are 6mm (nearest UK size P=6.1) for *P. molinae molinae* and *P. cruentata*. Note that 6.5mm rings can also be used for *cruentata*. Sizes N and P are used for *perlata*.

The age at which a chick is ringed can vary. Factors which influence the growth rate include the proficiency of the parents or the hand feeder, diet, ambient temperature and the number of chicks in the nest. The ages at which the oldest and youngest chicks are ringed could vary by as much as six days, thus the first and last chick could be ringed two weeks apart. Ringing usually takes place just before their eyes open at ten to fourteen days or up to sixteen days. There is variation because when chicks hatch over a period of one week or more initially the younger ones are not so well fed.

The rings of aviary birds should be examined regularly, also that of a new bird, and removed if it is too tight or too flimsy, after recording the numbers. Note that as the Blue-throated Conure is on Appendix I of CITES, exemption papers are required to offer it for sale in most countries. This means that a ring should not be removed unless a vet is present to micro-chip the bird.

A ring which is too large can be dangerous as a bird could become trapped by a small projecting piece of wire or by a small twig. A large ring suggests it might have been fitted when the bird was adult.

How to fit a closed ring

Inexperienced breeders might be apprehensive about fitting closed rings – but this is easy if carried out at the correct age. The ring is placed over the three longest toes and moved down until it meets the fourth. This toe should be gently eased through the ring, using a wooden toothpick or a sharpened matchstick.

If a chick is ringed too early it will immediately be apparent; the ring will be loose enough to slip off. It is better to remove the ring and wait a couple of days, or the ring might get lost in the nest litter. If ringing appears impossible because the chick's leg is already too large, smearing it with Vaseline (petroleum jelly) and gently easing the ring on might prove successful. On no account force the ring or the chick's leg could be broken. If necessary, use the next ring size. After ringing, the number should be recorded immediately.

Removing rings

If it becomes necessary to remove a ring, note that there are two types of ring cutters: for aluminium rings and for stainless steel. They cut vertically down the ring; ensure that the small recess in each blade is located at the top and bottom of the ring. Cut through the ring then repeat the process on the opposite side so that the two halves fall away. If the leg is swollen, first bathe it in distilled witch hazel to reduce the swelling. If there is any injury to the leg after removing the ring, bathe it to remove any impurities and apply an antiseptic or aloe vera gel.

Keeping records

Record keeping goes hand-in-hand with ringing chicks, either in the nest or by fitting split rings after they have fledged. If individual conures cannot be accurately and rapidly identified, record keeping is almost impossible and ineffective. The importance of keeping detailed records cannot be over-emphasised. Not to so do indicates an attitude to bird keeping that is casual, not serious. Good records provide the breeder with extremely valuable information, such as facts about the behaviour or performance of individual pairs that would otherwise be missed.

Records can be kept by hand or on the computer. Some breeders attach a record card to each nest-box. Others have a notebook or breeding register always at hand in the birdroom so that the latest events can be recorded immediately. They can later be transferred to the computer if desired. If stored only on the computer, they must always be backed up because to lose the entire records of a breeding stock would be disastrous.

Nest inspection

Nest inspection should be made without entering the aviary, from a service passage behind the nest-box. In a cage, the nest-box should be placed on the outside, or inside with an inspection door that coincides with one in the cage. If possible, wait until the female comes out, otherwise knock gently on the nest-box so that the birds inside are aware of your intention to open the inspection door. Some females tolerate nest inspection and stay in the nest. Others depart as soon as you tap on the door. One breeder told me that his females varied in their reactions. One female Crimson-bellied just moved aside while a female Yellow-sided would fly at his hand with the intention of biting.

It is advisable to keep nest inspection to a minimum when the female is incubating unless this can be achieved when she is out of the nest. However, it is important to establish the date on which the first or second egg is laid so that the hatching date can be calculated.

Fostering eggs and chicks

Experienced females with large clutches can hatch all the eggs and rear most of the young. The size difference between the first and last chicks is so great that the youngest one stands little chance of survival, so fostering might be the answer. Fostering of a single chick to a different species is not recommended. No behavioural problems are likely if young reared by different species are socialised with their own kind as soon as they are weaned.

Fostering chicks can be successful if carried out at a very early age and the fostered chick is placed in another *Pyrrhura* nest with chicks of a similar age. It can be the means of saving the last-hatched chick. In a pair of White-eared Conures that hatched six chicks over ten days, I transferred the very small youngest to the nest of another pair when it was three days old, the day before the foster parents' first chick hatched. When it was 16 days old and its foster parents had four chicks of their own, it was returned to its parents' nest.

Because Blue-throated Conures were inclined to break eggs when I was curator at Loro Parque, Tenerife, I fostered three eggs to the nest of Golden-capped Conures (*Aratinga auricapilla*) and the chicks were reared to independence along with one Golden-capped Conure. Two female Nanday Conures were also used for fostering, as no males were available, and they reared a Maroon-bellied Conure along with a Jenday Conure (*Aratinga jandaya*). I wish I had been able to follow up the breeding life of these birds to see if they were at all confused about their own identity. I no longer think it is advisable to foster chicks to different species and allow them to fledge with that species.

A very unusual fostering experiment was carried out by German breeder Armin Brockner. He removed an egg from an egg-breaking pair of Blue-throated Conures. Stella's Lorikeets (Charmosyna papou) were the only other parrots incubating so the two eggs were transferred to their nest. Stella's are primarily nectar-feeding species,yet the chicks thrived and were removed for hand-rearing at two weeks old. Considering how different are the food-soliciting calls of the two species, it was noteworthy that conure chicks were fed by lorikeets. Equally interesting, in Venezuela one egg from an Emma's Conure was placed with a clutch of Budgerigar eggs. The egg hatched and the chick was reared by the Budgies.

Breeders might wonder if Pyrrhuras can be used to rear chicks of other genera of neotropical parrots. The answer cannot be predicted because much depends on the circumstances and on the female foster parent. I fostered a day-old White-crowned Pionus (Pionus senilis) to the nest of a White-eared Conure who was feeding three recently hatched chicks. The Pionus chick was well-fed and removed at the age of three weeks for hand-rearing.

Breeding from trios

Breeding from trios has been recorded – for example, two female and one male Green-cheeked Conure. The male will usually fertilise the eggs of both females. This is only likely to be successful if the birds are introduced at the same time. On no account should a third bird be introduced when two others (regardless of gender) are already well established in an aviary. The newcomer would probably be killed.

Co-operative breeding

Gerhard Schmidt in Germany tried colony breeding with three pairs of Maroon-bellied Conures and six nest-boxes. After some difficulties three pairs attempted to breed but only the dominant pair reared young. More successful was co-operative breeding. The young were left with their parents and when the old pair hatched chicks in the following year, he believed that the offspring from the previous year helped to rear the youngsters, as often happens with Pyrrhuras in the wild. All the birds in the aviary used just one nest-box .

He stated of his Fiery-shouldered Conures (Pyrrhura egregia) that seven adult birds went into the nest-box to sleep in the evenings, along with four youngsters. They were reared without any problems. Of course, it was not possible to add some birds to a group. If it was necessary to remove a bird, the attempt to return it after some days was not successful. They chased the "new" bird and attacked it.

Continuous success

Some breeders find that after a few years the number of young reared by pairs gradually decreases. When I asked Jeff Hornsby about this he replied: "They get bored. I used to keep mine in a large indoor building, breeding them between October and May. When they were not breeding they were kept, dozens together, in large flights approximately 6m by 4.2m." Keeping them in groups outside the breeding season, stimulates breeding at the required time of year. Hornsby's *Pyrrhuras* proved to be totally hardy and in the coldest weather chicks were hatched and reared.

He told me about a remarkable female *griseipectus* that he bred. She was still producing ten chicks a year at the age of 23 – when she had a prolapse. He then gave her to a friend who retired her in an aviary. This indicates how long these birds can breed when properly cared for.

Quality – not quantity

Over-production is the breeder's worst enemy. Because *Pyrrhuras* can be so prolific, there is sometimes a glut of some species. Prices fall and breeders decide to acquire a different group of parrots. Inevitably, this has occurred with mutations of the Green-cheeked. This can affect the saleability of other less well-known members of the genus. One breeder told me that he was so successful with his *Pyrrhuras* that he sold them all, and went in for Amazons that are much harder to breed and never as prolific. However, a few years later he started to acquire *Pyrrhuras* again because they are such a pleasure to keep.

Most species will produce two or more clutches if the eggs do not hatch and some species will rear two broods of chicks; however, the Blue-throated Conure is usually single-brooded. Three nests of young of various *Pyrrhura* species can be produced in one year in indoor cages. This is not to be recommended and might be considered as over-production. The quality of young produced in one year is likely to deteriorate markedly in the third nest and if constant breeding is allowed to continue, the female's life will be cut short.

Breeders should not produce young just for the sake of it, but should recognise that some species are more or less in demand, or less readily available. In the case of the critically endangered Grey-breasted and Pfrimer's Conures, the day could come in the not too distant future, when the species are extinct in the wild due to almost total loss of habitat. Great care should be taken to produce excellent specimens, parent-reared and not cage-bred.

Endangered species

Finally, only someone totally without morals would seek or buy endangered endemic species, such as the Santa Marta and El Oro Conures, that are not in aviculture. If captive breeding is ever necessary, it will surely be carried out in the country of origin under the auspices of scientific organisations.

Hybridising

We are privileged to keep so many species of parrots in captivity. We should cherish those that we have and not try to "improve on nature". Some breeders produce hybrids just to breed something different that might have a higher price. The large macaws are the most notable example. Hybrid macaws should be worthless yet some breeders give them names as though they are a true species and sell them at a high price. Some of the macaws used are endangered species. The same could apply to endangered *Pyrrhura* species. If breeders deliberately hybridise with them, it gives the impression that aviculture is a disreputable pastime.

It is unethical because it produces birds of no use to serious aviculturists. A hybrid might resemble one parent so that it is not evident that it is carrying the genes of two species. Another breeder could thus unknowingly breed birds that are not true to the species.

Some breeders try to produce a colour mutation in a different species by hybridising. Thus some species in captivity become increasingly removed from the true, wild species. Our aim should always be to maintain a species as true to the wild type as possible.

Future breeding stock and ethics

Select future breeding birds with care.

- Discard individuals that are aggressive or that produce young with any defect that might be hereditary.
- If outcrosses are needed, bring in only young birds from known and reliable sources. Keep back sufficient own-bred females of the rarer species.
- Attempt to maintain the species as true to the wild type as possible.
- Do not seek to produce or perpetuate mutations in or hybridise with endemic species of conservation concern: *cruentata, griseipectus, leucotis, pfrimeri* and *lepida*. Within the lifetime of many readers of this book, one or more of these could be extinct in the wild. Aviculturists will be heavily criticised by conservation scientists if this valuable and precious genetic material is squandered. It is not only irresponsible, it could be described as a wildlife crime.

9. BREEDING PROBLEMS

ASSUMING that a pair consists of an adult male and female and that they are in good health, why would they not attempt to breed? The most likely reason is something stressful in the environment that makes them feel insecure. For this reason it is not advisable to house conures close to large parrots, macaws and cockatoos.

Egg peritonitis

Most laying problems can be attributed to poor diet, especially calcium deficiency, or lack of exercise. Rarely a female dies as a result of egg-related peritonitis which is usually fatal. This is the term for the ovum entering the abdomen instead of the open upper end of the oviduct. On looking at my breeding records for White-eared Conures at Palmitos Park, I found a curious fact. Of four young hatched in one nest in May 1989, three were females. One died in February 1993 when her second egg resulted in egg peritonitis. One of her sisters died in February 1994. On autopsy it was seen that an egg was forming. All birds that died were autopsied and no other egg-related deaths had been recorded among *Pyrrhuras*.

Egg-binding

The inability of females to lay an egg is a problem that claims many lives. It is probably most likely to occur in the coldest months. To prevent females, especially young ones, from laying, I would suggest that the nest-box is replaced with a small box with the top half of the front open and the floor replaced by a perch. This is perfect for roosting and provides the feeling of security that an ordinary perch lacks.

If a female lays in the winter, unless it is in a climate-controlled environment, it is advisable to remove the egg and the nest-box at once, and to separate male and female. If chicks hatch they will almost certainly need to be hand-reared because most females cease to brood after about two weeks – and the chicks will die. However, there could be a worse outcome than losing the chicks if the clutch proceeds.

When my female Rose-headed Conure was only 18 months old I was shocked to find her incubating an egg on December 31. The pair had a small nest-box for roosting. I made the mistake of allowing the clutch to proceed. Before she laid the third egg I thought she looked uncomfortable, shut all the birds in the inside quarters and placed two extra heaters by her cage to increase the temperature as much as possible. After she laid the fourth egg I saw the male bullying her back into the nest-box before she had a chance to feed. I removed the male and put him in a cage nearby. The female at once started to feed ravenously. On the day the fifth egg was due she spent most of the time out of the nest-box. Next day she had not laid and looked very sick.

By late afternoon she was too weak to take to a vet – and the stress of a long journey and handling would quite possibly have killed her. It was obvious that she was in a lot of pain and would die unless I took the last desperate measure. I caught her, felt for the egg which, of course, was near the cloaca, and exerted enough pressure on it to break it. This is a risky procedure but there was nothing to lose by this time. When handling her, I was shocked to find how much weight she had lost. Fortunately she passed the collapsed egg not long after. On veterinary advice I gave her the antibiotic Baytril for five days to prevent any infection. Much to my relief, she made a full recovery. I gave her calcium in a bread and nectar mixture for a few days afterwards. Ideally, high energy foods such as hemp should be offered at such a time. However, at first she just wanted to eat spray millet, bread and apple – and she spent a long time eating.

What treatment does a vet usually recommend in the case of an egg-bound female? He might try to massage the egg out. If that fails he is likely to break the egg and remove the fragments with forceps. Or he might insert a cotton bud into the cloaca, break the egg and withdraw its contents using a syringe. Perhaps it was just luck that resulted in my female passing the collapsed egg without any problems – but I feel that an invasive procedure, that of trying to remove the shell, is best avoided if possible. After all, the female has ensured some painful and stressful hours and, in my opinion, should be handled as little as possible.

Infertile eggs and death of embryos

There are many reasons for infertile eggs. The most common are that one or both birds of a pair is: too old or too young, not in breeding condition, or suffering from a nutritional deficiency. Poor health, including bacterial infections, could also be to blame. Incompatibility is another cause. A pair of Crimson-bellied belonging to a friend bred for several years successfully. Then, unusually, she laid her first clutch in December. Three infertile clutches were produced so that by April she had laid 18 clear eggs. She laid again in June, and when the nest-box was opened the male was fighting with the female who was on her back. Perhaps in this case the female had not allowed the male to copulate with her. My suggestion would be to split up the pair for several months.

There are many reasons why fertile eggs fail to hatch. These include incorrect humidity, dirty nest-boxes and bacterial infections such as *E.coli*, salmonella, pseudomonas and clamydia. Failure can also be caused by the fungal infection aspergillosis, viruses including PBFD, and paramyxovirus which causes 100%

mortality of embryos. Contamination with insecticides, herbicides and nicotine (smokers – please note) also cause embryo deaths.

Pet unfit to lay

Some pet owners buy a young pair even although they do not have the space for breeding. Two young males are likely to be compatible, if acquired at the same time but a male and a female will want to breed when mature. Only if they have a lot of flying exercise is this advisable; otherwise the female might not be fit enough to lay. If they are fit, they can be given a nest-box and eggs will probably be produced; it is advisable to let them carry out part of the breeding process. The eggs can be replaced with ceramic ones if the owner does not want to produce young. However, serious problems can occur when the female lays, either due to lack of exercise or poor diet. Most pet owners do not supplement the diet with a calcium product for birds. Cuttlefish bone is not adequate.

Here are two examples. A family was grieving over the loss of their Green-cheeked Conure who died after laying four eggs. I went to their house, soon after. The pair had been kept in a small cage, unsuitable for breeding, with a nest-box. The diet was not good and did not include calcium supplementation. The female must have died from egg-binding, egg-peritonitis or some other problem related to an unfit female laying. The owners were not knowledgeable enough to care for breeding birds.

Two articles in *Parrots* magazine, the first by James Hurford (February 2006) and the second by Erika Hurford (May, 2010) related the problem. When their Green-cheeked Conure was three years old, a baby hand-reared Maroon-bellied was acquired. As might be expected, there was a difficult period as the two adjusted to each other. A single bird that has been in residence for three years is almost certain to be jealous. Two actions were taken to relieve the tension between them. First, they were given "well diluted drops of Rescue Remedy to calm, comfort and reassure them – holly which helps reduce feelings of suspicion and jealousy between them, and walnut, which aids adjustment to new situations." The owners integrated the birds slowly, with them some time alone each day. This is a very important point where one bird has been in residence for a long time. In fact, it would be advisable to allow the birds to see each other for only a couple of hours daily, to start with.

Several years later, the Green-cheeked laid four eggs in a linen box on the landing. She had laid before but this time she became weak, exhausted, very unsteady on the perch and was not eating. Then she laid what appeared to be an egg without a shell, probably due to a calcium deficiency. The diet was described without any mention of a calcium additive. The female almost died but, interestingly, was revived when fed Manuka honey diluted in warm water. This was repeated on several occasions over the next few hours – and she survived.

Egg-breaking

Egg-eating is a common problem with Blue-throated Conures. If this occurs one suggestion is to construct a nest-box with a false bottom and replace the original box as soon as the problem is known. Make the box to resemble the normal one in every way except for a concave bottom with a hole in the centre just large enough for an egg to pass through. This might need to be reinforced with a large metal washer to prevent the pair from enlarging the hole. Make a false bottom about 7.5cm below and fill this to a depth of about 5cm with wood shavings. The egg can then be retrieved for incubation elsewhere.

On the other hand, changing the nest-box design to an L-shaped box might solve the problem. The end of the nest chamber is darker and, assuming that this is where the eggs are laid, the entering bird does not drop straight down on to the eggs. And if a small ledge is placed below the entrance perch, the male can rest there, look out and "defend his nest" without disturbing the female. Inverted L-shaped boxes in which the bird must climb UP to the nest chamber, might be even better

However, it might be possible to prevent the problem, if it is not an inherited one. Jörg Asmus told me that during the first two years his *cruentata* bred they broke their eggs. He then gave, on a regular basis, a multi-vitamin preparation for birds which contained Vitamin D3 in small quantities. In addition, he mixed powdered seashells with the eggfood and also sprinkled this over the fruit. He thought that a calcium deficiency was the cause as they then bred successfully for seven years.

At Palmitos Park I had a novel solution for egg-breaking in this species. In nests where I knew this had occurred, just before the female was due to lay I would give her an infertile egg of an Amazon parrot to incubate. This stopped her or the male from breaking her eggs as they were laid. I can only guess that a large egg was somehow a more compelling item to incubate. Instead of delaying incubation until the second egg was laid or laying several which were broken as laid, the female would start to incubate this large egg immediately, thus the male, if he was the culprit, had less opportunity to break eggs. This ruse was successful with several pairs.

Egg opened by parents

On occasions, a parrot will open an egg, perhaps because the chick is unable to hatch unaided. At Palmitos Park in 1992 an egg was opened by a White-eared Conure and this resulted in the parent removing most of the chick's upper mandible. The egg was not opened round the circumference but around its length.

The chick hatched and I photographed it when it was 25 days old. It looked very healthy and had three nest mates, two much younger. Obviously the parents had no difficulty in feeding this chick. Unfortunately, my records do not indicate what happened to it but similar occurrences with other species proved that the young bird could survive provided that it always had soft foods available.

Chicks not fed

Ian Price had a problem with his Rose-crowned Conures. Unlike his Green-cheeked, neither pair bred at one year old, and had difficulties knowing how to feed their first chicks when they bred for the first time when they were over two years old. When he fostered a three-day-old chick into the nest of one pair they soon got the message and fed the rest of the hatchlings. This is a ploy that can be used successfully with many parrot species. The more robust three day old chicks seem to stimulate their foster parents to feed them, and they then understand what is required of them!

Chicks not brooded

A common problem is that pairs cease to brood their young after about two weeks. This is not a problem in warm weather or when there are four or more chicks in the nest. Otherwise they could die, not only because they become chilled but because food digestion will cease. If this problem is anticipated, a special nest-box can be made. This has a compartment below the base that takes a light bulb with a cable that is plugged into a nearby power source. This keeps the base of the box warm. It should be tested before use with a reliable thermometer and bulbs of various wattage. Note that any wattage higher than 20 will overheat the box.

Death of chicks

Some birds have an excitable temperament which sometimes results in chicks being killed in the nest. In Amazon parrots, for example, killing of chicks and mutilation of toes and/or wing-tips can happen in excitable species like the Yellow-shouldered (*Amazona barbadensis*). In *Pyrrhuras*, killing of chicks is unfortunately not a rare occurrence. One breeder told me that as he was opening the nest-box, the female Crimson-bellied killed all three chicks. On rare occasions this does happen with other parrots due to misdirected (displaced) aggression: the bird is frightened and cannot attack the "intruder" so it turns on the chicks. This is why nest inspection should always be preceded by a warning, such as speaking and giving a light tap on the nest-box.

Another breeder told me that when his Fiery-shouldered Conures had four chicks in the nest, the pair killed three on bonfire night. It seemed that the disturbance caused by the fireworks was the reason. This might indicate that some *Pyrrhuras* are extremely susceptible to stress while rearing young and events usually unknown to the breeder cause them to kill their chicks.

Gerhard Schmidt believes that great care must be taken with nest inspection when there are youngsters in the nest-box. "Some pairs do not mind but others injure the youngsters or even kill them. The first days after hatching I do not control the nest box unless I can observe both adult birds in the outside aviary. Then I close the entrance so that I am able to inspect the nest without problems."

Robert Dietrich had an unfortunate experience with his established breeding pair of Yellow-sided Conures. It was not nest inspection that caused them to kill the chicks but the fact that he changed the nest litter. He did not normally do this but the nest was damp. The parents immediately entered the nest and killed two of the three chicks, the eldest of which was about 16 days old. Next day the third chick had been killed and the female laid again soon after. He realised that he should have put some of the soiled nest material on top of the new, to prevent this happening.

In the UK Ian Price said: "There are many factors that can influence behaviour. During the off season I constantly work with my birds to get them as used to me as possible. Most of my parent reared young from this year that I intend to keep will readily take food from the hand. I then find these birds become good breeders, with far less stress from nest-box inspections. Also they pass this calmer nature onto the next generation. Another trick I use is to place a hand-reared youngster with a batch of youngsters that have just left their parents. The parent-reared young soon realise that there is little to fear and become tame enough to feed by hand that much quicker. When I want to buy new stock I look for this year's youngsters. I then work with them to calm them down until they are ready to breed."

Feather plucking

Plucking of chicks in the nest is a common problem with many parrot species. There is no easy solution but placing a millet spray in the nest is worth trying. The areas plucked are usually the top of the head, scapulars and back and rump. In warm weather this is not a big problem as the young will feather up within about three weeks of leaving the nest. Tail and flight feathers are not plucked so young can fly on fledging.

Chicks pulled out of the nest

Several breeders have reported seeing males trying to pull feathered young out of the nest by the tail. I can only guess at the reason: that the male wants to nest again and is anxious to be rid of the young in the nest.

Constricted toes

At Loro Parque, Tenerife, vets treated a case of constricted toe syndrome in a Crimson-bellied Conure. At 27 days a front toe on the right foot was very swollen at the tip, preceded by a fibrotic area affecting the blood supply and causing a severe oedema. In this case the toe was bandaged for five days after surgery. Three weeks later the constriction line was still visible but the toe had healed perfectly (*Cyanopsitta*, 2010, no 96, 30-31).

This condition is quite often reported by parrot breeders in various species; the toe looks as though it has been tied with a very fine fibre. This condition is known in paedriatic medical literature (toe-tourniquet syndrome). The cause is unknown but an environment that is too dry has been suggested, also bacterial infections, hypersensitivity reactions, fungal toxins, viral infections and nutritional deficiencies! One or several deep incisions in the skin of the fibrotic ring will release the constriction. A hydroactive dressing should then be applied to prevent the formation of additional fibres or scabs. If there is severe loss of circulation, amputation of the toe might be necessary.

Inherited problems

In my view it is highly irresponsible to pair together brother and sister. One breeder told me he thought this was not a problem in the first generation. It is well known that in humans various harmful inherited conditions can occur when cousins marry, so such close pairing as brother and sister are much more likely to result in physical or mental defects, in humans and in birds. There may be problems that you cannot see. Just one brother to sister pairing might not be disastrous – but how does one know that the pair were not also bred from a brother and sister, because someone else had the same idea that it is not harmful? With parrots, information on parentage is not usually available! So pairing brother and sister could happen for several generations. I always find it shocking that many breeders do not keep proper records and given the ring number of a bird they bred, they are unable to tell you its parentage.

Remember, we are not breeding domesticated creatures that exist in the thousands – but in many cases with species that survive in the wild in only a few hundred individuals, or even fewer. Some of them are only one or two generations away from wild-caught stock. Or they are wild-caught. If we keep the gene pool pure (and this means eradicating mutations), we hold priceless resources in our hands. Given the on-going and relentless deforestation in the neotropics, some of the *Pyrrhura* species in aviculture might one day be the only ones in existence. We should take a totally different view to when breeding Budgerigars or Canaries, for example.

10. HAND-REARING AND WEANING

MOST *PYRRHURA* conures are excellent parents but intervention is sometimes necessary to save the lives of chicks. This can happen when five or more young are hatched and the youngest is (or are) neglected. It can also happen with pairs which, for an unknown reason, will rear only two chicks.

Specialist breeders of members of this genus are usually able to foster chicks to other nests with young. If this is carried out before the chick is ringed, it should be marked on the head with a spot of green food dye. *Pyrrhuras* are not the easiest parrots to hand-rear from the egg. Indeed, before the availability of commercial parrot hand-rearing formulas, successes were very rare. If chicks need to be hand-reared because there are too many in the nest, it is advisable to remove the eldest, provided that the smallest has not been severely neglected, because very young chicks are hard to rear. If a Green-cheeked, for example, is to be hand-fed for a pet, it can be taken as late as four weeks, although the optimum age is when the eyes are opening.

Rearing foods

As with all parrots, the first three feeds of newly hatched young should consist of electrolytes only. Hydration is of the utmost importance; after all, the chick's yolk sac will nourish it for the first two days. Whereas other neotropical parrots, such as Amazons, could be reared on home-made mixtures including baby cereals and liquidised fruit, *Pyrrhuras* were much more challenging. These days one commercial food in particular has been found invaluable for rearing these conures from the egg. For the first seven to ten days Harrison's Neonate formula has proved successful. Subsequently Kaytee Exact and other formulas have been used. It is the food given during the first week or so that is crucial.

Ray Berman had a female White-eared Conure that always laid up to fourteen eggs. Unfortunately, the pair would nip off the toes of the chicks if they were not removed as soon as they hatched. The chicks therefore had to be hand-reared from the egg. Kaytee Exact was used, sometimes with the addition of apple juice if the crop was slow to empty. Extraordinarily dedicated, for the first three weeks the chicks would be fed every hour, including during the night, he and his wife taking turns to get up! Many breeders find that very young chicks can survive with only one feed between midnight and 6am.

If chicks are removed from the nest in good health after the age of ten days, hand-rearing should not be difficult. A commercial hand-rearing product can be used, with the addition of liquidised papaya or other fruit. When they are older, a mixture can be made from equal parts of baby cereal and wheat germ cereal to form about 75% of the food with papaya or banana liquidised with bottled water as about 25%. Wheat germ cereal is suitable for spoon-feeding only.

Papaya is, in my experience, an ingredient without parallel. It aids digestion and prevents the impacted crop that can occur if the food offered is incorrect. It contains the digestive enzyme papain which breaks down proteins and turns them into the essential amino acids. It also has a high Vitamin A content (1090 iu in 100g).

However, the protein content of fruit is low so its use reduces the overall protein content of the diet. This is not a problem if wheat germ cereal (about 25% protein) is used. Chicks have the greatest need for protein soon after hatching and less after feather growth is complete.

Another essential component of the food is calcium which, combined with Vitamin D3, is needed for normal bone growth. Unfortunately, many parrot chicks of numerous species, hand-reared and parent-reared, suffer bone deformities,

The innocence and wide-eyed wonder of a young Rose-fronted Parakeet (*roseifrons*).
Photograph © Jason Wright

resulting in life-long disabilities, due to a calcium-deficient diet. Calcium products for birds (combined with Vitamin D3) are readily available. For chicks being hand-reared, they can be added directly to the food. For breeding pairs with young, the calcium supplement is best placed on the rearing food – not in water where it is most unlikely to be ingested in sufficient quantities.

Paul Stuart maintained his Blue-throated Conure chicks at a higher temperature for the first few days than that of some other parrot species: 37°C for three days, then at 36°C for the next four to five days. During this time the temperature of the food was 42°C – hotter than the 41° used for other parrots. At the age of seven weeks the young were placed in suspended cages (Stuart, 2003).

Behaviour towards other chicks

The temperament and personalities of different species are most apparent when the young are hand-reared. Not all *Pyrrhuras* can be trusted with other young chicks. I found Blue-throated Conures lacking in affection towards each other and towards the feeder (myself). One breeder had an experience with this species which should serve as a warning. *Five week old* Blue-throated chicks were kept with a Red-capped Parrot (*Pionopsitta pileata*), a quiet and gentle species. The *Pyrrhuras* attacked it and injured it so badly that it died. Although the other (smaller) members of the genus appear more gentle and affectionate, they should not necessarily be trusted with other species.

Close observation of chicks from the age of six weeks onwards is important. Whether kept with nest mates or with other species, aggression towards other young ones can occur. Aggressive individuals need to be separated from the others because, young as they are, they can inflict fatal injuries on other young birds. It might be that aggressive youngsters do not have pet potential. Many hand-reared *Pyrrhuras*, like other parrots, have no fear of humans so when they mature, they become nippy.

Young hand-reared Crimson-bellied: full of curiosity.
Photograph © Rosemary Low

Weaning

Suitable weaning foods for *Pyrrhuras* are frozen mixed vegetables (thawed), soaked and/or sprouted sunflower seed, sprouted lentils and cooked pulses, millet sprays, soaked figs and apple. These can be offered from the age of six weeks, to accustom them to nibbling at various items. I feed seeded batch bread (not white bread) dipped in lory nectar – but honey water would be an acceptable substitute.

This is relished. Each youngster should be treated as an individual and fed for as long as it needs it. Countless young parrots die ("unexplained" deaths) because mainly hard foods are offered as soon as the young appear to be independent. In the wild they would be fed by their parents for some weeks while they were learning to manipulate and open different food items. The weaning period is gradual and during this period young parrots eat, at first, soft items. As their parents regurgitate food to them less often over a period of many weeks, they become proficient at opening seeds and consuming harder foods. Despite this, most people expect young parrots to eat hard seeds or pellets within days of being weaned. Breeders of finches and Canaries know the importance of offering soaked seeds for a period after the young fledge. If these soft and easily digested items are not available, the young ones are likely to lose weight and die.

Breeders should educate the people to whom they sell young parrots, whether they are pet owners or pet shops, by giving them a leaflet with recommended soft foods. Furthermore, they should encourage them to continue spoon-feeding a hand-reared youngster for as long as it requests it. A hungry parrot is anxious and nippy – not the happy, gentle bird that owners are expecting. This behaviour starts a downward spiral in the relationship between human and parrot.

I prefer parent-reared young birds for breeding purposes. Sometimes, with females of the rarer species, there is no option but to acquire a hand-reared bird. When I bought a young female Crimson-bellied Conure (hatch date unknown) I was told she was weaned. Immediately I could see that she was hungry. In fact she was ravenous. The indoor part of her accommodation consisted of a 2.5cm square welded mesh flight. With a spoon with the sides bent inwards, I was able to feed her through the mesh, without the need to catch her up – initially five times a day. She pumped at the spoon so hard I had to hold it very securely. I gradually reduced the number of feeds, but nevertheless continued to spoon-feed her for five weeks.

This had several important benefits. One was that I added a calcium supplement to the food every day. The second was that after about three weeks, the young parent-reared male with her plucked up the courage to feed from the spoon. In this way he lost his nervousness and also received calcium supplementation. The third beneficial factor was my confidence that the female was properly weaned at this most important time of her life.

In the same circumstances, most people would probably have spoon-fed the female for a few days only. My policy has always been to continue supplementary feeding until the bird loses interest in it. Insufficient food in these early formative weeks can never be compensated later on. Some breeders are in too much of a hurry to sell hand-reared young and have little regard for their future.

Crimson-bellied chicks aged 27 (female 68g) and 29 (male 92g) days. Photograph © Rosemary Low

In 2012 the pair of Crimson-bellied bred for the first time. When the chicks were 23 and 25 days old I removed them from the nest because they were inadequately fed. They fed immediately from the spoon and seemed very hungry. There was a significant difference in their weights, the oldest weighing 92g and the smaller one only 68g.

They were silent and seemed quite nervous. Not until the third day did they make weak food soliciting calls. On the following day the eldest chick, who I was convinced was a male, was making loud calls and the next day the little one – a female, I thought – also made strong calls. (DNA feather sexing proved I was correct.) After that they were very vocal when being fed, making the short, rapid calls typical of chicks of the genus.

The male had already reached his peak weight, indicating he had been well fed. The female lost weight for five days. Her peak weight was only 77g at 40 days. I weighed them before the first (6.30am) and last (11pm) feeds of the day. Every day they lost weight overnight, usually 3g or 4g. I had a problem in that the minimum temperature in the brooder was too high so it was switched off and a heater was placed near it. Although it was June, it was quite cool at night. I continued to use the heater at night until the eldest was 41 days old by which time they were almost fully feathered except for the back and rump and the shorter tail; also the ear coverts were still in pin feathers.

At the age of 37 days the young male was vigorously flapping his wings. When he was 42 days old I put them in a small cage for a few hours during the day. By the age of 48 days they were both testing their wings and flying quite well in the kitchen. Indeed, when I let them out to fly they amused me by flying back to the brooder, a few feet away, going inside and settling down for their afternoon nap!

In the mornings they would fly on to the window sill and sit there quietly, staring out of the window as though fascinated. They could see the wild birds. I was not sure whether they could also see their parents whose outside cage was almost surrounded in growth from a fig tree.

By this time, aged 47 and 45 days, they refused food first thing in the morning and were becoming difficult to feed. As with all young parrots at this age, they wanted to fly first, and feed later. They nibbled at millet spray and green and seeding dock but ingested very little.

Within a few days they were eating soaked and sprouted sunflower seed, sweetcorn kernels and grapes. By the time they were nearly ten weeks old the young female was objecting to being caught to be returned to the cage. She would perch on the top of the kitchen units to evade capture. The male also perched there but allowed me to pick him up. She was more independent. He was slightly more attached to me, often flying to my head or shoulder. As I did not want to stress her by chasing her about, I moved the two to a 1.8m long cage in my kitchen.

Here they could fly and play – but they still fidgeted to come out and fly. This exercise had to be restricted to the evening. The brooder in which they had been reared was still in the kitchen. Right from the time I had moved them out of it to a small cage, they had put themselves back in it at night about 7.30pm – just as they would have used a nest-box had they been with their parents. The brooder was always covered with a towel at night so that they had eleven hours rest in a dark place. This is so important for young birds.

The two young ones slept in their brooder at night until they were three and a half months old. I let them out to fly in the evenings and they would always return to the brooder, rather than to the 2m (6ft) cage that they inhabited. A visit from my brother when they were four months old encouraged me to remove the brooder from the kitchen table so that we could eat in a civilised manner!

They will not enter their 2m long cage voluntarily so I can let them out only in the evenings. Then I turn out the light and gently pick them up. I still do this and they make no attempt to bite while held. They enjoy flying about so much, exploring every area of the kitchen, playing on me and hanging from my hair and drinking blackcurrant squash from my glass! They are totally captivating when flying free, swooping and diving at great speed. Surprisingly, they are extremely nervous of other people and of large objects, such as a mop, that I carry into the kitchen. This is in total contrast to their parents who seem afraid of nothing. Time will tell whether their temperament, which is so nippy, changes as they mature. Beautiful as they are, I suspect the temperament of some other members of the genus makes them a more suitable choice as a companion.

11. MUTATIONS AND GENETICS

MANY mutations have been developed since the mid-1990s, especially in the form of *molinae* known as the Yellow-sided Conure. These have added greatly to the appeal of *Pyrrhuras* for many breeders.

The "Yellow-sided" Conure is a naturally occurring form, which was formerly thought to be a separate species, and called *hypoxantha*. It was named from a female taken from a wild flock in the south-western Mato Grosso, in or before 1900. The other two, one of which, with the female, were taken for the American Museum of Natural History. The female is described on pages 130-131.

Parrot breeder Steve Garvin was working in a quarantine station in Los Angeles in the mid-1980s when he noticed two brightly coloured Green-cheeked Conures, imported from Argentina. He purchased them; both were females. The females bred from them resembled normally coloured birds. At the same time Denna Ferris also acquired two Yellow-sided females and bred from them with similar results. After several generations of line breeding she produced Yellow-sided females but it took several more generations before visual Yellow-sided males were produced. It is believed that this mutation is similar to the Opaline in the Budgerigar.

Breeding the Pineapple

The Pineapple mutation is a combination of the Yellow-sided and Cinnamon mutations. Males which look like Green-cheeks but are split for both mutations, when paired with a Cinnamon female, will produce visual Cinnamons and visual Yellow-sided females in approximately equal numbers. Occasionally a Pineapple female will result from this pairing. The males bred from males which are split for both mutations, when paired with a Cinnamon female, will be Cinnamon and normal Green-cheeks. Any males will be visual Cinnamon and split for Pineapple. According to Gary Clayton, they look different from normal Cinnamons and are sometimes referred to as the Lime mutation (Clayton, 2006).

When a male split for Cinnamon and Yellow-sided is paired with a normal Green-cheeked female, most of the males produced are split for Cinnamon, Yellow-sided or Pineapple; some could be pure Green-cheek. The genetics of each male can be proved only by test pairings. The females from this pairing are nearly all either visual Cinnamon or visual Yellow-sided, with about 10% Pineapple. Rarely, a normal female will be produced.

The male Pineapple is a very striking bird, more colourful than the female. To produce a male Pineapple, a male that is split for Cinnamon and Yellow-sided should be paired with a female Pineapple. Nearly all the males produced will be split for Pineapple but visually they will be either Cinnamon (split also for Yellow-sided) or Yellow-sided (split also for Cinnamon). However, about 10% will be visual Pineapple. A male Pineapple can also be produced (50% chance) by pairing a Cinnamon male split for Yellow-sided to a Pineapple female.

If two visual Pineapples are paired together, all the young will be like their parents.

Dilute mutation

Steve Garvin was also involved in establishing the recessive American Dilute. It first appeared in California – from a normal pair. When the breeder retired, Steve Duncan and Steve Garvin bought his stock. In this mutation the pigment is reduced even more than in the Pineapple – about a 75% reduction in melanin (Duncan, 2007), that is, it is a lighter shade of yellow-green, with a lighter head. The tail is *bright* red. It has dark eyes, beak and feet, yellow breast,

Green-cheeked Conure chicks – three Cinnamons and three normals. The parents were a Cinnamon male and a Yellow-sided female. Photograph © Mark Scrivener

dark orange-red abdomen, silver-grey crown and lime coloured back. In contrast the Cinnamon has ruby-coloured eyes and lighter feet and beak. When a visual Dilute is paired to a normal, all the young produced will be normal split for Dilute. Normal/Dilute x Dilute produces 50% Dilutes and 50% normal/Dilute.

Grey-breasted Conure

The Dilute mutation has also been bred in the Grey-breasted Conure *(P. griseipectus)*. Its plumage is lighter throughout; the green is approaching yellow-green. In view of the fact that this species is CRITICALLY ENDANGERED and very seriously threatened by habitat loss, I would urge breeders not to develop mutations.

Many combinations in *molinae*

Combining mutations has led to the availability of countless colours in the Green-cheeked. These include the Cinnamon Dilute (mainly yellow), Red Opaline (cheeks and underparts infused with red – darker on the abdomen), Turquoise Cinnamon, Turquoise Cinnamon Violet, Turquoise Opaline Violet, Turquoise

Opaline Cinnamon Dilute (pale yellow and white), Turquoise Opaline in various forms, including Violet, and Turquoise Opaline Violet (blue above and pale yellow below). Those interested can search online where they will find many photographs, also information on inheritance. This aspect of their breeding is constantly being updated.

Blue mutations

In the first edition I wrote the following – but note that the Blue mutation is now called the Turquoise.

In the Green-cheeked Conure it appears that the Blue mutation arose in Belgium about 1995, according to Geert Vannieuwenhuyse. The manner of inheritance was recessive. He bought the stock of the breeder of the first Blues: the parents (brother

Pineapple mutation and normal Green-cheeked Conures.
Photograph © Rosemary Low

and sister), the grandparents and some split Blue young. By 1997 he had bred the Blue mutation to the second generation. He described it as having the green areas replaced by blue, the scalloped feathers of the throat and breast as white with darker margins and the tail a striking rust-red, fading into grey-blue (Vannieuwenhuyse, 1997). It appeared to be the Parblue mutation.

The name Blue is a little misleading; perhaps Parblue is the correct term. The gene that creates the blue mutation can be partially activated to create a colour that is intermediate between green and blue, as in this mutation, which is recessive in its manner of inheritance. The wings are bluish-green, also the cheeks, and the ear coverts and breast markings are mainly whitish. The underparts are bluish green, tinged brown on the abdomen, or, in the Opaline Blue form, they are whitish.

Sex-linked mutations such as Cinnamon and Pineapple can, of course, be combined with the Blue mutation. Among the combination mutations now being bred are Cinnamon Blue and Cinnamon Dilute.

If a Blue male is paired with a Pineapple female, the males produced will be normal split for Pineapple and for Blue. The females are normal split for Blue. If a male Pineapple is paired with a Blue female all the males will be normal split for Pineapple and for Blue, and the females will be Pineapple split for Blue.

In Denmark Claus Nielsen bred a similar Blue mutation in a Painted Conure.

In his book *The Avis Brasilis Field Guide to the birds of Brasil* (2009), Tomas Sigrist illustrates a Blue mutation – a "true" blue, such as we see in a Cobalt Budgerigar, for example. The skin of this Maroon-bellied Conure, that served as a model to the plate, belongs to the Museum of Zoology of the University of São Paulo and according to the label, the bird was collected in the wild near the city of Santos, São Paulo State in December 1970. It was mainly blue, darker above, with pale brown ear coverts and white and grey breast markings. The under wing coverts were white and blue.

Painted Conure

In the Painted Conure, at least two mutations are known: the Pied and the Blue. In 1996 a striking pied was bred in the UK from a *wild-caught* Pied male (with a bright red rump) and a normal female. Until the first moult, this bird had normal plumage; during the moult yellow feathers covered the shoulders, back, part of the wings, sides and flanks. The yellow markings were much more extensive than in the male parent. The entire lower part of the breast, the abdomen and the rump were bright red – not dull maroon as in a normally-plumaged bird. The head coloration was normal.

In the same nest as the Pied male, were two normally-coloured males. The anonymous owner of these birds believed that this mutation was the equivalent of the Yellow-sided Green-cheeked Conure ("*hypoxantha*") (Anon, 2000). Photographs of the front and side appearance of this bird appeared in the January 2000 *Magazine of the Parrot Society*, page 16.

Also in the UK, Steve Beaver bred Pied *roseifrons* (pied with yellow) with red feathers extending beyond the eye.

Black-capped Conure

In the USA Howard Voren acquired some Black-capped Conures *(P. rupicola)* in the late 1980s which had the abdomen variably marked with crimson and the feathers of the sides of the upper breast suffused with yellow. They were all females. Within five years males were produced with similar markings; even more intensely coloured birds were bred when they were paired together. However, many were infertile and, furthermore, most lost much of the colour when they were mature.

In the UK, Jeff Hornsby, who stated he had bred both sub-species, recalled producing one nest of five young in which the amount of bright buttercup yellow in the plumage varied from 50% to 90%. This might have been due to some metabolic disorder because, unusually, they all died at about four months old.

Abnormally marked Black-capped Conure at a clay lick in Peru.
Photograph © Karl Heinz Lambert

Karl Heinz Lambert photographed an unusual Black-capped Conure at a clay lick with a number of normally-coloured birds. The back view shows a bird with pale greenish cheeks, brown wings with some green feathers (reminiscent of opaline markings), some primaries dark and some light coloured, with normal dark tail and white nuchal collar, also white crown.

Dark factor mutations

The "Misty" appears to be a dark factor and has appeared in several *Pyrrhura* species. In Australia, in the Green-cheeked Conure, it is known by the name Khaki, also as the Jade, and is described as an incomplete dominant mutation. The dark factor, as in Budgerigars, can appear as Dark Green or Olive, as in the Rose-crowned Conure *(P. rhodocephala)* in which the Olive mutation is established. According to Les Waring: "Mutations have appeared in the Rose-crowned, mainly in Europe, such as the dark factor in which dark green and olive are being produced."

Steve Beaver acquired a pair of Maroon-bellied Conures whose ancestors had been bred in eastern Europe. They were very dark in colour and he thought they might have been single dark factor birds (equivalent to the dark green mutation in the Budgerigar). They were surgically sexed but for three years produced huge clutches – all infertile. He then had them DNA-sexed which confirmed that they were a true pair. They never produced a fertile egg, either because they were closely in-bred or perhaps possessed a lethal gene. He also kept and bred the Olive. The Fallow mutation has been bred in Europe.

Abnormal colours developed by breeders

Many breeders retain birds showing abnormal or exceptionally bright colours in the hope of developing new forms, usually by in-breeding. One example of unusual coloration occurred in the aviaries of Barry Butcher in the UK. One of two Crimson-bellied Conures left the nest with dull blue plumage on breast, nape and wings. Also in his aviaries is an unusually coloured Fiery-shouldered Conure. It has scarlet feathers on the abdomen and extended areas of orange-red on the under wing coverts. Birds such as these can be *developed* over the years into new varieties. They should not be called mutations as they are acquired by selective breeding.

A spread in the red head colour has occurred in many parrot species and perhaps is often associated with very mature birds.

12. FOOD SOURCES IN NATURE

A DAY in the life of a *Pyrrhura* conure goes like this. It emerges from its roost – a cavity in a tree or perhaps a crevice in a rock face or a frond at the base of a palm – soon after first light. It spent the night inside with its companions – possibly as many as ten other birds. They settle nearby in a tree canopy and look around suspiciously. If there is nothing threatening in view, they take off to a food tree, which is probably quite close.

They feed quietly, hardly pausing between finishing one seed or berry and taking the next. All the while the sentinel in their group, posted to warn of danger, has been looking around intently. If danger threatens, the sentinel makes a certain call, to which the other flock members respond with a specific vocalisation. Suddenly it gives a squawk and the whole flock departs as a single bird. Any human in the area would be surprised as he did not know they were there.

They fly a little way and find another food source or, after a few minutes, return to the same tree. This could be a fruiting fig, a *Cecropia* with seeds or catkins or a tree such as *Trema micrantha* that produces little berries. In the rainforest they will seek trees with large flowers, to take the nectar. They continue feeding until their crops are full. Then they settle down in the shade of a tall forest tree which protects them from the glare of the morning sun, or from a heavy downpour.

If it is raining, they ruffle their feathers to welcome the moisture on their plumage, perhaps hanging upside down and opening their wings to become thoroughly drenched. They enjoy the feel of the rain and instinctively know the importance of keeping their plumage in superb condition. They spend a long time preening themselves or the bird perched near them. By this time, if they are lowland birds, it is hot. They doze contentedly, undetected by most other creatures, protected by the dense canopy.

If they are birds of the mountains, the temperature is not too high for them to venture out again, taking off like a little squadron of fighters. In a second they are out of sight. Now they can move around to a number of locations in their search for food, which might not be as plentiful in the mountains as in the rainforest.

Unless it has been raining the conures might have a strong desire to find water. They might search epiphytic plants, such as the bromeliad *Tillandsia calloura*. If the weather has been dry they will fly to small rock pools, or even to a waterfall.

The mid to late afternoon is time for another feeding session. And then they seek the shelter of their roost site.

Seeds, nuts and fruits

Pyrrhura conures feed on small berries, seeds and the seeds and pulp of fruits such as figs, also on flowers. The fruits of palm trees are also important in their diet, such as those of the palmetto fruit *(Euterpe edulis)*. In Brazil Maroon-bellied Conures feed on araucaria nuts and, in the Atlantic forests on nuts from a species of *Virola* tree. Also favoured are the nuts (seeds) in the cones of the slash pine *(Pinus elliotii)*.

Favoured by White-breasted Conures is the seed of *Mollia gracilis* inside spherical pods 1cm in diameter, attached to branches by stalks 2cm long. While searching for the pods the conures move upwards along branches, periodically descending to repeat the search. Green seed pods are preferred, as opposed to the older yellow or brown ones. Only the body of the seed is eaten, the seed wings and pods being discarded. The bill is used to remove the pod from the branch and the pod is then usually transferred to the foot. If it is in an awkward location the conure bites at it directly to remove the seeds (Toyne *et al*, 1992).

In Guyana Painted Conures eat the orange-red, berry-like drupes of kabukalli *(Goupia glabra)*. Each drupe is about 5mm in width and contains five to ten seeds. According to Sick (1993), Maroon-bellied Conures "like so many other birds is fond of the hot pepper *Capsicum fructescens*." Note that parrots are said not to detect the strong, hot taste.

In one study (Ragusa-Netto, 2007), it was found that fig seeds and pulp comprised 70% of the diet of Green-cheeked Conures *(P. molinae)* at one site and were the only foods available throughout the year. In the arid-rain-shadowed valleys in La Paz, Bolivia, Green-cheeked Conures were observed feeding on the fruits and flowers of *Cassia*. They frequented peach orchards in the Inquisivi area, consuming so many peaches that they were said to be too heavy to fly and were easy to catch. Or perhaps they were drunk on the fermenting juices? It would be very unusual for any bird to eat so much it was unable to fly.

The feeding ecology of *molinae* was studied in the Yungas sub-tropical forest of Argentina. Of the 18 plant species consumed, 31% of feeding bouts were from the iguana hackberry *(Celtis iguanaea* – used by humans as medicine and food) and 22% related to the Jamaican nettletree *(Trema micrantha)*. Overall fruits (67%) were the most consumed items, followed by seeds (17%) and flowers (10%) and, to a lesser extent, nectar and leaves. Like other *Pyrrhuras*, the Green-cheeked has a flexible diet that is adjusted to seasonal availability (Benavidez *et al*, 2021).

Most *Pyrrhuras* shun human habitation. One exception is the Maroon-bellied. It visits parks, also bird tables and feeders in gardens in Brazil.

In Colombia, species of the *picta* complex, including *caeruleiceps* and *lucianii*, have been documented feeding on 25 different plant species.

The fruits of palm trees of various species are an important part of the diet of Madeira Parakeets.

Photograph © Bent Pedersen

A Maroon-bellied Conure in a park in the centre of Rio de Janeiro was feeding on dropped fruits of the African oil palm (*Elaeis guineensis*).

Photograph © Rosemary Low

For example, *caeruleiceps* feeds on the fruits of a croton (Euphorbiaceae), on guavas, on *Cecropia peltata* (Cecropiaceae); flowers of *Tillandsia* species, on the ice cream bean *(Inga spectabilis)*, leaves of hibiscus (Malvaceae) and on the bark of the trunk of the avocado *Persea americana* (Lauraceae).

The second most important food item (33%) of the endangered Pfrimer's Conures was the immature seed of *Hyptis* species (Olmos *et al*, 1995). They had to descend to the ground to take these, and several sentinels were posted while the other birds fed. The researchers were surprised to see *pfrimeri* feeding on the ground (as does *calliptera* in the Andes of Colombia) but this has advantages in the seasonal dry forest where resources are limited. They have access to additional foods at ground level. Other items eaten by *pfrimeri* were *Cecropia* catkins, figs and guavas (pulp, not seeds). All the figs opened were heavily infested by wasps; these probably contributed protein to the diet when the conures had dependent fledglings.

In October and November Pfrimer's Conures fed mainly on the fruits of the fig *Ficus gomeleira* (72%), and more than 120 conures would congregate around the one fruiting tree. They also consumed the fruit pulp of a *Pouteria* species. Olmos explained why Pfrimer's Conure, which belongs to a genus of primarily rainforest-dwelling birds, can exist in a seasonal, even dry habitat. It is because of the abundance of nectar-rich species and of fig trees in the surrounding *cerrado* vegetation.

Flowers

In eastern Brazil, Pfrimer's Conure was studied in 1995, in June (46 feeding bouts) and October (25 feeding observations). There were striking differences in the foods eaten during these periods. Flowers of *Tabebuia impetiginosa* were eaten in 43% of all feeding bouts observed. "The conures spent hours picking one flower at a time, chewing around its base, discarding it and repeating the process, usually ignoring the approach of an observer right to the base of the food tree" (Olmos *et al* 1995).

The flowers of *Maclura tinctoria* and a *Bauhinia* species were also eaten. Flowers were an important food source in a season when there were few alternatives, and accounted for 53% of feeding bouts in June. After *Tabebuia* had finished flowering, some of the common trees of the dry forest were flowering.

Olmos *et al* (1997) commented (with references): "Flowers, mainly large ones with abundant nectar, have been recorded as a food item of some importance for the rainforest *Pyrrhura picta*, and *P. perlata* and *P. albipectus*, and as making 25% of

Grey-breasted Parakeets feeding on the native fruits of siriguela (*Spondias purpurea*). Photograph © AQUASIS/www.aquasis.org

Pyrrhuras, such as these Painted Conures in Guyana's Kanuku Mountains, often feed on *Cecropia* catkins. Photograph © www.wildparrotsupclose

the diet of *P. frontalis,* but were absent from the diet of *P. leucotis* in the lowland humid forests of Espirito Santo, where it was found to feed only on soft fruit and seeds, especially *Cecropia* spp., suggesting an interesting ecological difference between *leucotis* and *pfrimeri.*"

In the study of Green-cheeked Conures in the dry forests of western Brazil, it was estimated that flowers formed 10% of their diet at one particular location, especially the nectar of *Tabebuia impetiginosa.*

Fieldwork by Hugo Oliveros-Salas between November 2004 and June 2005 suggested that the flowers of *Croton bogotanus* were the principal food source of the Santa Marta Conure. For a detailed study of the foraging and food preferences of this species, refer to Botero Delgadillo *et al,* 2010.

In Venezuela, Blood-eared Parakeets *(P. hoematosis)* were observed in the Yacambu National Park. The main items consumed, based on the number of feeding bouts, were arillate [with a fleshy covering – often brightly coloured] seeds of Euphorbiaceae, from mature fruits of *Tetrorchidium rubrivenium* and *Alchornea triplinervia*, and immature fruits of *Sapium stylare*. Capsules of these tree species were less than 10mm in diameter and contained one to three arillate seeds that turned red when ripe. Other items eaten were seeds of *Croton gossypifolius* (Euphorbiaceae), flowers of *Erythrina* and *Ocotea*, and fleshy fruits of *Geonoma undata* (Arecaceae), *Cecropia angustifolia* (Urticaceae) and *Guettarda crispiflora* (Rubiaceae). Blood-eared Parakeets also included *Inga oerstediana* pods in their diet. They used thirteen species of plants and their diet consisted principally of arillate seeds, but also included fleshy fruits and flowers (Buitron-Jurado and Sanz, 2016).

Clay licks

Clay licks occur in Brazil, Peru, Bolivia, Ecuador and Paraguay and attract many parrots. These soil banks are concentrated in the Amazon rainforest along the eastern base of the Andes. Their situation is within tropical and sub-tropical broad-leafed forest, typically by a river or a stream. Clay licks have been positively correlated with distance from the ocean (Lee, 2010). It is now believed that parrots are searching for sodium, not soil that protects against dietary toxins, as formerly suggested. (See photograph on page 92)

Several species are known to visit clay licks, including White-necked Conures in Zamora-Chinchipe Province, Ecuador. In south-eastern Peru many bird watchers have seen Rose-fronted *(roseifrons)* and Black-capped Conures at a clay lick. Except at these sites or in a prolifically fruiting tree, *Pyrrhuras* are not usually seen in association with other parrots. In the Rio Cristalino reserve in the rainforest of north-western Mato Grosso, Crimson-bellied and Snethlage's Conures visit patches of bare ground during the dry season to eat the exposed sodium-containing earth. Pfrimer's Conures have been observed scraping at limestone rocks and ingesting the sediment. One such sighting occurred close to the opening of the Terra Ronca II cave in the municipality of São Domingos, in Goiás state. A flock of about 20 *pfrimeri* were observed clustered against a distant limestone wall at a height of approximately 8m (26ft), making frantic scraping motions with their beaks (Dornas *et al*, 2016). See also photograph page 92.

Our knowledge of the dietary habits of this genus is minimal. From what has been recorded so far, it seems that figs, *Cecropia* catkins, flowers, green seeds and berries form the diet of most species.

13. LIFE IN THE WILD

THERE IS a great deal to learn about the way *Pyrrhuras* live. Especially in the Andes, there was little knowledge – so little, that in August 1980 three ornithologists from the Department of Ornithology of the Academy of Natural Sciences, Philadelphia, made an astounding discovery. A new species! One of them was the renowned Robert Ridgely, author of some of the most important works on neotropical avifauna published in the 20th century. The men were investigating remnant patches of cloud forest in El Oro province, Ecuador, on the western slope of the Andes. Suddenly, nine small parrots, clearly *Pyrrhuras*, landed in the canopy. But they had no scalloped plumage on the breast. What could they be? Imagine how intrigued they were!

Not until nearly five years later was the Academy able to organise a return expedition. Its members spent three weeks in the region, acquiring a lot of information. The parakeets were relatively numerous. Thus a species hitherto unknown to science was described and named as the El Oro Parakeet (*Pyrrhura orcesi*.) This was tremendously exciting – after all, most *Pyrrhura* species were named between 1648 and 1881! How could this one have been overlooked? It has a very limited range, being found in only three areas, in the humid, upper tropical zone forest, between 600m and 1,100m.

Except for the most endangered species which are being intensively studied, *Pyrrhura* biology is not well known. There are two reasons: their secretive habits and the fact that some of the regions they inhabit are almost inaccessible. There are many areas where ornithologists cannot go. According to Robin Restall, formerly research associate at the Natural History Museum in Caracas, birders are the main source of information these days regarding the status of birds in Venezuela. They are far more restricted than in even Colombia or Ecuador because of the many no-go areas due to drug-running, timber theft, FARC encampments, kidnapping, murder and robbery.

It is not necessarily the case that the natural history of species with a wide range is well known – quite the reverse: there is little incentive to study those which are numerous. The Green-cheeked Conure might be described as the most successful species because it has adapted to various habitat types over its large range yet we know rather little about it.

Habitats and altitudes
Most *Pyrrhuras* occur in wet forests, and members of the genus can be found from sea level up to 3,100m. Only a few inhabit the tropical zone.

Cloud forest species tolerate climates that are as cold, wet and foggy as northern Europe in winter and the páramo is an even bleaker habitat. The table below shows the type of habitat from which different species originate. It indicates that most species come from the sub-tropical zone.

Species	Tropical Up to 300m 1,000ft	Sub-tropical 300m-1,800m 1,000-6,000ft	Cloud forest 1,800m-3,000m 6,000-10,000ft	Páramo 3,000m-4,500m 10,000-15,000ft
Albipectus		X		
Amazonum	X	X		
Frontalis/devillei	X	X		
Caeruleiceps		X	X	
Calliptera		X	X	X
Chapmani	X	X	X	
Coerulescens/perlata	X	X	X	
Cruentata	X	X		
Egregia		X	X	
Eisenmanni		X		
Emma/auricularis		X		
Griseipectus	X	X		
Hoffmanni		X	X	
Hoematotis		X	X	
Leucotis	X			
Lucianii	X	X		
Melanura	X	X	X	
Molinae	X	X	X	
Orcesi		X		
Pacifica		X		
Peruviana		X		
Pfrimeri	X	X		
Picta/roseifrons	X			
Rhodocephala		X	X	
Rupicola	X			
Snethlageae	X			
Viridicata		X	X	

Most if not all *Pyrrhura* species have traditional roosting/nesting trees, which have been used for decades by small groups of up to 10 birds and probably limit their dispersive abilities. They mainly use living trees such as *Albizia polycephala* and *Inga* species, the absence of which appears to be a significant limiting factor in the ability of birds to occupy otherwise seemingly suitable habitat. The specific habitat requirements of most of the Peruvian *Pyrrhura* species are incompletely known, but it seems that many populations require intact mountain rainforest with tall tree species. They forage at lower elevations in more fragmented areas at certain times of the year, but are generally absent from forested areas which have been affected by human activities. This suggests special habitat requirements, which result in localised occurrence (Arndt & Wink, 2017).

In Brazil

The distribution map for the genus shows a huge empty space within the enormous country of Brazil. Much of this is dry *cerrado* habitat. Olmos *et al* (1997) noted that although the dry forests of the Serra Geral from Minas Gerais to

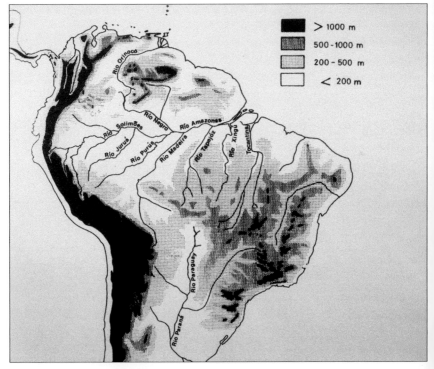

South America: altitudes above sea level and major rivers.

Bahia have been ornithologically explored since the 19th century, no *Pyrrhura* has been found there. They commented: "This is puzzling considering that the taxon geographically closest to *P. pfrimeri* is *P. leucotis* from eastern Brazil's coastal forests and some related taxa linking them would be expected to occur in the intervening area east of the Serra Geral, especially with the similarities between the forests there and to the west."

However, they also point out that in north-eastern Brazil rainforest with Atlantic affinities was at one time much more extensive further inland than it is today and this may have been the source of the ancestral stock from which *P. pfrimeri* originated. The more arid climate in the dry forests east of the Serra Geral might explain the absence of a *Pyrrhura* there because the dry season is too long for a forest parakeet to survive.

Two similar-looking species inhabit areas in excess of one thousand kilometres apart, with the intervening area devoid of any *Pyrrhura* despite the presence of Atlantic forest. The White-eared Conure *(leucotis)* inhabits the eastern lowland Atlantic forest from southern Bahia to Rio de Janeiro whereas the Grey-breasted

The habitat of species from the Andes, such as the Chingaza Natural National Park in Colombia where the Flame-winged Parakeet occurs, is very different to that of species from lowland rainforests. Photograph © Rene Wust

Conure *(P. griseipectus)* is restricted to montane forest areas that have strong Amazonian affinities in otherwise semi-arid Ceará and Pernambuco.

General habits

Pyrrhura conures are highly social birds. They are observed in groups of a dozen or so, and in larger flocks, but only occasionally of more than sixty individuals. They spend much time perched in leafy trees in small groups, indulging in preening and mutual preening. There is much physical contact, especially between pairs and family members who usually sit close together, touching. In many respects they remind me of the lorikeets of the Pacific region. As well as the habits just mentioned, they share the characteristics of being highly inquisitive and very fast in flight. Like lories, they feed a lot on flowers, adopting acrobatic manoeuvres or hanging upside down from slender branches to reach the blossoms.

In *Birds of Venezuela* Steven Hilty writes of the Fiery-shouldered Conure: "Flies in small, tight, fast-flying flocks of 3-25 (usually about 6-10) that thread and twist their way through forest canopy or lower with amazing speed and agility, then suddenly settle into a canopy tree and 'disappear'. Typically very silent and watchful when feeding on fruit or seeds, but usually utter a few scratchy calls immediately before taking flight" (Hilty, 2003). This well observed description could apply to any member of the genus. He too emphasises their amazing flight skills.

Donald Brightsmith (1999) noted of *Pyrrhura* conures in general their "...habit of perching silently in a tree then calling briefly just before taking flight is common. The calls seem to synchronize the departure of the flock. I have discovered a frustrating side-effect of this is that I often spot the birds just as they take off and speed away."

Flight

Observations of these conures in flight are often brief. Unlike some parrots, a group that has been quietly feeding or resting in a tree does not depart leisurely or continuously: they call to each other for a couple of seconds, apparently indicating departure, and they take flight and are gone in the bat of an eyelid.

The speed and skill of *Pyrrhura* conures is amazing in view of the fact that they form such tight-knit groups in flight. Unlike most parrots, they fly below canopy level. In my book *Go West for Parrots*, I wrote about a sighting of Maroon-tailed (Black-tailed) Conures in Ecuador which 'sped through the trees screeching *kree kree*. I scarcely had time to take in their dark green plumage, barred breast and the red bend of the wing. Parakeets of this genus are difficult to observe, being fast and wary and flying in tight formation. Unlike the *Aratinga* conures, more than a fleeting glimpse is exceptional' (Low, 2009).

One comes across them unexpectedly – and they are gone in a flash making their rapid, chattering calls. Flying below canopy level at great speed requires remarkable precision especially as they can fly as low as 2m above the ground.

Bathing

These parakeets are enthusiastic bathers, using vegetation after rain, river edges, rock pools and even puddles. Roth recorded that "Painted Conures" (now classified as *snethlageae*), came every day during the dry season in the Mato Grosso, to watercourses to bathe and changed the location only when water levels receded. They were also seen bathing at a rocky cliff in the spray from a waterfall (in Forshaw, 1989).

Donald Brightsmith (1999) recalled watching a flock of Painted Conures (the form now known as Rose-fronted). The sky was a brilliant blue, and the early morning sun was just reaching the tops of the dripping wet trees. He was amazed to see the bizarre antics of one conure as it apparently tried to land on the surface of single leaf which could not support its weight. The conure fell fluttering through the leaves before landing on a solid branch. He thought it was a young bird just learning to fly, then he saw another conure, then another, behaving in the same way. When he spotted a bird on a branch covered with moss and lichen leaning down into a soaking wet clump of moss and ruffling its feathers, all became clear: the entire flock of birds was bathing in the sun on rain-moistened leaves over 23m above the ground! It was certainly safer than descending to find a puddle.

Nest sites and breeding season

Most *Pyrrhuras* nest in tree cavities, including those in palm trees, but nesting in holes in cliffs also occurs. In Brazil, in Santa Catarina, pairs of Maroon-bellied Conures, perhaps the only species that does not shun human habitation, were observed nesting under a tile roof, gnawing through a slat to gain entry. This is not unusual. On the island of São Sebastião (Ilhabela), on the coast of south-east Brazil, this is a problem that has been addressed by the organisation Cambaquara. An education programme aims to prevent the use of such nesting sites and to rear and release young birds that are illegally removed from them.

In many populations reproduction must be limited by lack of nest sites. Perhaps this is how co-operative breeding (see below) originated. Where nest-boxes have been erected for endangered *Pyrrhura* species, they are usually immediately occupied, with successful outcomes.

The most threatened species have been studied, especially in the Andes of Colombia, thus it is known that the Santa Marta Conure has two periods of reproduction. Copulation is seen in December and January, inspection of nests in February and March, laying in March and April and rearing of young in May and June. In the second breeding period nest inspection occurs between March and June, laying between July and August and rearing of young in September and October.

Co-operative breeding and young helpers at nests

In Ecuador, Fundación Jocotoco monitored nest-boxes erected for the El Oro Conure. It was discovered that the nest was visited by various members of a group four to five times a day, each visit lasting from 12 to 20 minutes.

Donald Brightsmith was one of the first ornithologists to record that more than two birds attend one nest. He spent long periods at the Tambopata Research Centre in south-eastern Peru. One day he observed a group of four Rose-fronted Conures in a tree on the side of a trail. He admired their agility as they flew off in tight formation through the branches. A few hours later he paused in the same spot and heard the same quiet yet distinctive calls. At a height of 9m four conures were clinging to a thin, bare, vertical vine. The birds were watching him, then quickly flew off.

He moved around the tree and saw a 5cm diameter hole in the side. He returned to camp for his climbing gear and was soon hanging 9m up with a dental mirror and a flashlight at the entrance of the cavity that had formed where a branch had broken off. The open hole was surrounded with a thick layer of new live wood making the entrance extremely hard and nearly unbreakable. The inside of the cavity was 30cm deep and extended up and to the side out of sight. He discovered a newly hatched chick and three eggs.

The clutch size of four suggested that only one female was involved. Could it be that young from previous years stayed to help raise the new brood, he asked himself? At least one of the birds had much less red on the head.

Fooling a nest predator

One day, as he sat by the nest, at about 5pm, he heard the birds calling quietly as they arrived. They perched about 18m north of the nest. To the south-east a group of Brown Capuchin Monkeys were jumping through the trees. In a few minutes the four conures moved to the canopy of the tree above the nest then all four descended until they were perched on a vine within 1.8m of the hole. Two birds quickly hopped inside, then the third entered, leaving one outside watching the approaching monkeys.

At this point the monkeys (voracious nest predators) were within 9m of the nest. The lone conure outside then flew up to the safety of the canopy, calling quietly. Two of the birds left the tree cavity and perched on the vines near the nest entrance. Then a monkey, less than 6m away, started down a vine that would bring it within a few feet of the nest. With this, one of the conures flew up to a branch only 4.5m above the nest and hung awkwardly upside down calling loudly as though trapped, tangled in the leaves. The monkey spotted it and immediately sprung forward in an attempt to capture it, covering the remaining distance in a few rapid leaps. In this instant, all four conures quickly took flight and weaved off through the trees. The excited monkey, having missed its prize, bounded off in the direction the birds had flown and did not see the nest cavity (Brightsmith, 1999). If anyone doubts that small parrots can think through solutions to problems, this incident should dispel that doubt!

Predator avoidance

Comparing members of the genus with other parrots, in the wild and in captivity, many *Pyrrhuras* show exceptional vigilance and, as already mentioned, are very fast to react to danger. Watching a group of Crimson-bellied Conures in the Rio Cristalino reserve, I was amazed at the extreme caution and patience of

Adult and young Grey-breasted Parakeets at one of the many nest boxes which were responsible for the rapid population increases. Photograph © Aquasis

the sentinel bird as the small group sat high in the canopy, waiting to come down to the saliero (earth containing sodium).

Alan Lee told me: "I am most familiar with the Black-capped parakeet *(Pyrrhura rupicola)* and a bit with *P. roseifrons*. Both of these visited clay licks in south-eastern Peru. I don't think any of my team witnessed a predation event on these species. Mealy Parrot and Cobalt-winged Parakeet were taken by Ornate Hawk Eagle and Ocelot respectively, Black Hawk Eagles were observed attacking larger macaws, and Orange-breasted Falcon attacks were observed on Red-bellied Macaw and Blue-headed Parrot.

"The interesting thing about the *Pyrrhuras* was that they did not use clay licks like the other parrot species. They made greater use of mammal clay licks within forest and were only observed on a few typical riverside clay licks. They normally fed in small groups, occasionally with Cobalt-winged Parakeets. When they made use of the 'normal' clay licks they arrived quietly, and would eat soil only from behind the shelter of vegetation. They were thus quite hard to pick up on – sometimes one would be aware of their presence only when they flushed for whatever reason. I am sure their feeding strategy is based on predator avoidance."

Does predation occur in other circumstances? The instinctive urge to flee is triggered in less time than it takes to bat an eyelid, by the alarm call of another flock member. (In captive birds a sudden, loud sound has the same effect.) Their rapid reflexes, and the fact they are such extremely fast and skilful flyers, makes it seem likely that only a newly fledged bird would be taken by a raptor. Probably conures are at their most vulnerable in their roost/nest site when they could be attacked by monkeys, toucans or tree snakes.

It is known, for the El Oro Conure, for example, that when forest trees are destroyed these birds are forced to nest in isolated trees in open pasture and on the forest edge. These nests were more exposed to predation, especially by Crimson-rumped Toucanets *(Aulacorhynchus haematopygus)*.

Roosting

Pyrrhuras prefer to roost in cavities where these are available. The Santa Marta Conure roosts in fronds of the palm *Ceroxylon ceriferum*. In the Colombian Andes, Paul Salaman reported that nocturnal inspections revealed that roosting Flame-winged Conure flocks are not "huddling together at the bottom of the cavity, but hanging upside down from the roof like bats!"

Sick (1993) wrote (contradicting the head position): "With captive *Pyrrhura* one can also see that they usually sleep not perched but clinging head up to a vertical cloth or similar substrate."

Roost sites have also been seen in rock crevices. In December 1993 three birds of the *flavoptera* sub-species of the Green-cheeked Conure were observed in La Paz, Bolivia. Every evening they arrived, screeching, just before dusk, then perched on a small shrub on a rock face for fifteen to thirty minutes while producing "peculiar calls". These were described as a loud, drawn-out *kEEEE-eh*. Finally, they would fly a few metres to an overhanging section of the rock face where they disappeared for the night (Maijer, *et al*, 1998). (No signs of breeding were observed.)

Hybrids

Captive breeding has shown, as one would expect, that various species can hybridise; it seems likely that, in this closely related group of parakeets, any two could produce young. Wild hybrids are known. In the 1970s the renowned neotropical ornithologist Ted Parker reported that a hybrid between the Black-capped Conure (*rupicola*) and the Green-cheeked (*P. molinae*) had been taken in Puno, Peru.

Some White-breasted Conures observed in a flock of Black-tailed Conures in Ecuador at an altitude of 1,000m to 1,200m were said to show some plumage differences from individuals seen at a higher altitude but it was not known whether the differences were age-related or due to *albipectus x melanura* hybridization. Perhaps they were not hybrids as White-breasted and Black-tailed Parakeets remain separated during the breeding season, each utilizing a different

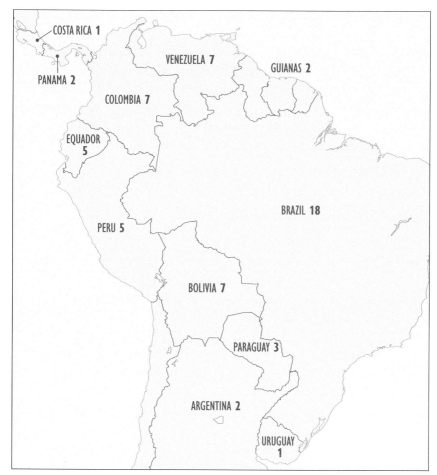

The number of *Pyrrhura* species per country, as known in 2021 – but always subject to revision.

altitudinal range, but outside the breeding season they form mixed flocks (Robbins *et al.* 1987).

There is plenty of scope for ornithologists and bird watchers to record (especially with images) new information about these fascinating birds.

Range of *Pyrrhura* conures by country

* denotes endemic species

Argentina (2): *frontalis* and *molinae*.

Bolivia (6 or 7): *devillei?, molinae, perlata, peruviana, roseifrons, rupicola* and *snethlageae/pallescens*.

Brazil (18): *amazonum*, coerulescens*, cruentata*, devillei, egregia, frontalis, griseipectus*, leucotis*, lucianii*, melanura, molinae, perlata, pfrimeri*, picta, roseifrons, rupicola* and *snethlageae*.

Colombia (7): *caeruleiceps, calliptera*, chapmani*, melanura, pacifica, subandina** and *viridicata**.

Costa Rica (1): *hoffmanni*.

Ecuador (5): *albipectus, melanura, orcesi*, pacifica* and *peruviana*.

Guianas (2): *egregia* and *picta*.

Panama (2): *hoffmanni* and *eisenmanni**.

Paraguay (3): *devillei, frontalis* and *molinae*.

Peru (6): *albipectus, melanura, parvifrons, peruviana, roseifrons* and *rupicola*.

Venezuela (7): *caeruleiceps, egregia, emma*, hoematotis*, melanura, picta* and *rhodocephala**.

Uruguay (1): *frontalis*.

14. AVICULTURE AND CONSERVATION POTENTIAL

IN EUROPE and the USA breeders were fortunate to obtain frequent stocks of some *Pyrrhura* species until permanent import bans were imposed on wild-caught birds. The history of Hoffmann's Conure in aviculture is a very interesting one because it demonstrates how species are lost in aviculture without concerted attempts to maintain them.

In 1980 veterinarian Dr Nathan Gale was working in Panama, a country which had ceased to allow the export of its birds. He was able to acquire a special permit for thirty-six Hoffmann's Conures, the first and only group ever to be exported legally. They were received by a USDA approved quarantine station. At the completion of quarantine, all but one pair went to two breeders in Arizona. The first captive breeding was achieved by Chris Rowley in 1982.

What happened over the next decade was sadly not unusual when a new species enters aviculture in limited numbers. By 1992 only eleven birds were known, some of which were captive-bred. These eleven birds were sent to Dale Thompson, a leading aviculturist in California, who became the director of a consortium project. Even although the group included one breeding pair, all were shipped in one container without any records – not an auspicious start for the consortium. They therefore had to be surgically sexed, indicating seven males and four females.

All the birds were placed in one flight. The breeding pair was quickly identified by the close bond. They were removed and the other pairs were observed. During the first breeding season the aim was to obtain as many young as possible, regardless of genetic diversity. As it happened, the known bonded pair produced most of the young. All were removed for hand-rearing – a total of 26 young.

After the first season Dale Thompson sought the advice of genetics experts. The theory is that six pairs of any species are needed to maintain genetic diversity. Ideally, unrelated stock is continually paired. This was impossible with the group of Hoffmann's Conures. Two of the males were sixteen plus years old. One of them did breed but he died the following winter. The other old male was paired with every female over a period of four breeding seasons but no fertile eggs were produced.

After the first year, parent-rearing was the aim. Most of the early clutches contained only two or three eggs. All offspring were kept and paired in the best way to maintain genetic diversity. Each female was moved on to another male but only two reproduced very well, the others being reluctant to accept new males, sometimes not breeding for two years and producing only one offspring.

The next problem was the early lack of females produced: only three in the first two years, with 14 males reared. During the third and fourth year, the ratio of females increased greatly. The fourth generation was the first to produce more females than males – but by one only. By 1998 (eighteen years after they were received) all the founder stock had died.

After four years the pairs were starting to produce some four-egg clutches and the chicks were consistently bigger in size and weight. The number of clutches produced each year also increased. During the fifth year, the 14 males bred by the original bonded pair at last were given the opportunity to breed, paired with one-year-old females. Dale Thompson wrote: "They had excellent fertile clutches and were consistently the best parents of any of the pairs within the consortium. We believe this was due to their maturity and being mostly parent-reared. They were also housed together during the previous years in a very large flight and were very well socialized" Christian and Thompson, 2007 *Pyrrhura* Breeders newsletter).

By the fifth year the females were laying eggs in the food dishes at only 12 months of age so they were given nest-boxes – earlier than had occurred in the past. When the consortium started to sell young, a minimum of three pairs were sold to each breeder, the aim being to maintain genetic diversity. All the birds were ringed and were sent to seven overseas countries, with instructions regarding which birds should be paired together. By 1998 their offspring were being sold as single pairs – which was not desirable. However, by 1999 more than 350 young had been reared and Hoffman's Conure had been established in aviculture.

The outome could have been very different. Hoffmann's Conure could have been lost to aviculture by or before the end of the 1990s had Dale Thompson not set up a consortium and adhered strictly to the guidelines. If, in the future, any *Pyrrhura* species with small populations in their natural habitat are brought into captivity, the Hoffmann's Conure story must be studied with care. It has very important implications for conservation.

Looking to the future

Will the day ever come when captive breeding is considered as a last resort to save a species of *Pyrrhura* or when a few birds are taken to try to build up a captive population? These days captive breeding as part of a conservation programme for an endangered species seldom occurs and normally only *in situ* – not in the hands of private aviculturists. Because of their adaptability and prolificacy, captive breeding of rare *Pyrrhura* conures might be seen as the solution. What is not generally realised, however, is that species with a small gene pool or those that have become isolated in small populations due to loss of habitat, are likely to be more difficult to reproduce in captivity than widespread and common conures such as the Green-cheeked and the Maroon-bellied.

So breeders, please don't yearn after White-breasted Conures when the current range of species in aviculture provides such beauty and variety. It is only human nature to desire that which is rare – but where endangered species with small populations are concerned, whose capture is illegal, it would be immoral and unethical to try to acquire the threatened endemics.

Hybridisation is deplored

Captive breeding might have conservation applications with members of the genus *Pyrrhura* already established in aviculture and to jeopardise that possibility by producing hybrids and mutations would be disastrous.

Catherine A. Toft, of the Department of Zoology, University of California - Davis, wrote:

Hybridization is the fastest and surest way to destroy the genetic make-up of a species. It breaks up complexes and genes that allow species to be adapted to the natural environment and to be recognised as a potential mate.

Breeding mutations

In my view this is acceptable for popular, free-breeding species not of conservation concern, such as the Green-cheeked Conure. At the time of writing, the most endangered species in aviculture are the Brazilian endemics, *leucotis, griseipectus* and *pfrimeri*. Mutations are already being bred of the first two species. **To encourage this is akin to recognising that aviculturists can never contribute to conservation by producing captive populations that might be of value if the species becomes extinct in the wild.**

15. CONSERVATION: PRESENT AND FUTURE

THROUGHOUT the world, bird and animal species with small ranges are the most vulnerable to extinction, due to habitat loss and degradation. Only two species of *Pyrrhuras* have large ranges in South America: the Green-cheeked in the southern-central area, including Brazil, Bolivia and Paraguay, and the Black-tailed in the west and north. The Black-tailed Conure is numerous and may even have benefited from deforestation. Seventeen species have extremely small ranges in the wild and most of them are declining rapidly and/or are endangered due to clearance of habitat. This is especially the case in Brazil and in the Andes of Colombia and Ecuador where deforestation has been severe.

Summary of IUCN threat status at 2020

CRITICAL/POSSIBLY EXTINCT
Sinú Parakeet (*P. subandina*)

ENDANGERED
Grey-breasted Parakeet (*P. griseipectus*)
Pfrimer's Parakeet (*P. pfrimeri*)
Azuero Parakeet (*P. eisenmanni*)
Perija Parakeet (*P. caeruleiceps*)
Santarem Parakeet (*P. amazonum*)
Santa Marta Parakeet (*P. viridicata*)
El Oro Parakeet (*P. orcesi*)

VULNERABLE
Pearly Parakeet (*P. coerulescens*)
Crimson-bellied Parakeet (*P. perlata*)
White-eared Parakeet (*P. leucotis*)
Madeira Parakeet (*P. snethlageae/pallescens*)
White-necked Parakeet (*P. albipectus*)
Flame-winged Parakeet (*P. calliptera*)
Blue-throated Parakeet (*P. cruentata*)

NEAR THREATENED
Blaze-winged Parakeet (*P. devillei*)

LEAST CONCERN
All other *Pyrrhura* species, including Black-capped Parakeet (*P. rupicola*) which was down-listed in 2020.

Note that some of the above species might be down-listed. In 2022 the following (using IUCN nomenclature) were proposed for a lower level of threat category: *devillei, perlata, lepida, eisenmanni, amazonum* and *snethlageae/pallescens*. This was due to reassessment of rates of forest cover loss within their ranges. It is perhaps surprising that down-listing is considered based solely on a mathematical prediction.

Categories of threat

The most widely accepted criteria for objective evaluation of the status of species are those used by the International Union for the Conservation of Nature (IUCN)/ BirdLife International Red List of threatened species (BirdLife International, IUCN) to classify bird species according to the relative level of threat, from Least Concern to Extinct.

LC Least Concern (the species is believed to be safe).
NT Near Threatened (close to qualifying as Vulnerable).
V Vulnerable (faces a high risk of extinction in the medium-term future).
EN Endangered (faces a high risk of extinction in the near future).
CR Critically Endangered (faces extremely high risk of extinction in the immediate future).
EW Extinct in the Wild (survives only in captivity or in a naturalised population).
EX Extinct

When *Threatened Birds of the World* was published in 2000 only seven *Pyrrhura* species were listed as of conservation concern. The El Oro and Santa Marta Conures were classified as Endangered and the Blue-throated, White-necked and Flame-winged as Vulnerable. The Pearly Conure was placed in the Near-threatened category.

Two decades later, as the result of greatly increased research and field work, the situation looked much more serious with more species in threat categories. See notes under **Status** for each species.

Habitat loss is the biggest threat

The populations and ranges of most of the world's parrots have declined in the 21st century due to habitat loss. This is of particular concern for *Pyrrhuras* as flocks of most species are localised. The birds do not move long distances and cannot survive in areas of despoiled habitat. The situation for some species was exacerbated by the catastrophic fires of 2019 and 2020 which raged in Brazil and elsewhere over much of the habitat of *Pyrrhura* species.

The anti-environmental policies of Brazil's President Jair Bolsonaro, who took office in January 2019, proved catastrophic for the Amazon rainforest. From August 2019 to July 2020 a vast expanse, seven times larger than Greater London, was destroyed as deforestation surged to a 12-year high. Figures released by the Brazilian space institute, Inpe, on November 30 2020, showed that at least 11,088km^2 of rainforest was razed between August 2019 and July 2020. This was the highest figure since 2008. Destruction of these primary forests are incalculable in terms of biodiversity loss, ecosystem function and carbon sequestration.

The Prodes satellite system showed that most of the devastation was occurring in four regions: Pará state, the north of Mato Grosso state, the south of Amazonas state and Rondônia. Pará, a long-time deforestation hotspot, was by far the worst-affected, accounting for almost 47% of the total deforestation. The Pearly Conure (*P. coerulescens*), already classified as Vulnerable, is likely to be pushed further towards extinction in this highly degraded area. Rondônia and the northern part of Mato Grosso were also badly affected; these three states are occupied by the Crimson-bellied Conure, another IUCN Vulnerable species. The Painted Conure (*P. picta*) is also found in Pará but is less vulnerable due to its much wider distribution.

Conservation projects start
Many parrots were known to be endangered in the wild by the 1990s. The first conservation projects focused on the large charismatic macaws of South America and the threatened Amazons parrots of the Caribbean islands. When it was known that some small and inconspicuous parakeets were also threatened, would any organisation be willing to fund their survival?

Loro Parque, Tenerife, in the Canary Islands, has the most comprehensive collection of parrots that has ever existed – 350 species and sub-species. It was most timely that the Loro Parque Fundación (LPF) was founded in 1994 to assist the conservation of threatened and endangered parrots. At that time 95 species out of the approximate total of 330 were at risk of extinction. By 2011, LPF has directed about US$10 million to save species and their habitats. In 2011 it budgeted US$1.23 million for conservation projects including four species of *Pyrrhura* in Colombia, one in Brazil and one in Ecuador. In 2012 the budget was again substantial – US$1.1 million. By 2021 LPF had donated US$19 million to conservation – and more than half to projects to benefit parrots. By 2021 it had donated US$688,719 to the projects to support *Pyrrhura* parakeets.

Habitat protection in Ecuador
The first species to attract the attention of conservation biologists was the El Oro Conure (*orcesi*), found only in south-western Ecuador. It was not known to science until 1980 and was named as a "new" species in 1985. Because of its restricted

habitat in an area where serious forest fragmentation had occurred and where there were rapid rates of logging during the late 1980s, continuing into the 1990s, it was immediately classified as Endangered.

Starting the in the early 1960s the Ecuadorian government had established the Ecuadorian National System of Protected Areas (SNAP). By 2020 it comprised about 60 areas covering more than 80 million hectares, more than 13% of Ecuador's territory.

In 1999 the Buenaventura Reserve was established with the conure as the flagship species. Owned by the NGO Fundacíon Jocotoco, the reserve covers 3,700 acres with future hopes of increasing the area to 10,000 acres. Its reforestation is part of the World Land Trust's Carbon Balanced Program. A sight to gladden the heart of any conservationist is the photograph (see page 226) of nine El Oro Conures at one of many nest-boxes erected by Jocotoco which has allowed the population to make a significant increase. Without the intervention of conservationists soon after it was discovered, this conure might not have survived to this day.

Despite management issues, such as private land inside the protected areas, most Ecuadorian bird species receive formal protection. Unfortunately, most of the protected areas are located in northern Ecuador. The southern Andean habitats, so important for the *Pyrhura* species, are under-represented. However, throughout Ecuador there are about 160 areas with the status of Protected Forest (Bosque Protector). Almost half of these are owned by the Ecuadorian government, even when they are not part of the SNAP. The others consist of about one hundred private protected areas extending over approximately 70,000 hectares (173,000 acres). Again, the majority lie in the northern half of the country.

In Ecuador, Fundación Jocotoco (founded in 1998) has helped to protect the habitat of the El Oro Conure. Loro Parque Fundación supports further research by the University of Freiburg (Germany) and the Ecuadorean Museum of Natural Sciences (MECN) to identify other important sub-populations within its geographical range, and to evaluate the genetic effect of isolation of sub-populations due to fragmentation of the forest. Jocotoco successfully acquires and restores degraded habitats. It started reforestation projects in 2004, focused mainly on the reserves of Tapichalaca, Buenaventura, Jorupe and Yanacocha. The foundation uses only local native species. It has successfully planted more than 1.4 million native trees of 130 species, restoring more than 3,000ha (7,400 acres) of key habitat for countless birds and becoming a leading organisation in ecosystem restoration in Ecuador.

Conservation, education and research in Colombia

In 1991 Paul Salaman went to Colombia to carry out field work, as part of his PhD studies at Oxford University. He found the Yellow-eared Parrot *(Ognorhynchus icterotis)* on the edge of extinction. With funding from Loro Parque Fundacion and with a small number of Colombian field workers, he founded ProAves in 2000. This organisation is dedicated to saving the birds and their habitats in Colombia. Their project with the Yellow-eared Parrot, which has seen the population increase from fewer than 100 to 1,500 birds, is the most successful worldwide in parrot conservation to date. Now it is the smaller parrots, *Pyrrhuras*, and small parrots of the genus *Hapalopsittaca*, that are more desperately receiving their attention.

The publication of an important document in 2010 drew attention to it. This was the *Colombian Threatened Parrot Conservation Action Plan 2010-2020: Progress, Achievements & Prospects* (Botero–Delgadillo and Páez, 2010). The authors pointed out that urgent action needed to be taken to investigate the conservation status of the Pacific Black-tailed *(pacifica)*, the Perija or Todd's Conure *(caeruleiceps)* and the Sinú Conure *(P. subandina)*.

Colombia is very important in *Pyrrhura* conservation and research, due to the dedicated field workers among ProAves personnel. I have seen them in action and was very impressed. SELVA, an offshoot, was formed in 2009 for research purposes, especially to determine the geographic distribution of *Pyrrhuras* in Colombia and to identify conservation priorities. Study of these aspects was urgently needed – as indeed they are in other parts of South America.

In Colombia, the Santa Marta Conure *(P. viridicata)* is listed as Endangered. It can be found in the El Dorado Bird Reserve, which forms part of the Alliance for Zero Extinction (AZE) site. These sites protect the last known location of one or more of the world's most endangered species – those classified as Endangered or Critically Endangered by IUCN. The El Dorado Reserve is another site where the erection of nest-boxes has played a major part in saving a *Pyrrhura* conure, reduced to a small population, from extinction. Here the work is carried out by the Colombian NGO ProAves. Loro Parque Fundacíon, the American Bird Conservancy and Conservation International have been major contributors financially. Aviculturists were involved with a donation from the International Conure Association (USA).

In Germany, the Zoological Society for the Conservation of Species and Populations (ZGAP) set up a working group in 1989, Fonds für bedrohte Papageien (FbP) (Funds for Endangered Parrots). Working group members examine and evaluate project applications, in the same way as Loro Parque Fundación. One of the projects supported by FbP is within the same site in Colombia of the Alliance for Critical Ecosystems. It promotes close co-operation with the Indians living in the Sierra Nevada de Santa Marta. The conure there acts as a key species in educating the people about the unique flora and fauna of their mountain range. They also take part in field work.

During the first decade of the 21st century, a small number of people, scientists and field workers, made an enormous difference to our knowledge of these birds. In the past little was known about the breeding biology of *Pyrrhura* conures. Now it is known that in some species, including the Flame-winged (*calliptera*), a Colombian endemic, it is a group of from three to nine birds, not a pair, that attends the nest. The helpers are likely to be the young from the previous nest. This work is part of Project *Pyrrhura* of Fundación ProAves and Loro Parque Fundación. Until little more than a decade previously no small parrots featured on the list of neotropical parrots of conservation concern. The only conure that had received much attention regarding field projects was the iconic Golden or Queen of Bavaria's Conure (*Guaruba guarouba*).

Without the support of LPF, the American Bird Conservancy (ABC) and some other organisations, several *Pyrrhura* species might be extinct by now or their habitat irretrievably lost. Loro Parque Fundación's Project *Pyrrhura*, working with NGO personnel in Colombia, Brazil and Ecuador, has revolutionised knowledge of the habits of and threats to these birds and made enormous strides towards safeguarding their habitats. Awareness campaigns to educate local people regarding the uniqueness and rarity of what, were to them, just little green parrots, has been extremely successful.

Nest-box programmes

Perhaps the most important factor in reversing the decline of endangered *Pyrrhuras* is the erection of nest-boxes. In some cases this has resulted in very rapid results.

The nest-box programme for the Grey-breasted Conure was so successful that within four years the species was downlisted from Critically Endangered to Endangered. This became an extraordinary success story, with 1,553 young fledged from nest-boxes by the end of 2020.
© AQUASIS/www.aquasis.org

In the Andes of Colombia, Flame-winged Conures (*P. calliptera*) demonstrated their urgent need for nest-sites. In 2005 forty-eight vertical nest-boxes were erected, modelled on the deep natural cavities used, where the birds enter through a natural crack, often well hidden by bromeliads. Breeders of *Pyrrhura* conures know they are very inquisitive and unlike most parrots will enter a new nest-box quickly. This is exactly what happened and sixteen days later five nest-boxes were occupied. By the end of October forty-five eggs had been laid.

Education programmes

In Colombia, Fundación ProAves runs education programmes with their fieldwork and research. This is very important for the threatened endemic species such as the Flame-winged Conure. An education programme was carried out, in the field and at a local college, to teach people about the threats facing this parakeet. In the tropics some people believe that parrots occur throughout the world and most people have no idea that a certain rare or endemic species is found only in their locality. With this information, it is much easier to instil in them a sense of pride in their unique species. In 2005 ProAves launched its LoroBus which travels around the Colombian Andes, visiting schools and communities to spread the conservation message. By 2011 the bus had visited 2,392 educational institutions and travelled more than 80,000km in Colombia – a remarkable achievement.

The work promoted by the LoroBus includes discouraging children from killing birds (including threatened species of conures) with catapults or sling shots. ProAves launched a campaign against this activity. By 2011, 326 sling shots and twenty air guns had been handed over. In exchange, children received T-shirts and educational material, plus free membership of *Amigos de las Aves* (Friends of the Birds), an ecological group within ProAves. This has demonstrated the ability of children to respond to environmental messages and will, hopefully, destroy the tradition of killing birds and lacking respect for nature.

In Ecuador, the educational outreach work of the El Oro Parakeet project supported by LPF has also achieved successes, notably that the City of Piñas, the nearest large urban area to Buenaventura Reserve, has officially adopted the parakeet as the city mascot, called "Pirry". A large metal sculpture of it has been erected within the city boundary.

The Amazon basin

In 2012 the status of the Black-capped Conure *(P. rupicola)* was uplisted to Near Threatened. Considering its large range, extending over parts of Peru, Brazil and Bolivia, this was unexpected. The change was based on a model of future deforestation in the Amazon basin. However, BirdLife International state that proposed changes to the Brazilian Forest Code reduce the percentage of land a

Fabio Nunes outside the Aquasis office in Guaramiranga, Baturité.
Photograph © Fabio Nunes, Aquasis

private landowner is legally required to maintain as forest (including, critically, a reduction in the width of forest buffers alongside perennial steams). The Code will include an amnesty for landowners who deforested before July 2008 (who would subsequently be absolved of the need to reforest illegally cleared land).

In Brazil, virtually confined to the Serra de Baturité in the north-east state of Ceará, is the Grey-breasted Conure. The Brazilian NGO Aquasis, supported by LPF, ZGAP and Chester Zoo, is fighting to save this species. The extensive field work, surveys and resulting publications are impressive and are a model of what can be achieved. Interviews with dozens of people indicate that the Grey-breasted Conure has recently (past forty years) become extinct in certain areas. An interview with a 44-year old farmer elicited the response that his grandmother had described the bird for him. He never saw it.

Aquasis, led by the dynamic Fabio Nunes, has made this conure the regional flagship species for conservation. When he started in 2010, only approximately 100 Grey-breasted Parakeets survived and it was considered to be one of the most endangered birds in Brazil, with Critically Endangered status (IUCN). The awareness campaign and the extremely successful nest-box programme led to a rapid increase in numbers, and in 2014 it was downlisted to Endangered. The number of breeding pairs had increased dramatically to between 200 and 300.

In Brazil, the future for the most endangered species hangs in the balance, especially that of Pfrimer's Conure. Those with a small range in areas where deforestation has been rapid and is continuing, are among the most vulnerable parrots of the neotropics. My fear is of the sudden realisation that a species' numbers have plummeted to the brink of extinction and it is too late to halt the decline.

Two other *Pyrrhuras* endemic to Brazil are of conservation concern but there are no projects to investigate their current plight. It has been known for a long time that the Blue-throated Conure (classified as Vulnerable) is endangered by loss of habitat.

The Pearly Conure, Near-threatened, has more recently been found to have declined for the same reason and is believed extinct in part of its range. Field work is needed to find out more – before it is too late.

The recent emphasis in Colombia, Ecuador and Brazil on members of the genus at last gives some hope for their long-term survival. But conservation projects are expensive to fund and deserve the attention of everyone who is sufficiently interested in the genus to read this book!

Supporting conservation

No matter how strong the will, conservation efforts will not succeed without sufficient funding. Throughout the world thousands of people are privileged to enjoy the company of *Pyrrhura* conures in their homes and aviaries. This is possible only because the ancestors of these birds were taken from the wild. Many other people are privileged to travel in order to observe them in the wild. To assist the conservation and future survival of these captivating conures, please donate to one of the following organisations that support *Pyrrhura* conservation projects:

LORO PARQUE FUNDACIÓN (Tenerife) www.loroparque-fundacion.org
AMERICAN BIRD CONSERVANCY (USA) www.abcbirds.org
AQUASIS (Brazil) www.aquasis.org
CHESTER ZOO (UK) www.actforwildlife.org.uk
FUNDACION JOCOTOCO (Ecuador) www.fjocotoco.org/donations
FUNDACION PROAVES (Colombia) www.proaves.org
ZOOLOGISCHE GESELLSCHAFT FÜR ARTEN- UND POPULATIONSSCHUTZ (Germany) www.zgap.de

PART TWO: THE SPECIES

KNOWLEDGE of what constitutes a species or a sub-species in the genus *Pyrrhura* is in a state of flux. In the first decade of the 21st century perceptions changed, mainly as a result of studies based on mitochondrial DNA. The South American Classification Committee makes the decisions regarding this genus. However, they must look at more than DNA sequencing. As is explained under Painted Conure, a number of former sub-species are now considered as species. Furthermore, there is not always a clear definition between one species and another.

In 1982 George Smith was far ahead of his time when he wrote of this genus: **"...the species of *Pyrrhura* seem to form a winding chain where adjacent species have such a strong resemblance to each other that they make the whole into a merging sequence."** This is especially the case with *picta* and *leucotis*.

Individual variation

Many bird keepers expect individuals of the same species to look alike but there can be significant plumage variation. This is especially the case in species which cover a large area of the huge South American sub-continent, such as the Black-tailed Conure *(melanura)* and the Green-cheeked *(molinae)*. It can therefore be difficult or impossible to assign captive birds to one sub-species because the area from which they or their ancestors originated is unknown. (See Black-tailed Conure for further explanation.)

The maroon patch on the abdomen can vary from that described for a certain species and might even appear in a reduced form in species supposedly without it. Possibly it is an atavistic feature, found in the ancestral *Pyrrhura*.

More *Pyrrhura* species occur in Brazil than in any other country. The maps on the following two pages show their approximate range.

Distribution of *Pyrrhuras* species in Brazil – Group 1

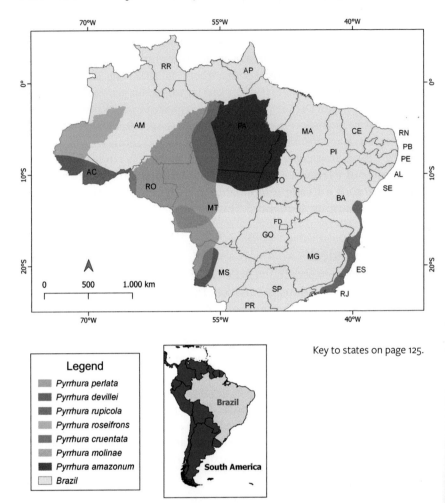

Key to states on page 125.

Map generously drawn by Raphael Sabongi Lúcio Marcelino.

Distribution of *Pyrrhuras* species in Brazil – Group 2

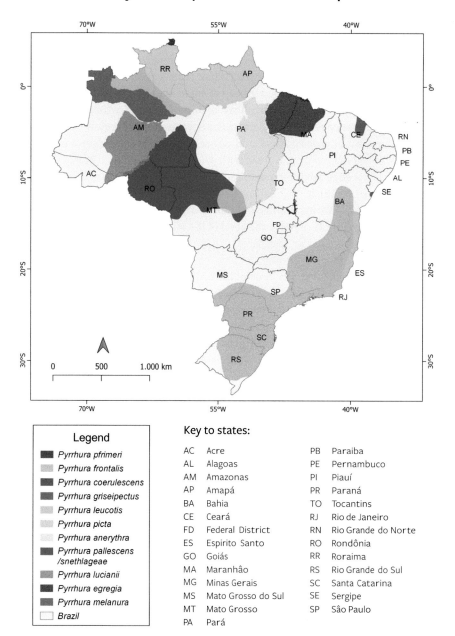

Legend

- Pyrrhura pfrimeri
- Pyrrhura frontalis
- Pyrrhura coerulescens
- Pyrrhura griseipectus
- Pyrrhura leucotis
- Pyrrhura picta
- Pyrrhura anerythra
- Pyrrhura pallescens /snethlageae
- Pyrrhura lucianii
- Pyrrhura egregia
- Pyrrhura melanura
- Brazil

Key to states:

AC	Acre	PB	Paraiba
AL	Alagoas	PE	Pernambuco
AM	Amazonas	PI	Piauí
AP	Amapá	PR	Paraná
BA	Bahia	TO	Tocantins
CE	Ceará	RJ	Rio de Janeiro
FD	Federal District	RN	Rio Grande do Norte
ES	Espirito Santo	RO	Rondônia
GO	Goiás	RR	Roraima
MA	Maranhâo	RS	Rio Grande do Sul
MG	Minas Gerais	SC	Santa Catarina
MS	Mato Grosso do Sul	SE	Sergipe
MT	Mato Grosso	SP	Sâo Paulo
PA	Pará		

Map generously drawn by Raphael Sabongi Lúcio Marcelino.

GREEN-CHEEKED CONURE *(Pyrrhura molinae)*

Origin of name: named for abbot Giovanni Molina, Chilean/Italian naturalist (1740-1829).

Local names: Argentina and Bolivia *Chiripepé de cabeza gris*; Argentina and Uruguay *Chiripepé cabeza parda*; Brazil *Tiriba-de-cara-suja*.

Description: crown: brown (entire top of head is green in Maroon-bellied). Tail – upper side maroon, with base of four central feathers green and underside coppery-red. Cheeks green, ear coverts greyish-brown, nape brown, tinged blue. Throat, sides of neck and upper breast light brown (or with green tinge), each feather broadly margined with pale grey-buff and with scarcely visible blackish-brown edge. Abdomen: maroon patch. Under tail coverts: green tinged blue. Bill: dark brownish.

UK breeder Les Waring pointed out that many examples of *molinae*, of various sub-species, have flecks of red at the bend of the wing or even more extensive red along the carpal edge, as in *flavoptera*.

Length: 26-27cm. **Weight:** 85-90g.

Problems with identification in aviculture. The sub-species can be difficult to identify, especially as hybridising between them has occurred, (by breeders not familiar with the different forms, or possibly attempting to breed mutations into other sub-species). The situation is further confused by photographs in avicultural literature wrongly accredited to a certain sub-species, and compounded by *restricta* intergrading with *molinae* in the western part of the Santa Cruz province (Bolivia) if such birds reached breeders.

In the UK, Jeff Hornsby believed he kept all sub-species except *flavoptera*. One form, probably the nominate, was appreciably larger, approaching *cruentata* in size, with a longer body and longer tail compared with the other sub-species.

Immature birds have slightly duller plumage with little or no red on the abdomen. The tail is shorter.

Range: central South America in south-western Brazil at a few sites in Mato Grosso and Mato Gross do Sul, mainly near the border with Bolivia (Silveira and Brettas, 2015), Bolivia, northern Paraguay and north-western Argentina.

Range of nominate race: Eastern Bolivia, highlands.

Status and threats: Least Concern. CITES Appendix II. Common; however, extensive areas of its habitat have been cleared for pasture and for crops.

Habitats: A wider range of woodland habitats than any other member of the genus, from lowlands to above 2,000m, including grasslands (Pantanal). It might be described as the most successful species, in its adaptability to habitats and altitudes. It is found in the dry forests of the Mato Grosso to montane cloud forest. The montane forests of north-western Argentina are disappearing at an alarming rate: 1.1% annually – much higher than for many other tropical forests (FAO 1993).

Habits: A common species, yet little has been recorded. In February 2001 Natalia Politi and Luis Rivera studied patterns and abundances of the six parrot species along an elevational gradient in the montane forests of the Calilegua National Park in Jujuy province, north-western Argentina. The study area was divided into four forest types (from low to high altitude: foothills, transition to montane, montane, and transition to cloud forest). The transition to cloud forest had

Approximate range of *molinae*. See map on page 124 for range in Brazil.

the lowest number of species. Yellow-collared Macaws *(Propyrrhura auricollis)*, Scaly-headed Parrots *(Pionus maximiliani)* and Green-cheeked Conures occurred in three forest types at the lower end of the elevational gradient. Mitred Parakeets *(A. mitrata)* occupied montane and transition to cloud forest.

The Green-cheeked was observed most often in groups of six (Politi and Rivera, 2005).

In Brazil the Green-cheeked Conure mainly inhabits the dry forests of Mato Grosso and Mato Grosso do Sul. It had never been studied until J.Ragusa-Netto from the Federal University of Mato Grosso do Sul researched its feeding ecology in semi-deciduous and highly deciduous forests in the Urucum mountain chain in Mato Grosso do Sul. Its flexible diet consisted of sixteen tree species, from which it consumed flowers, seeds, the fruit pulp or aril of four species and both pulp and seeds of six species. In the semi-deciduous forest a wide range of fleshy fruits were eaten, especially the catkins of *Cecropia pachystachya*. In the highly deciduous forest the conures foraged extensively for figs, which made up about 70% of the diet. They also consumed nectar and seeds from dry fruits (Ragusa-Netto, 2007).

Aviculture: In Europe, the sub-species *australis* and *restricta* are well represented. The Green-cheeked Conure was almost unknown until the late 1970s. The first recorded breeding occurred in the aviaries of Dr Romauld Burkard in Switzerland who kept 14 birds in adjoining aviaries in the early 1970s. One pair nested on the

Flowers are an important part of the diet of all *Pyrrhuras*, such as the Green-cheeked. Photograph © Steve Brookes www.wildparrotsupclose.com

ground in a metre-long tunnel. In the UK the first breeder was George Smith of Peterborough in 1979. Four birds were kept together and two females laid in the same nest-box. Four eggs placed in an incubator hatched after 22 days while those left in the nest took 22 to 24 days to hatch. The three incubator-hatched chicks were returned to the nest together with a Hawk-headed Parrot chick that was removed at 24 days. In 1984 George Smith hand-reared 30 young Green-cheeked Conures from two pairs.

It soon proved to be the most prolific member of the genus, with the average clutch being five and some pairs double-brooded. Within twenty years it ranked alongside the Cockatiel, Peach-faced Lovebird and Indian Ringneck Parakeet for prolificacy leading to numerous mutations being produced in large numbers. Its popularity as a companion bird soared.

This is the ideal species for the beginner with *Pyrrhuras*, although a watch needs to be kept in case the male is aggressive towards the female. Some Green-cheeked Conures start to breed at one year. They are usually fairly tolerant to disturbance, less susceptible to nesting failure for this reason than most members of the genus. In *Bird Keeper* magazine, February 1999, a letter was published from R. Curtis of Kent demonstrating how amenable these birds can be. Mr Curtis went to a breeder's house, having arranged to buy a pair of Green-cheeks that had to go that day, although the female was incubating one egg. The birds were placed in a carrier, the egg was wrapped in tissue paper and the nest-box was removed. On reaching home, the pair was immediately placed in a flight with the nest-box. Two hours later the conures had not entered so the nest-box was removed to the same position it had occupied in the previous aviary. The female went straight inside and two days later she laid again. Including the egg laid in the first location there were five and all hatched! Eventually the chicks were removed for hand-rearing.

Birders: Calilegua National Park (lower elevations), Jujuy, Argentina; Amboró National Park (Refugio Los Volcanes), Santa Cruz department, Bolivia.

P. m. australis

Description: paler than the nominate race; more extensive brown-red patch on abdomen, with the centre of the breast suffused with dull yellow.

Range: Southern Bolivia and north-western Argentina.

Identifying the sub-species of *molinae* in aviculture can be difficult due to the pairing together of different sub-species over the years. This is *australis*.

Photograph © Ron and Val Moat

P. m. restricta

Description: Differs from nominate race in the **feathers of neck and breast being more uniformly barred:** each feather is brownish-grey with a clear, broad white sub-terminal band. The crown is darker brown (no green tinge). **The green cheeks are tinged with blue and there is a blue collar on the hind neck. The flanks and under tail coverts are suffused with blue.** On the abdomen there are only a few reddish-brown feathers.

Range: Eastern Bolivia in Santa Cruz province.

P. m. sordida

Description: differs from *restricta* in **indistinct barring on breast and sides of neck:** the feathers are brown, tinged with greyish-white towards the tips. **There is a yellow suffusion on flanks and under tail coverts.Range:** Southern Brazil and north-western Paraguay.

YELLOW-SIDED CONURE
(formerly *P. molinae hypoxantha*)

Description: The so-called "yellow morph" is an opaline mutation of *sordida* and was considered to be a separate sub-species, *hypoxantha*, for many years. The type specimen, a female, was taken in the south-western Mato Grosso of Brazil. It was described as follows: crown brown, darker on the forehead; ear coverts pale greyish-brown; nape feathers brown edged with buff, cheeks green. Feathers of sides of neck, throat and upper breast yellowish-white, those of lower breast yellow, all of these narrowly tipped with pale brown, with an orange-red patch in the

Young parent-reared Yellow-sided mutation of the Green-cheeked Conure
Photograph © Rosemary Low

centre. Flanks and thighs yellow, each feather faintly margined with green. Under tail coverts: yellow. Lower back, rump and upper tail coverts green marked with yellow. The legs were said to be grey. Note that Yellow-sided Conures in aviculture do not always adhere to this description, also that under wing coverts are yellow.

Length: 25cm.

Aviculture: The Yellow-sided Conure enjoys enormous popularity, especially among breeders whose interest lies in breeding and developing mutations. The production of this mutation (See Chapter 11) changed the history of *Pyrrhura* breeding. A pretty bird, with a nice temperament, it has become very popular as a companion. People love the pastel colours of the Pineapple mutation, for example. In South Africa, Terry Irwin recorded: "They lay large clutches, up to eight eggs, but five is the norm. They are excellent parents and can safely be left to rear their own chicks. If chicks are removed for hand-rearing after about ten days they will re-clutch, sometimes three times a year, depending on how early in the season they start...but even when left to rear their own chick I usually get two clutches per year. In Zululand they start breeding soon after the first rains in August and can continue until May." (Irwin 2007/2008).

P. m. phoenicura

Description: Differs from nominate race in having the **tail green towards the base** on the upper side, extending just beyond the upper tail coverts.

Range: Southern Brazil and north-eastern Bolivia.

P. m. flavoptera

In 1998 this was the last sub-species to be described, also perhaps the most distinctive.

Description: Bend of wing and carpal edge orange-red. **Striking yellow marginal coverts along leading edge of wing or a variable number of yellow, salmon-coloured or scarlet feathers along wing bend. The small stiffened feathers of the alula are blue and yellowish-white** (Maijer *et al*, 1998).

Range: estimated at 1,000 to 1,500km^2 in northern Bolivia in the Cochabamba-La Paz border. It occurs at altitudes between 1,250m and 3,000m in any available habitat in rain-shadowed valleys. However, only *flavoptera* was present in the Rio Khatu valley, whereas in the La Paz valley *flavoptera* was found primarily in the upper part at 2,000m to 3,000m; nominate race occupied a wider elevational range from at least 1,500m to 3,000m further east. *P. m. flavoptera* might have evolved in the Rio Khatu valley in isolation and later dispersed. Hybridisation with *P. m. molinae*, especially if induced by man-made habitat changes, could eventually lead to the extinction of *flavoptera*. But if both forms have been in contact with only limited hybridisation, they might represent separate evolutionary populations (Maijer *et al*, 1998).

Status: Locally common. The total population is believed to be "a few thousand birds". Because *flavoptera* seemed to cope well with habitat degradation, it was not considered to be under immediate threat from habitat destruction (Maijer *et al*, 1998). Apparently hybridisation between the nominate sub-species and *flavoptera* occurs. A detailed study of the degree of hybridisation in the La Paz and Cotacajes area is needed to establish the taxonomic and conservation status of *flavoptera*.

Habitat: deciduous and semi-deciduous forest including *Acacia*; also tall cacti such as *Cereus* species. The forests varied in height from 5m to 10m and were severely degraded by cattle grazing, timber extraction and occasional burning. Much of the area had been degraded to scrubland dominated by *Dodonaea viscosa* (an evergreen shrub). Small patches of evergreen vegetation were found along creeks and rivers, where *Erythrina* (coral tree species), *Piper* and *Acacia macracantha* dominated. Scattered throughout the area were agricultural fields, orchards and plantations of *Eucalyptus globulus*. A group of six birds was seen in evergreen montane forest at 3,000m – but this was not the preferred habitat of *flavoptera* (Maijer *et al*, 1998).

Aviculture: unknown or unrecognised.

MAROON-BELLIED CONURE *(Pyrrhura frontalis)*

Synonyms: Red-bellied Conure, Reddish-bellied Conure
Origin of name: *frontalis* = relating to the forehead.
Local names: Argentina *Chiripepé de cabeza verde*; Brazil *Tiriba-de-testa-vermelha*; Paraguay and Uruguay *Chiripepé*.
Description: Forehead: maroon; **crown dark green,** feathers of nape with lighter margins. **Ear coverts light buff-brown;** cheeks dark green. Feathers of sides of neck and upper breast with typical scalloped appearance, olive on breast, edged with yellowish or whitish-yellow on sides of neck. These markings vary considerably. (One bird that I kept was golden-yellow on the upper breast.) Abdomen: an irregular patch of maroon. Upper parts dark green with some maroon on the lower back, well defined in some birds. Tail: feathers reddish and green at base; underside maroon.
Length: 26cm **Weight:** 70g.
Immature birds: the plumage is duller.
Range: Uruguay and south-eastern Brazil, to eastern Paraguay and northern Argentina. This is perhaps the most extensive continuous range, from north to south, of any *Pyrrhura*. The nominate race occurs in south-eastern Brazil in

Maroon-bellied (left) and Green-cheeked Conures for comparison. The crown colour is a rapid aid to identification. Photograph © Rosemary Low

lowlands and mountains up to 1,400m, from Bahia, southwards through the states of Minas Gerais, Espirito Santo, Rio de Janeiro, São Paulo and Paraná to Rio Grande do Sul.

Status: CITES Appendix II. Listed as Least Concern due to large range and apparently stable population (BirdLife International). Common; in many areas of south-eastern Brazil it is the most common parakeet.

The Maroon-bellied Conure was described as common in Paraguay in the literature but, in 2008, 228,000ha (563,400 acres or 2,280km^2) of the Chaco were bulldozed for agriculture, mainly cattle ranching. It occurs in eastern Paraguay, and part of Uruguay and Argentina. This is an adaptable species, found in large urban parks and around human habitation.

In Brazil these parakeets have become an urban problem in some areas, making nests in roofs, damaging wooden structures and electrical wires and vocalising during the night. This nesting habit is not popular with local people. Often nests are destroyed or the chicks are illegally removed for pets. They can then be confiscated by the local authorities. On the island of São Sebastião (Ilhabela), in the Atlantic Forest, since 2014 confiscated chicks have been taken to the rescue organisation ASM Cambaquara to be hand-reared and released.

Habitat: Often associated with *Araucaria* forest, it also occurs in the Atlantic forests. Tolerant of habitat disturbance, it occasionally visits city parks and orchards, mainly during the winter. In December 2003 I saw *chiripepe* and other presumably escaped parrot species, in a park in the centre of Buenos Aires, Argentina.

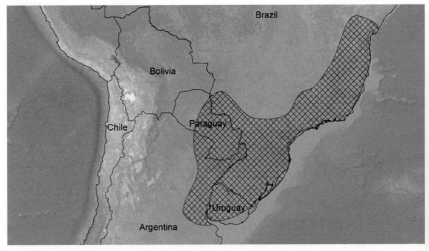

Approximate range of the Maroon-bellied Conure (*frontalis* and *chiripepe*).

Map courtesy of Alex Bovo, Centro Nacional de Pesquisa e Conservação de Aves Silvestres – CEMAVE

Habits: Fruits of the palmetto (*Euterpe edulis*) and those of *ucuúba* (*Virola* species) are eaten, also those of cinnamon trees (genera *Nectandra* and *Ocotea*), and nuts of *Pinus ellioti* (Sigrist, 2009). In 1988 I observed a small group of Maroon-bellied Conures at the Iguazú Falls. They flew over the thundering waters of this world-famous tourist attraction, to land in trees at the water's edge. After bathing in a small rock pool, they flew back to the trees to preen their plumage dry in the sun. One bird entered a hole in the rock face. Others fed in the trees on small seeds. Sick (1993) observed them at the Iguazu Falls in Paraná (Brazilian side) among the Podostemonaceae growing on rocks under a thin layer of running water. He noted that parrots elsewhere also descend on these "peculiar plants" to feed on small creatures found there.

Trade: Between 1981, when it was listed on CITES Appendix II, and 2004, 52,523 wild-caught birds were recorded in international trade.

Aviculture: For decades this was the only well-known member of the genus. It was bred in the UK as long ago as 1925, in Japan in 1928 and in Australia in 1954. One of the most prolific species and an attractive and usually friendly aviary bird, it is perfect for the beginner with *Pyrrhuras* – as I was in the 1960s. My two proved to be males and after acquiring (and returning) several birds bought as females, I finally acquired a female in 1971. I was enchanted by my first two and wrote, in the notes I kept at the time, that I thought them "the most charming, delightful and intelligent" birds I had ever kept.

One breeder in the UK described their tolerant nature (*Magazine of the Parrot Society*, October 1971). C. Bowden bought a newly imported pair of Maroon-bellied – probably young birds – in the spring of 1969. They were housed in an aviary 6m long by 90cm wide; a tangled mass of uncut weeds covered the ground. At the end of April 1971 mating was observed. At the end of June two chicks and one egg were seen in the nest-box. The two young left the nest on July 26. Ten days later they were feeding themselves. Throughout this period they had shared their aviary peacefully with a pair of Moustache Parakeets. When the young left the nest they were attacked through the wire by the Jenday Conures in the next aviary so the Maroon-bellied family was moved to the aviary on the other side which contained a pair of Abyssinian Lovebirds. Again, they co-existed peacefully with these birds. Other *Pyrrhura* species are unlikely to be so tolerant!

My diary entries for one pair at Loro Parque, Tenerife, in 1988, read: First nest, one chick hatched, gone by January 26. Second nest, two eggs by February 8, two chicks on March 5, five chicks by March 28. On April 6 there was one new egg and five chicks. (Note the strange laying of one egg when chicks had hatched one month previously.) The first young one left the nest on April 21 and the second on April 25. On May 2 all five chicks had fledged but one died two days later after a nearby firework display. On May 20 all four young were removed. Third nest,

Young Maroon-bellied Conures, received as confiscated chicks, return to the feeders after being released by Cambaquara.
Photograph © Rosemary Low

six eggs by June 6. June 10: one chick plus a newly hatched White-capped Pionus (*P. senilis*) that was transferred to the nest and fed for ten days until removed. The parents reared four; one chick was reared by foster parents. Fourth nest, three eggs laid by October 4, total of five eggs; there were three chicks by October 27. Four chicks were reared, thus the total for the year was twelve young.

Although colony breeding is not recommended with members of this genus, it is perhaps more likely to be successful with the Maroon-bellied. In 1953 three young were reared in a group of four birds belonging to A.A.Prestwich (secretary of the Avicultural Society). All the birds roosted in one box, even while breeding. In the twenty-first

Chicks removed from a roof to be hand-reared by staff at Cambaquara.
Photograph © Cambaquara ASM

century, Gerhard Schmidt reported on his attempt at colony breeding in Germany: "I tried in a large aviary with three pairs of *Pyrrhura frontalis*. I offered six nest-boxes. After some difficulties all three pairs were breeding but just the dominant pair raised their youngsters."

Birders: Argentina: Iguazú National Park, Misiones; Brazil: Rio de Janeiro Botanical Gardens, Intervales State Park, São Paulo; Serra dos Tucanos Lodge, Atlantic forest; Paraguay: San Rafael National Park.

Azara's Conure (*Pyrrhura frontalis chiripepe*)

Range: northern Argentina (provinces of Salta, Chaco, Formosa, Corrientes and Misiones), Uruguay and southern Paraguay.

A review of museum collection specimens suggests that distinctions used to describe the sub-species *in Brazil* might be due to morphological variation (Somenzari *et al.*, Taxonomic review of *Pyrrhura frontalis* complex, in prep.). There is variation in the colour of the tail. This is the feature often used to define the sub-species *chiripepe*. There might be clinal variation with the birds from the southern part of the range, including extreme southern Brazil, having the tail olive-green or almost golden in colour, in contrast with the dark red markings of those from further north. Individual variation in tail colour is great. For example, in three birds (museum specimens) from Minas Gerais, one had reddish markings on one side of the shaft, greenish markings on the other. A second had mainly green tail feathers, but more golden green on one side of the shaft. In the third the tail was golden-green on the lower part, mainly green on the basal part of the tail. Distinctive tail colour is sometimes suggested in describing *chiripepe* and even *kriegi*. The latter is not recognised by most authorities.

Aviculture: In 2013 there was discussion among Dutch and Belgian aviculturists regarding the existence of pure *chiripepe* in Europe. After visiting a number of breeders, Daniel Nuijten believed that pure *chiripepe* might be more numerous than pure *Pyrrhura frontalis frontalis* as, he said, hybrids between both sub-species look like the nominate form.

Pyrrhura frontalis kriegi

No longer recognised by most authorities. Said to differ in having the tail very narrowly tipped with brownish-red. Appearance is intermediate between the two recognised forms whose ranges are to the north – nominate – and to the south and west.

BLAZE-WINGED CONURE (*Pyrrhura devillei*)

Origin of name: named for Emile Deville, French ornithologist.

Local name: Bolivia *Periquito alianaranjado*; Brazil *Tiriba Fogo*.

Taxonomy: Ridgely (1981) wrote: "In Paraguay *P. devillei* has been reported to 'interbreed at least sporadically' with *P. frontalis* (Short 1975), and in July 1977 I noted a few apparent hybrids among flocks of *P. devillei* seen along the Rio Apa on the Mato Grosso border (the hybrids showing little or no colour on the under wing-coverts). The two forms are quite likely conspecific."

Perhaps the "apparent hybrids" seen by Ridgely were juvenile birds. Perhaps Short made the same error. If so, there is no evidence that hybridisation occurs in the wild. This is important because the existence of hybrids between *chiripepe* and *devillei* in the Apa mountains, along the Paraguayan border with Brazil, is given as the reason why *devillei* should be classified as a sub-species of *frontalis* (Arndt, 2007). Even if these two forms are conspecific, in view of the Near Threatened status of *devillei* (see below), maintaining them as separate species would have conservation advantages for *devillei*.

Description: Differs from frontalis in the **scarlet bend of the wing and under wing coverts,** and in the brown crown. The area of maroon on the abdomen is usually reduced. The tail is invariably described as olive above but in the birds I saw (in Aquiduana in 2019) they were golden yellow on the upper side; the feathers of the underside of the tail were dull red, margined with grey-olive.

Blaze-winged Conure; the upper surface of the tail is golden-yellow.

Photograph © Rosemary Low

Habitat of the Blaze-winged Parakeet along the Aquiduana River.
Photograph © Rosemary Low

Length: 26cm. **Weight:** about 70g.

Immature birds: "Undescribed", according to Forshaw (1989 and 2006). In 2008 in the vicinity of the Caiman reserve in the Brazilian Pantanal, I observed a young one shivering its wings as it was fed by a parent. I was able to see the scarlet carpal edge of the wing. Immature birds could be recognised by the **small amount of red** on the bend of the wing and the under wing coverts.

Range: northern Paraguay and southern Brazil. In Paraguay it has a very restricted range in north-western Concepción and south-eastern Alto Paraguay in gallery forest along the Rio Apa. In southern Brazil it occurs in south-western Mato Grosso do Sul, the Pantanal lowlands, and along the Taboco river (municipality of Aquiduana). Possibly it also occurs in south-eastern Bolivia although alteration to the border could mean that this area is now part of Paraguay. See map on page 124 for range in Brazil.

Status and threats: Near Threatened (2010 IUCN Red List). CITES Appendix II. A moderately rapid decline is suspected because its habitat is increasingly fragmented and degraded by conversion for agriculture and charcoal production. It is believed to approach the threshold for classification as Vulnerable (BirdLife International 2010 Species fact sheet). Locally common but generally uncommon, its population size is unknown. No conservation action has occurred.

Habitat: deciduous and gallery woodland, savannah and scrub.

Aviculture: Unknown (or unrecognised).

Birders: Caiman Ecological Refuge, near Miranda, Pousada Agape and Serra da Bodoquena National Park – Mato Grosso do Sul (Pantanal), Brazil.

PEARLY CONURE
(Pyrrhura coerulescens formerly *P. lepida)*

Origin of name: *coerulescens* = bluish
Local name: *Tiriba-pérola*
When the first edition of this book was published the species *lepida* was included with two sub-species, *coerulescens* and *anerythra*. At that time there had been no taxonomic investigation into these forms. In 2015 a paper was published that justified a revision. It described the morphological variation and revised their taxonomy and geographic distribution. (Somenzari and Silveira, 2015):
Morphological analysis, according to patterns of plumage of 174 specimens [in eight museums], resulted in the recognition of only three valid taxa that should be treated as full species: *P. perlata*, *P. anerythra* and *P. coerulescens*. A small hybrid zone between the latter two species was detected west of the mouth of the Tocantins River, and its establishment seems to be related to an already known geological shift in the course of the Tocantins River.

These species are of conservation concern, they are known in aviculture and their identification was formerly difficult to discern, so I quote at length:
"The *Pyrrhura lepida* species complex currently consists of four taxa: *P. l. lepida*, *P. l. coerulescens*, *P. l. anerythra*, and *P. perlata*. It occurs south of the Amazon River, and is distinguished within the genus by a dark red upper tail and black under tail, as well as by having wider rectrices.
Description of *P. coerulescens*: Distinguished by the green abdomen. "Distinguished from *P. anerythra* by red underwing coverts. Pileum colour ranges between light to dark brown. Whitish tipped feathers mainly in post-orbital region. Hindneck marked by a blue stripe; forehead has a barely noticeable narrow anterior dark red stripe followed by a discrete posterior blue one. Whitish ear coverts forming a single ear spot. Greenish upper cheeks and bluish lower cheeks whose feathers extend until the throat. Sides of neck, throat and upper breast are characterised by the presence of pale-coloured feathers with narrow margins of lighter colour, generally whitish, providing a scaled pattern; main colour of these feathers ranges between grey and blue and tip colour can be pinkish hued. Overall, the back, rump and wings are characterised by having a greenish colouration. The primaries and alula are black, with external vane and base of the internal vane cobalt blue. Bright red under and at bend of wing coverts. Green abdomen. Flanks, thighs and crissum range from green to bluish. Brownish-red upper tail and blackish under tail. Bill and legs black; dark brown iris and whitish bare periophthalmic skin" (Somenzari and Silveira, 2015).
Length: 24cm. **Weight:** 70g.

Immature birds: On fledging the first young I reared in 1966 had dark grey feathers of the back of the head and the nape were only very faintly margined with buff. They otherwise resembled adults except for the beak which was grey – dark or silvery-grey (Low, 1967).

Range: North-eastern Brazil, limited to the west by the Tocantins River. It occurs in the states of Tocantins, Maranhão and Pará, including the forested portion (western) of Marajó island. Restricted to the south of the Amazon River, its distribution follows Amazon biome boundaries. It also occurs in the city of Recife, Pernambuco State, owing to escaped captive birds (Somenzari and Silveira, 2015). See map on page 125.

Status and threats: It occurs in the most deforested areas in Amazonia, including Pará (one of the first to be degraded) and is listed (under *P. lepida*) as Vulnerable on the IUCN (since 2012) and Brazilian red lists. CITES Appendix II. It still occurs in small flocks in the few remaining protected areas.

The Pearly Conure is probably close to extinction in coastal areas of northern Maranhão, owing to large-scale deforestation (Birdlife species fact sheet). It inhabits some "protected" areas where illegal logging occurs.

Habitat: lowland humid forest, also clearings and second growth forest.

Habits: Brazilian photographer Edson Endrigo told me: "I saw *P. lepida* in Carajás National Forest, Pará state; they are not very common, but I saw them twice feeding on flowers of what I imagine to be *Erythrina*."

Aviculture: This species was occasionally available from the 1960s and is established. However, it has been over-shadowed by the availability of the Crimson-bellied Conure. Now that the price gap is closing in Europe, *lepida* could be in danger of being lost from aviculture except in Australia where the price of the Crimson-bellied is many times higher and *lepida* is well established.

While the Pearly Conure might be perceived as just lacking the crimson abdomen, in fact head and breast coloration is different. It is equally delightful as an aviary bird but I fear interest in it will decline. The Crimson-bellied Conure has a large range, unlike the Pearly Conure. Aviculturists need to pay more attention to this also beautiful bird.

Probably the first breeding in the UK occurred in 1963 when Brian Killick of Northampton reared five young. Five more fledged in 1965. Mr Killick believed that they were White-eared Conures until he saw the plate in Seth-Smith's book *Parrakeets*. (In that era only a couple of illustrated parrot books were available and they were more or less collectors' items.)

My first "pair" of Pearly Conures was acquired in 1965. In that era there was no means of determining the gender of birds and then, as now, more males were available. Then sellers did not purposely mislead buyers about gender – they just did not know. So the first two were males. When I came across a true pair I could see the difference: "One was far bolder about the head and its upper mandible was wider" (Low, 1967). Fortunately, I was able to buy this pair and placed them in an outdoor aviary, 3.6m long, with an open-fronted shelter. They were very fond of millet spray (though refused loose millet) and they would "bite off a section and fly on to a perch where they eat it held in the foot, or, as often happens, one bird will hold the millet and both will feed from it. Seeding grasses are eaten in the same manner."

Several months later, on July 23, the pair was observed mating. The female started to spend long periods inside the nest-box, which measured 31cm high by 25cm square. By August 5 there were three eggs and on August 27 I heard a youngster being fed. In those days of wild caught birds the general opinion was that the nest-box should not be inspected when the chicks were very young, for fear of causing the parents to desert or even kill their chicks. I contained my impatience for three weeks, then the hen's continuous absence from the box caused me to fear that something was amiss, although the quantity of food taken was still increasing. Inspection revealed three plump youngsters and one soiled egg. It was normal for the female to cease to brood the young at this age.

I then inspected the nest at weekly intervals as the parents showed no concern. The female apparently entered the box only to feed the young and to roost at night with the male. At the last inspection on October 8 the eldest youngster, which was almost fully feathered, adopted the same threatening attitude as the adults when disturbed in their box: ruffling up the head feathers, stretching the neck and swaying from side to side. Later that day it was looking out of the nest hole.

Early in the morning of October 18 I watched one youngster emerge from the box and fly to the perch at the opposite end of the aviary. A few minutes later the second one emerged, flying equally well, so they probably left the nest on the previous day. They fed themselves on apple and seed almost immediately and followed the adults into the nest at night. The third youngster, which had probably hatched several days after the second, left the nest six days later and was noticeably smaller.

Five days after they left the nest-box, I witnessed an interesting incident. "The

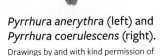

Pyrrhura anerythra (left) and *Pyrrhura coerulescens* (right).
Drawings by and with kind permission of Barbara Tomotani.

eldest youngster begged for food from the cock, dropping its wings, then flapping them vigorously whilst being fed. It then immediately disappeared into the nest-box and judging from the sounds coming from within, it was feeding its nest-mate!"

The following year, 1967, the pair bred even later in the year. The first of four eggs was laid on August 24. One chick had hatched by September 16 and three by the 23rd. They fledged during the second week in November.

In 1969, another female laid at the beginning of February, when several inches of snow lay on the ground. When there were two eggs in the nest the female appeared to be in pain. I brought her indoors and about ten minutes later she became paralysed in one leg, then in the other. She panted at a speed that frightened me. I thought her last hour had

Pyrrhura coerulescens, on exhibit at Loro Parque, Tenerife. The green central area and abdomen and red under wing coverts distinguish them from *anerythra.*

Photograph © Rosemary Low

come. I was wrong. After about ten minutes she laid the egg, and five minutes later she regained the use of her feet and was up on the perch. Meanwhile the male was in the nest box but the eggs were cold, so I removed them. I did not want her to lay again during the cold weather. The pair went to nest later in the year. Four eggs were laid; one chick hatched and was reared.

They gave me my first lesson in the Houdini-antics of the members of this genus. As I recorded in *The Parrots of South America*: "I returned from two weeks holiday to find the aviary empty: a rat had burrowed into the floor and the Pearlies, unable to resist the temptation to explore, had made their exit via this hole. However, I soon heard them calling in the distance and before long they alighted in a large apple tree in the garden. I opened the birdroom door and they returned almost at once."

I should comment that it is several decades since a rat had the opportunity to enter any of my aviaries and I would be deeply ashamed of my management if such occurred today.

It is a strange fact that information about the Pearly Conure is almost non-existent in the avicultural literature.

Birders: Gurupi Biological Reserve, Maranhão; Agropalma Forest Reserves, Tailândia, Pará.

SCALY-BELLIED CONURE (*Pyrrhura anerythra*)

Origin of name: *anerythra* = lacking red.
Local name: Tiriba-pérola-do-Xingu
Description: distinguished from *coerulescens* by having bluish green underwing coverts and at bend of wing. Greenish abdomen with main part of central region feathers dark red, providing scaled appearance and depending on wear of feather tips, their dark red colour becomes more evident, eventually forming a central dark red spot on the abdomen. Colour range of flanks, thighs and under tail coverts is from green to bluish. Brownish-red upper tail and blackish under tail. Bill and legs black; dark brown iris and whitish bare periophthalmic skin (Somenzari and Silveira, 2015).
Range: Brazil, restricted to the southern bank of the Amazon River. It occurs in Pará and Mato Grosso State, limited to the east by the Tocantins River and to the south by transition to Cerrado biome. The western boundary remains uncertain (Somenzari and Silveira, 2015). See map on page 125.
Status: Classified as Vulnerable in Brazil, due to the high rates of deforestation in the area in which it occurs (Silveira and Brettas, 2015). It is found in low densities in areas under severe logging pressure, with few recent records (Somenzari and Silveira, 2015). However, between 2009 and 2021 scientists produced an inventory of wildlife at Fazenda Fartura, on the border of the states of Pará (to the north), Mato Grosso to the south and Tocantins to the east. The fazenda covered 53,078ha, 35,108ha of which included areas of remnant forest and wetlands. Prof. Luis Fabio Silveira, who led the research, reported in 2022: "The population there is stable, and growing slowly. It was rare in some places, but in the last years, we found some good populations at Fazenda Fartura, in groups of a maximum of eight to ten birds" (pers. comm, 2022).

CRIMSON-BELLIED CONURE (*Pyrrhura perlata*)

Origin of name: *perlata* = pearl-shaped markings
Local name: Brazil *Tiriba-de-barriga-vermelha*
Taxonomy: Formerly *P. rhodogaster* before the discovery that *perlata* was described from an immature Crimson-bellied Conure, found in captivity by Spix. Now usually treated as a separate species rather than forming one species with the Pearly Conure *P. lepida*, *anerythra* and *coerulescens*. As the latter are all of conservation concern, it seems important to treat this as a separate species.
Description: Unmistakeable with **intense crimson underparts, from lower breast nearly to vent.** Bend of wing and lesser under wing coverts are also crimson. Upperparts: olive green variably marked with blue; some birds, perhaps originating from a certain area, have much more blue on the back than others. Thighs, sides and under tail coverts: blue; upper tail coverts green, with blue feathers on outer coverts. Forehead: bluish with very narrow line of reddish-brown above cere; crown feathers brown, margined with buff; nape: bluish. Cheeks: olive-green towards lores and blue-green on lower part. Scalloped feathers below throat: whitish, margined with grey, and blue, black and white at back of head. Primary coverts and secondary coverts are blue on outer edge. Under side of tail: black; upper surface maroon.

Crimson-bellied Conures at 15 weeks. Flash photography appears to have bleached their plumage slightly. Photograph © Rosemary Low

The crimson feathers of the breast start to appear at four and a half to five months. Interestingly, some of these feathers were moulted before the age of one year, starting at ten months in two young under very close observation.

Length: 24-25cm. **Weight:** 80-85g.

Immature birds: colours duller and greener; feathers of abdomen green, tinged blue, with a few scattered red feathers. Lores: greyish, merging into olive green; lower part of cheeks mixture of dull green and blue. Young birds without red on abdomen can be distinguished from *coerulescens* by the colours of cheeks and ear coverts: grey and white in *perlata*. The beak is horn-coloured with grey at base, becoming pale grey; cere whitish. Rarely, breeders have reported young fledging with lower breast and abdomen crimson. Young differ from adults in the dark skin (not white) surrounding the eye. Barry Butcher noted of young bred from one pair that males had dark feet, while those of females were much lighter. This was apparent for several weeks after fledging.

Range: Central and southern Amazon river basin in Brazil and neighbouring north-eastern Bolivia up to 600m. Its north-south range probably occupies at least 800 miles (1,287km). See map on page 124 and note that range extends marginally into north-eastern Bolivia.

Status: CITES II. Uplisted to Vulnerable (2012). Based on a model of future deforestation in the Amazon basin, and its "susceptibility to hunting", a rapid population decline is predicted over the next three generations (18 years), during which it is projected to lose 23% to 30% of suitable habitat (BirdLife International Species fact sheet, 2013). Described as fairly common, its population is believed to be stable.

Threats: Deforestation for cattle ranching and soy production, and road-building. Proposed change to Brazilian law regarding forest in private ownership (including narrower buffer zone along streams) could also result in loss of habitat.

Habitat: humid lowland forest; said to prefer dense vegetation at the forest edge, also secondary growth. *Protection*: Amazonia National Park, Pará.

Habits: On the Upper Aripuana River in north-western Mato Grosso, Crimson-bellied Conures were often observed (July 1977 to July 1979) where *Trema micrantha*, a favoured food plant, was prevalent. This was usually in the middle to lower stages of the forest, rather than in the canopy (Forshaw, 1989). Their diet consists mainly of fruit, of *Trema micrantha* and various palms, also *Cecropia* catkins, and the large yellow-white flowers of the Brazil nut tree *(Bertholettia excelsa)* and *Dioclea glabra* (BirdLife International Species fact sheet, 2013).

In the early 1990s American ornithologist John O'Neill was making a bird survey in the Noel Kempff Mercado, a fairly new national park in Bolivia. He informed me: "The most common parrot is *Pyrrhura rhodogaster*, probably the prettiest of

Crimson-bellied Conures, at Paradise Park in Cornwall. Each one is busy eating except the upper bird. Is he the sentinel? Photograph © Rosemary Low

the New World Parrots, at least for me! We often saw fifty to sixty per day, even trying not to count certain flocks more than once."

Aviculture: These beautiful birds were first recorded in the UK in 1927 when London Zoo received a pair. They were then almost unheard of until the 1960s. A pair brought from Brazil was exhibited at the World Show (COM) of bird breeders in Rotterdam in 1965 where they aroused much admiration. (They were at Rotterdam Zoo when I visited in 1971.) Then the species was bred by the Spenkelink family in the Netherlands and subsequently at Rotterdam Zoo in 1966. Young bred there in the following years were distributed to several European zoos.

Robert Ridgely, one of the most important neotropical ornithologists, wrote: "The Crimson-bellied Conure is extremely rare in captivity, though as it is perhaps the most beautiful of the *Pyrrhura* conures, it would quickly become popular were it to become available (fortunately this seems unlikely, given Brazil's total prohibition on the commercial export of its fauna)" (Ridgely, in Pasquier 1980). He was wrong about its availability (due to Brazilian birds smuggled into Europe and through legal acquisition and exchanges by mainstream zoos) but right about its popularity.

Some European birds originated from a private owner in Brazil via a breeder who caught them in Maués, in the Amazon, on his *guaraná* plantation. Later I saw the pair sent from Brazil to the C.O.M. World Show in Lisbon, Portugal, in 1970. Their beauty made a deep impression on me. Because I grew up knowing so many parrot species (London Zoo had a multitude!) I cannot recall the first time I saw most parrots – but this was my first sight of the Crimson-bellied – and I was enchanted. Now that I see them daily, I am no less impressed! When you see the sun shining on the blue of their flanks, under tail coverts and wings, adjacent to the crimson belly, they are breath-taking!

Few, if any conures, can equal their beauty. At the very first glance, the impact of the crimson belly, set off against the more subtle intermingled blues and greens, the olive cheeks and greyish-white scalloping of the neck and upper breast, is unforgettable. To my eyes, it is by far the most beautiful member of the genus, with an outgoing personality that matches its gorgeous plumage.

This conure was well established in aviculture by the 1990s. It is now frequently bred in all countries where aviculture is popular. The usual clutch size is five or six eggs. In the UK the first breeding success occurred at Chester Zoo in 1976, in an off-exhibit aviary. The female always laid during the early part of June, until the male died of visceral gout in 1980.

My first experience was at Loro Parque, Tenerife. Two birds there at the beginning of 1987 were surgically sexed as males. In 1988 four females were acquired so it was decided to set up trios. The three birds on exhibit nested immediately. There was only one nest-box and, by the end of September, both females were incubating side by side. The male paired with one female then, after a few days, the second female entered the nest. Two chicks from the first female hatched on October 14 and 16 (26 days after the second egg was laid: either the first egg did not hatch or the female did not incubate until the second egg was laid). The incubation period was probably 24 days.

By October 23 two chicks had hatched from the second female. The first young one left the nest on November 29 after only 46 days, the second on December 1, and the third and fourth on December 6. The colour of the abdomen was green. They gave me great pleasure because their plumage was immaculate and they were so tame. These young were the first of many. The other trio at Loro Parque was not then successful. One chick hatched but had died by the following day. One female was removed and the pair nested again.

In the UK, *Pyrrhura* breeder Jeff Hornsby had a lot to say about the temperament of this species – none of it complimentary. In his experience killing of chicks would have been frequent if he had not hand-reared the young. In one nest, the female killed the four chicks as he opened the nest-box. (See also *Killing of chicks, Chapter 9, Breeding Problems*). Note that it is advisable to inspect the nest only when the female is not inside, or to give warning by gently knocking on the nest-box. However, some species are naturally more aggressive than others and the Crimson-bellied does not have the best temperament among members of the genus.

They are seldom kept as pets, probably due to the high price until about 2011. In August 2010 I acquired two young from different sources and put them together at once. Five days later – sunny, after showers and gloom – I opened the hatch to the outside cage and the male was out in five minutes. The female followed about half an hour later. She was more active and adventurous in the outside cage whereas he wanted to sit and look and take in everything. When I hosed down the fig tree that filled half their cage, she bathed in the leaves. The male suddenly became protective and preened her dry! That was the first time I had seen mutual preening.

This extremely compatible pair, who seldom spend more than a few seconds out of touching distance, bred for the first time in 2012 (see *Chapter 10, Hand-rearing*). I hand-reared the resulting two young. Living in a 2m long cage in my kitchen, they are a never-ending source of amusement and joy. They play on vertical twigs and swing on a steel fruit holder or on miniature logs on a chain that hang from the roof. Often they play-fight, the female on her back, feet in the air, and the male pouncing on top of her. My delight in their behaviour occasionally turned to concern after the female bathed, until they were about seven months old. Then the male chased her; on occasions I had to catch him and place him in the identical cage below for several hours. This behaviour diminished as they matured.

What seems to me to be marked in this species, is its intense wariness and alertness to danger. This is, unusually, equally apparent in hand-reared birds – more so than in any parrots I know which have never had the benefit of being taught by their parents.

Birders: Brazil: Cristalino Jungle Lodge, Cristalino State Park, northern Mato Grosso; Bolivia: Noel Kempff Mercado National Park, Santa Cruz.

Crimson-bellied Conures enjoying fresh-cut branches in the author's aviaries.
Photograph © Rosemary Low

WHITE-EARED CONURE (*Pyrrhura leucotis*)

Origin of name: Greek – *leukos* = white; *otis* = eared.
Local names: *Tiriba-de-orelha-branca, Fura-mato-pequeno*; in Espirito Santo *Querequetê*.
Description: Forehead: tinged **with blue;** top of head light brown. Lores and cheeks: rich shade of dark brown. **Breast feathers are greenish, margined with white or yellow following the contour of the feather – not V-shaped as in *picta*.** Lower part of upper breast: green feathers margined with dull yellow; abdomen: large maroon patch in middle; another maroon patch from lower back to upper tail coverts. Bend of wing and under wing coverts: scarlet. Tail: maroon above except green at base; coppery-red below.
***P. griseipectus* is distinguished from the White-eared Conure by the purer white, more conspicuous white ear coverts, by underlying breast colour which is grey with white margins to feathers more conspicuous and appearing closer together.** Nape: light grey-brown, whereas in *leucotis* nape darker brown and forehead tinged with blue; both have blue on nape.

Length: 22cm – the smallest member of the genus.

Weight: Males 54-56g, females 49-52g (wild-caught captive birds weighed by author).

Immature *leucotis* differ from adults in softer overall coloration, less pronounced barring on breast and in some birds, duller and less extensive maroon patch on abdomen. Cere and eye skin is whitish in newly fledged young, gradually becoming grey. The beak is lighter grey.

Range: Brazil, east of the coastal range, from southern Bahia south to Espirito Santo and eastern Minas Gerais; formerly occurred in Rio de Janeiro state, just south of the city. The

Deforestation has greatly reduced the available habitat for the White-eared Conure. Photograph © Agnes Coenen

southern-most present day locality is Serra do Tinguá, near Rio de Janeiro; record of it as far as Sâo Paulo is in error (Olmos *et al*, 1997). See map on page 125.

Status and threats: Near-threatened. CITES Appendix II.

Threats: extensive forest clearance throughout range has resulted in a significant decline. In southern Bahia it was found in only four of thirty areas surveyed (BirdLife Species fact sheet).

Habitat: Lowland and foothills below 500m in fragmented humid forest.

Habits: Unlike some members of the genus, flowers were not noted in the diet of White-eared Conures in the lowland humid forests of Espirito Santo, where it was seen to consume only soft fruits and seeds, especially those of *Cecropia* species. There is a record of a *leucotis* with a full crop of insects – a valuable protein source.

Aviculture: a long history, being imported into Europe fairly often from the 1880s until about 1956. Along with *frontalis*, it was the best known member of the genus. It could no longer be exported legally after 1967 when Brazil prohibited bird export. As a Brazilian endemic, by the 1970s it was already becoming rare in aviculture. By the 1980s there was a growing trade in smuggling birds out of Brazil, thus once again White-eared Conures became available.

Reports of early breeding successes in Europe include what was probably the first reported, in 1886, in Tours, France, when M. Barnsby's pair had seven eggs

Family of White-eared Conures bred by Claus Nielsen in Denmark in 2013. The male parent is the third from the left and the female third from the right.

Photograph © Claus Nielsen

and reared four young. In Britain the first breeder was E. J. Brook in 1906. Eight eggs were laid and seven hatched. The young differed from the adults in having the inner web of the flight feathers and larger wing coverts yellow. This was not a characteristic of immature birds but probably due to an inadequate diet resulting in a lysine deficiency.

In the 1960s it was bred in Denmark by Carl Wentrup whose pair reared nine young in one nest! The last youngster fledged one month after the first, the younger chicks having been less well fed. While it is not unusual for the last-hatched in a large nest to fledge two weeks after the first one, four weeks is exceptional. Previously the pair reared five in 1966 and then six in 1969.

When I was first in charge of the birds at Palmitos Park, Gran Canaria, there were nine birds in the breeding centre, kept in one aviary: three pairs and three surplus males. In 1989, the pairs were placed in suspended cages measuring 1.5m x 1m x 1m high. One pair nested that year and hatched chicks on May 13, 14, 17 and 19. All fledged, two on July 4. In 1990, three pairs nested. Pair number one had four eggs, three of which hatched on March 12, 14 and 15. They were ringed aged 14, 16 and 18 days with 6mm closed rings. The young left the nest on April 24, 25 and 27 (aged 43, 42 and 43 days). They were independent and removed from the cage on May 17. By that time the female had three eggs, and three more were laid. Three chicks had hatched by June 8 and a fourth on June 9. All were successfully reared.

In 1991 the female laid even earlier, on January 10, 12, 14 and 17; date of fifth egg was not recorded. Two chicks hatched on February 4 and the others on February 6, 8 and 11, to give incubation periods of 23 and 22 days. The third chick died within a few minutes of hatching and the fifth died when it was five days old – perhaps too small to compete. The total production of this pair in three seasons was 16 eggs, and 16 chicks of which 14 were reared.

Pair number two produced six fertile eggs in 1990 which hatched on April 6, 8, 11, 12, 14 and 16. The incubation period for the first three eggs was 24 days. The first two chicks left the nest on May 21 and five had left by May 29. Because the sixth chick was so much smaller and had difficulty in competing for food, it was transferred to the nest of pair number three at three days old. When it was 16 days old it was returned to its parents' nest and eventually fledged successfully.

In 1991 the first of six eggs was laid on March 3. All six hatched but the youngest was much smaller so I transferred it to the nest of a *cruentata* pair where it was the eldest, and well fed. At the age of 22 days it was transferred back to its parents' nest. The six chicks left the nest between May 11 and 20 and were removed on June 7. The female laid the five eggs of her second clutch between June 10 and 18. Unfortunately, she deserted the nest due to a small injury just above her leg; the eggs were transferred to an incubator. Up to that time, the pair had reared 12 young from 12 eggs in two clutches during a period of 12 months.

Pair number three first nested in April 1990 and produced seven eggs. Six were fertile and hatched on April 20, 22, 24, 29 and May 2 and 6. Five chicks were reared and the first two left the nest on June 6 and 7. Two eggs were badly soiled by the chicks' faeces and were removed to an incubator. One newly hatched chick was returned to the nest where the eldest chick had died at 13 days, reason unknown. The other was hand-fed on hatching but died at the age of three days.

In 1991 the female laid nine eggs at intervals of two and three days, between April 7 and 29. The first and second eggs hatched after 24 and 23 days, the ninth after 23 days and the others after 21 and 22 days. One chick hatched in an incubator and another under a different pair of *cruentata*. The latter chick was removed at eleven days and hand-reared. The second chick appeared dehydrated at ten days and was also removed to be hand-fed. On June 7 these two chicks were returned to their parents' nest, as the sixth and ninth chicks had died, so they then had seven in the nest, six of which had fledged by June 29. In a period of 13 months this female had produced 15 eggs in two clutches, all of which hatched and of which eleven were reared. These (presumably) wild-caught pairs and their offspring proved to be very prolific.

To sum up, five pairs nesting over one, two or three seasons produced 54 eggs, of which 51 hatched and 44 young were reared. Two pairs reared young from every egg laid. During a period of 29 months the original eight birds increased to 51. One young bird died suddenly when a few months old but no other losses of young or adults occurred (Low, 1991).

Unfortunately, the White-eared Conure is not doing so well in Europe in the 21st century and some of those produced are not good specimens. There are few breeders concentrating on them. Claus Nielsen in Denmark and Horst Mayer in Germany are among the most successful breeders.

Birders: Linhares Reserve and Sooretama Biological Reserve, Espírito Santo; Tinguá Biological Reserve, Rio de Janeiro.

PFRIMER'S CONURE (*Pyrrhura pfrimeri*)

Synonyms: Goiás Conure, Maroon-faced Conure
Local name: *Tiriba-de-Pfrimer*
Origin of name: named for Rudolf Pfrimer, a professional bird skin collector who worked in Brazil in 1910.
Taxonomy: Split from *Pyrrhura leucotis* in 2005 on the basis of its distinctive appearance, geographically isolated range and significant ecological differences.
Description: This is one of the most outstandingly beautiful members of the genus. **The most striking characteristic is the contrast between the dark red face and the light blue head.** It differs from *leucotis* in **lacking the light ear coverts** and in possessing blue forehead, crown, (including rear of crown) and nape, with this colour spreading to sides of neck and throat before merging into green on lower breast. It lacks almost entirely the dark narrow terminal band of the breast feathers of *leucotis* (Olmos *et al*, 1997). Underside of tail is attractive – nearer to red than maroon with dark outer edge of feathers.
Length: 22cm (Hodel, 2012b). **Weight:** three males 51g, 52g, and 55g, one female 47g (captive-bred in 2020 and 2021 by Horst Mayer).
Immature birds: duller plumage, with less blue on forehead, crown and nape, and less well defined breast markings. There is much less red on the bend of the wing. See photograph on page 159.
Range: north-central Brazil near the Serra Geral in the states of Goiás and Tocantins, up to 600m. Its range is one of the smallest of any neotropical parrot. See map on page 125.
Status: ENDANGERED (IUCN: 2006 not evaluated, 2007 Endangered). CITES Appendix II. It was listed only as Vulnerable on the Brazilian Red List. Generally it is scarce, and fairly common within its very restricted range wherever dry forest exists. Considering the fact that widespread deforestation is recent, **the isolated groups of Pfrimer's Conures that exist will not survive long term, especially as such remnants are vulnerable to fire and continue to be selectively logged** (Olmos *et al*, 1997).
Threats: habitat destruction, especially logging (trees like *Tabebuia impetiginosa* and *Astronium urundeuva* for fence poles). Only 40% of the forest remains and most of it continues to be logged. Forest burning was widespread; most of the fires originated from logging camps and from attempts to improve the local pasture. The loggers were removing all *Tabebuia* trees over 50cm in diameter, effectively depleting the conures' food supply. Fire killed all saplings and damaged thin-barked species like fig trees. Most of the forest in the flatter areas had been destroyed and the remnants were being selectively logged. The riverine forests were badly damaged and dominated by bamboo, second growth and liana-covered

Pfrimer's Conures on a rock face in the Terra Ronca state park.
Photograph © Agnes Coenen

trees. Trapping is believed to occur at a low level. Olmos *et al* (1997) wrote that although forests on the limestone outcrops are usually spared "the proximity of a major developing center at the country's capital Brasilia makes one wonder how long it will take for a cement company to become established in the area."

Population: Not estimated – but small and declining. In 1998 its population was estimated to be about 162,000 to 202,500 individuals but such general estimates are usually based on assuming that suitable habitat survives throughout a range. Given its small range, only 2,185 km², much of it seriously deforested and fragmented, it seems inconceivable that such a large figure was arrived at. By 2011 this estimate had been reduced to 20,000 to 49,999 individuals, a figure that still seems inordinately large in view of the rapidly disappearing forests in Goiás and Tocantins, the only states in which it occurs. So little is known about some species that it can be unwise to extrapolate facts to suggest an estimate.

Habitat and habits: restricted to semi-deciduous (riverine) or deciduous (dry) forests growing on limestone outcrops or limestone-derived soil patches. It occurs from Taguatinga de Goias south to Iaciara, a stretch of about 300km and, at some points, only 30km wide, along the foothills west of the Serra Geral massif.

The climate is seasonal, with a dry season from May to September and an average rainfall of about 1,300mm. The more fertile limestone-derived soils support forests presenting an almost continuous canopy 15-20m high, with a dense undergrowth of lianas and, in some disturbed areas, bamboo. On rocky outcrops several tall species of cacti and terrestrial bromeliads occur. This type of habitat has been considered as an arboreal type of caatinga, therefore this is a caatinga forest island amid the *cerrado*.

In one study (Olmos *et al*, 1997) Pfrimer's Conure was not seen in the latter habitat although it could have reached it less than one kilometre away. Many fruiting mango trees attracted hundreds of Canary-winged Parakeets (*Brotogeris versicolorus*) that came from the forest and spent the whole day there. The conures' reluctance to visit the mango trees was surprising because that month, November, the forest was almost completely dry and there were few fruiting trees. Cultivated crops were eaten by Pfrimer's Conures, including rice. In October and November most or all of those at Nova Roma gathered to feed in one fig tree (*Ficus gomelleira*).

Group size in June ranged from two to thirty-two (averaging 12.6) over 36 sightings. Food soliciting young were observed only in June. The probable total population at Nova Roma was 120-150 individuals for the whole area of forest, that covered about 2 km² (Olmos *et al*, 1997).

Pfrimer's Conure was found in every patch of dry forest surveyed, even in some degraded areas, so its distribution is probably continuous wherever forest survives. Interestingly, it was found that the two species of *Eupsittula* conures there (*aurea* and *cactorum*) avoided continuous forest.

Pfrimer's Conures always flew towards exposed limestone outcrops during sunset; they probably nested and roosted in the numerous rock cavities. Breeding probably occurred in the late rainy season to early dry season (April to May) but the rains could be delayed by several months. Pairs were observed with two or three young. Fledglings made up 20.6% of the individuals of the six groups that could be positively identified, suggesting that most pairs had not bred during the 1994-1995 season of drought.

Protection: Occurs within the proposed Terra Ronca State Park which reaches the Serra Geral, but the park is not yet fully implemented.Other parts of its range are not protected. The flatlands of the Mata Grande National Forest, where it formerly occurred, have been mainly deforested. Fragments of forest survive only on karst limestone outcrops.

Conservation: Not until 2005 was Pfrimer's Conure considered to be a species, not a sub-species of *leucotis*, therefore it was previously treated as of no conservation concern. Fábio Olmos referred to skin specimens in the São Paulo Natural History Museum to discern localities where *pfrimeri* had occurred (Olmos, 1997). In June 1995 and October (to November 3) 1995 he and other researchers visited all these areas plus intervening zones. Most time was spent at Nova Roma and São Domingos to obtain ecological data and to walk transects through patches of natural vegetation and adjacent disturbed areas.

Aviculture: Brasilia Zoo started a breeding programme in 2001 with ten birds but six years later none had survived. In 2010 Carlos Keller informed me that it was well established in Brazil and was bred in some of the big breeding centres (with government permission). However, only registered commercial breeders can keep it. If a small breeder buys a pair the law states that the eggs or chicks must be destroyed as small breeders are allowed to breed only lovebirds, Bourke's Parakeets, Cockatiels and Budgerigars. The other problem was that the number of males reared very greatly outnumbered the females – but, of course, this could change.

In Europe this species is bred in Denmark, Germany and the Netherlands in very small numbers. Most of the stock originated from seven birds that were imported into Switzerland and bred successfully. One male died after three years. This captive population might one day be of great significance. I would urge breeders to discard for breeding purposes any mutations that might occur, which is quite likely if closely related birds are paired together.

In Denmark the first breeding occurred in 2009 when three young fledged. The pair reared two in 2010 and two more in 2011. A specialist breeder of *Pyrrhuras* who has 18 species had six young fledge from one nest in 2011. One keeper told me that *pfrimeri* is a rather nervous bird, even those that are captive-bred.

In Switzerland Jörg Hodel first bred this species in 2010, using a nest-box measuring 35cm x 17cm x 17cm, with a 5cm entrance hole. Four eggs were laid but only one was fertile. The chick was ringed with a 4.5mm ring and left the nest after about 50 days. A second pair produced infertile eggs. One egg measured 25.4mm x 17.8mm (Hodel, 2012b).

Claus Nielsen made an interesting observation about *pfrimeri*, it can make a circular flight from a perch, vibrating the wings like a hummingbird and producing a similar sound. This is usually repeated, then the circular flight occurs again but without the vibrating sound.

Birders: Goiás: Terra Ronca State Park; the road from Nova Roma to Iaciara (first 10km).

EMMA'S CONURE (*Pyrrhura emma*)

Synonym: Venezuelan Parakeet
Origin of name: Uncertain, possibly Emma Jourdan (according to A.A.Prestwich) or perhaps Emma, wife of German ornithologist Graf von Berlepsch.
Local name: *Perico pintado*
Formerly considered to be a sub-species of the White-eared Conure *(leucotis)* but isolated from it by about 4,000km.
Description: Differs from *leucotis* in **blue plumage of head, from forehead to middle of crown** where it is marked with dark brown, and continuing to nape and sides of hind-neck. Scalloped feathers of upper breast are suffused with blue, with white margins. It differs from *picta* in the scalloped feathers lacking the grey chevrons (arrow-shaped markings). See photo on page 159.
Length: 23cm. **Weight:** about 55g.
Immature birds have duller blue markings on the head and less prominent and less extensive scalloping on the upper breast.
Range: disjunct areas of northern Venezuela in the coastal mountains from the states of Yaracu and Carabobo, just west of Caracas, to Distrito Federal, east of Caracas, also interior mountains of Aragua, Miranda and Anzoátegui. There is little or no range overlap with *hoematotis*.
Habitat: Coastal mountains and interior mountains up to 1,700m, but more often at low elevations; in humid and wet forest and forest borders.
Habits: In the Guatopo National Park *emma* has been observed eating the flowers and nectar of balsa (*Ochroma*), according to C.Parrish. Its flight call is described as a loud, harsh *Kik-Kik-Kik-Kik* and its angry or distress call *wa-Ké-Ké-Ké-ka* (Hilty, 2003).
Status: IUCN Least Concern. CITES Appendix II.

Approximate distribution of *emma* (west) and *auricularis* (eastern part of range).

From left to right: Pfrimer's (young), White-eared, Emma's and Grey-breasted Conures (*pfrimeri, leucotis, emma* and *griseipectus*).

Photograph © Horst Mayer

Aviculture: Probably unknown until 1929 when a small number of birds were received by an importer in England. Venezuela banned the export of wild-caught birds in 1970 so the species again became unknown in aviculture (except locally) for a couple of decades until a Venezuelan breeder exported a number of captive-bred birds to Europe. Availability quickly increased as a result of their prolific nature. In 2000 I saw a nest containing seven young at NiederRhein Park Plantaria, near Kevelaer in Germany. Their ages ranged between three and eighteen days.

Robin Restall, ornithologist, author and illustrator of field guides, informed me that the illegal trade in wild-caught birds in Venezuela results in some birds being smuggled across the border to Guyana. (It is therefore quite likely that *emma* has been exported as *picta*.) He lives in Caracas. In 2003 he acquired two wild-caught adult Emma's Conures, recently trapped just south of Caracas, together with three Painted Conures. The wholesale price was the equivalent of £6 per pair. They had been fed on sunflower seed and plantain. He told me: "Right now all five are in a cage on the kitchen table. They have kept up the most enchanting conversation of little chucks, *chwarks*, and budgie-like notes. I gave them some plantain, which they all sampled immediately, some watermelon – which they haven't touched – and a dish of pine seeds and pumpkin seeds. In the morning I will get them sunflower seed and a selection of fruits. They smell bad – the result of living in filthy small cages with no bathing water."

Sadly, the conditions in which they had been kept are typical of those which wild-caught birds might have to endure. Most are not long-lived. When I mentioned the Houdini escape skills of these birds, he wrote: "Both my friend and the trader confirmed that they are real Houdinis. They loved that expression! And true to form, within a few minutes of feeding each one was exploring every corner of the cage, testing the wires, looking for holes. It seems that they are lost to people here because of their habit of thrusting their heads through holes in order to find a way through, and they get stuck and die before they are found."

Probably they were kept in cages with Canary cage fronts which have small holes where food dishes and drinkers are hooked on the outside. This is a warning not to use such cages for *Pyrrhuras*.

Birders: Parque Nacional El Avila, Caracas.

P. e. auricularis

The validity of the sub-species is in dispute.

Description: supposedly differs from *emma* in the whiter ear coverts. The back and upper tail coverts are said to be darker green. Cere and eye ring are grey (not white).

Range: north-eastern Venezuela in eastern Anzoátegui, Sucre and northern Monagas to Caripe, east of the nominate race.

Habitat: mountains up to 1,700m.

Aviculture: It has been imported into Europe and exists in small numbers – but perhaps has not always been distinguished from *emma*. A breeder in Denmark wrote about his breeding pair in *Dansk Fuglehold* (1/2008). The photographs published with this article clearly show the dark grey cere and lighter grey eye ring.

Birders: Guatapo National Park, northern Venezuela.

GREY-BREASTED CONURE (*Pyrrhura griseipectus*)

ENDANGERED 2017 (Critically Endangered 2007).
CITES Appendix II.

Synonym: Salvadori's Parakeet.
Origin of name: *grisei* = grey, *pectus* = breast.
Local names: *periquito-do-talhardo* (cliff parakeet), *periquito cara-suja, gangarra cara-suja*.
Taxonomy: Formerly a sub-species of White-eared (*P. leucotis*). In 2005 the South American Classification Committee passed proposal #181 to split *griseipectus* and *pfrimeri* from *leucotis*: "All three possess distinctive morphology, habitats and ecology, wholly allopatric ranges and complete lack of intermediate or contact zones, and can be considered full species under any concept available." Following DNA sequencing in 2006, the Committee decided to reverse this decision but currently it is again considered as a distinct species. For conservation reasons this is an important decision.
Description: differs from *leucotis* in **brighter, denser white ear coverts, lack of blue on forehead and the scalloped breast feathers which are grey, prominently scalloped with white**. *P. griseipectus* differs from *leucotis* or *pfrimeri* in the following: *leucotis* has blue suffusion on the forehead (sometimes extending above eyes), nape and sides of neck, the rest of head being buffy-grey; *griseipectus* has blue suffusion only on sides of neck, the crown being entirely grey. Ear coverts are cream to yellowish in *leucotis* (usually tinged buff) but pure white to cream, and notably larger, in *griseipectus*, in which ear-patch connects with the pale breast. Breast feathers in *leucotis* are green with blue suffusion, more intense near neck, with broad pale grey or buff sub-terminal band and black terminal one; in *griseipectus* breast feathers are dusky grey with broad cream to pale buff terminal band.

Bare skin around eye is dark blue in *leucotis* but variable (ranging from whitish to slaty) in *griseipectus* (Olmos *et al*. 1997, 2005). *P. griseipectus* has a significantly longer bill and broader and deeper mandible (Olmos *et al*. 1997).
Length: 23cm. **Weight:** about 52g.
Immature plumage: duller than adults'. Cere and bare skin surrounding eye whitish; beak grey-black.
Range: a very small area of north-eastern Brazil in forest of Serra de Baturité (a small cluster of mountains) in Ceará State. Ranges of hills above about 500m receive sufficient rain to support humid forest in an otherwise semi-arid area. Several new populations have been discovered: in March 2010 in Quixadá, Ceará, in 2014 five birds in Serra Azul (Ibaretama) and in August 2018 in the Serra

do Parafuso (in Canindé). These discoveries were made due to funding from a Conservation Leadership Programme award. In September 2019 a remarkable find occurred in the state of Bahía, far from the range of *griseipectus*, closer to the White-eared Conure. A photo had appeared on the Wikiaves website incorrectly identified as *leucotis*. The isolated population lived in mangroves close to the ocean; 54 individuals were counted, including about 15 pairs. The Aquasis team captured five birds and took DNA samples, and released them. Fabio Nunes told me: 'They look like *griseipectus* but the voice is a little different and some individuals have blue in the front and on the chest (as in *leucotis*).'

Former range: In the recent past it also occurred in the Serra Negra Biological Reserve. Its original range probably extended further south in the states of Pernambuco and Alagoas. In 1978, Galileu Coelho (Federal University of Pernambuco) collected three specimens in Serra Negra, a small moist forest enclave in the dry interior of Pernambuco State, near the border with Ceará State. This represents the only known documented records outside Ceará State. In five small towns of the Serra da Ibiapaba, two of the 147 people interviewed gave accurate descriptions of the parakeet – extinct there at least 20 years ago. Known locally as Cliff Parakeet, it was associated with slope and cliff habitat. Interviewees from Serra do Machado stated that about 60 years ago flocks of up to 100 individuals could be seen there. About 20 years ago the flocks consisted of only two to five individuals (AQUASIS unpublished report, 2008, Conservation of the Grey-breasted Parakeet *Pyrrhura griseipectus*).

Reason for local extinctions: In the Serra do Machado, Ceará state, few forest fragments remain. The area now produces maize, beans and cassava. João Evangelista told field workers about flocks of seventy birds in the 1960s. It was common to see people shooting them because they ate maize. He said: "With one shot, up to 10 birds could be killed".

Status and populations: IUCN Endangered since 2017; previously Critically Endangered CITES Appendix II. The population has increased rapidly in recent years (see page 165) due to the provision of nest-boxes and the local education campaigns by Aquasis which have reduced trapping. In December 2017 a simultaneous count took place in Baturité with nearly 100 volunteers at roost sites over two days (same time, same places mapped during the last two years). The official count was 314 individuals; 467 were counted in roosting places, but only 314 stayed there. This was a minimum because not all roosting sites were known, the territory has increased and some pairs had already started to breed. In addition, there were 52 in Quixadá and seven in Ibaretama.

More than 150 volunteers took part in the 2019 census and 657 parakeets were simultaneously counted at the roosting sites. This represented a 30% increase on the previous year. With the populations in Ibaretama, Quixadá and Caninde, the

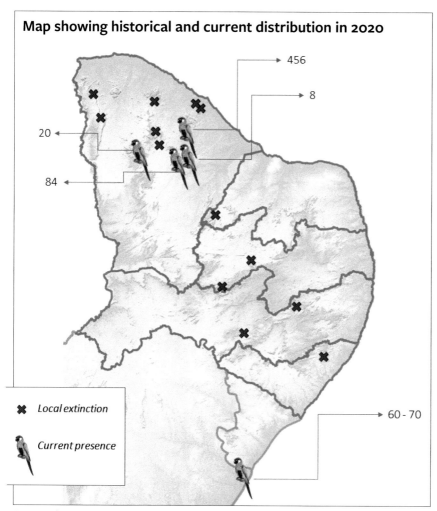

Map showing historical and current distribution in 2020

456

8

20

84

✖ *Local extinction*

🦜 *Current presence*

60 - 70

© AQUASIS/www.aquasis.org

known total of Grey-breasted Parakeets in the wild was 771. At the end of 2020 Fabio Nunes believed the number of breeding pairs had increased from about 10 in 2017, to between 200 and 300 pairs in 2019, including about 20 pairs in the Serra do Mel but only one pair in Ibaretama.

Although the Grey-breasted Parakeet's status was down-listed to Endangered, poaching activities were still the main threat and habitat change also had a serious negative impact. However, the remarkable work of Fabio Nunes and his colleagues offers confidence that the populations will continue to grow.

Threats: extensive destruction of habitat since the early 1970s; by 1996 original forest cover had been reduced to 13% and replaced by coffee plantations. Lack of sufficient trees large enough for nesting cavities stunted the population growth.
Protection: Above 600m it occurs in the Serra de Baturité Environmental Protection area which is not managed for conservation by state authorities but for sustainable use, with small towns and farms within its boundaries. Several landowners have supported habitat conservation of the Grey-breasted Conure and allowing the placement of nest-boxes, thus numbers have increased. Several private reserves have been created in the Baturité mountains, the first in 2010. A decree for a protected area, known as Refúgio de Vida Silvestre Periquito Cara-suja, was signed in August 2018 in Guaramiranga, Baturité. The government provided Aquasis with a rent-free office there and a field base.
Habitat: Unique moist forests above 500m and sometimes dryer forests in isolated mountain ranges in otherwise low-lying semi-arid *caatinga*,[1] north of the Sao Francisco River (and formerly Pernambuco). The humid forest enclaves, described as wet "sky islands" (locally called *brejos*), are restricted to upland granite or sandstone areas, and grade into semi-deciduous forest and eventually into dry *caatinga*. These montane forest enclaves have strong Amazonian affinities. The more robust bill and the larger head of *griseipectus* compared to *leucotis* reflect the different habitats and biogeographical settings in which they live. Another difference is the call, that of *griseipectus* is of a higher frequency.
Habits: Food includes fruits native to tropical America, and locally called "siriguela" *(Spondias purpurea)*, sometimes called red mombin and/or purple mombin (see page 105).
Conservation started in 2007, with searches for other populations, it is led by AQUASIS (Brazilian NGO), and supported by Loro Parque Fundación, Chester Zoo (UK), Act for Nature and ZGAP. (Anon, 2007).

By 2010 sixty nest-boxes had been installed. PVC boxes were ignored. In March 2010 four chicks hatched in one of the wooden boxes, at a height of 8m. Just before they were due to fledge, the box was invaded by carnivorous wasps. Two young ones managed to fly away but one chick was severely stung and died (its body could be used for DNA studies).

Fortunately, the field team intervened and, with the help of local people, smoked out the wasps and returned one young bird one hour later. More nest-boxes were hung with the support of Loro Parque Fundación, Chester Zoo (UK), and ZGAP.

---

1 Highly seasonal deciduous forest with a prolonged dry season, dominated by spiny trees and shrubs, found extensively in north-eastern Brazil.

Fledging success in nest-boxes

	Annual number of fledglings from nest boxes	Number of estimated individuals	Number of individuals counted	Accumulated number of fledglings from nest boxes
2010	3	96		0
2011	33	115		36
2012	70	137		106
2013	42	162		148
2014	74	190		222
2015	96	224		318
2016	124	264		442
2017	165		314	607
2018	234		456	841
2019	324		687	1165
2020	388		890	1553
2021	414			1967

Source: Fabio Nunes/Aquasis.

The availability of nest sites was enormously successful in driving the population increase. It was possible to ring 56 of the 191 chicks that hatched, enabling future identification of individual birds to add to the knowledge of this rare species.

The success of the 2010 nest was reported on television, with the result that a farmer in Quixadá (a straight-line distance of 70km) informed the AQUASIS field team of a small population in a secluded valley on his property. They immediately went to the locality and filmed about fifty parakeets. This population was roosting in cavities in vertical rocky cliffs and foraging in dry forest at the base of the cliffs. (For more information about the conservation Project visit www.aquasis.org or contact Fábio Nunes fabio@aquasis.org. Ongoing studies investigate factors influencing the survival rate of nestlings. Colour-ringing adults and juveniles has resulted in population genetics studies. In the future, DNA techniques may be used as a deterrent against illegal collection of wild birds. The illegal trade is local:

poor people trying to make money. When environmental police were employed in Baturité, more than 400 illegal animals were confiscated in two weeks, including nine Grey-breasted Parakeets. Two with clipped wing feathers were found in the woods. With the news of confiscations some people relinquished or released animals.

It is not difficult to buy legally-bred Grey-breasted Parakeets from three officially recognised facilities. At first prices were very high, which was why the illegal trade continued. The price fell to 350 reais (about U$85), but it is still expensive compared to the illegal trade price of U$22 (F. Nunes, pers. comm., 2018). The release of birds bred in captivity in Brazil, to populate unoccupied areas, was being prepared as this book went to press.

Aviculture: As a result of a few birds imported during the late 1980s, there are a number of breeders in Europe. At that time Jeff Hornsby in the UK found single birds in collections in various European countries, some of which were captive-bred. He placed all in one large aviary and let them choose their own mates. In this way he formed twelve pairs, all of which produced young. They were allowed two nests a year, so it was not unusual to breed between six and fourteen young from each pair.

The inspirational work of the NGO Aquasis has resulted in a rapid population increase. Photograph © AQUASIS/www.aquasis.org

Some pairs regularly reared seven young in a nest. In this way the Grey-breasted Conure reached many breeders, not only in the UK but worldwide – exported by one dealer. Of all his *Pyrrhuras*, these were his favourites – he called them his "soldiers" for their upright stance. Recently, when a pair of these conures were bought by another breeder, he checked their rings and found that they were two of his young that he had sold nineteen years previously!

In Germany, Horst Mayer bred *griseipectus* in 2000. Eight eggs were laid, the average size being 21.6mm x 17.7mm. Five chicks hatched after 22 to 24 days. They were ringed at only ten or eleven days with 4.5mm rings (Mayer, 2001). One female reared 87 young from 2003 to 2013! Loro Parque, Tenerife, acquired six captive-bred birds from Germany in 2002. By 2009 there were five breeding pairs and by 2011 seventy young had been ringed. As an example of the readiness to nest of this species, Danish breeder Claus Nielsen bought a pair from the Netherlands in December 2013. The male was hatched in 2009 and the female in 2011. They hatched their first chick on March 31 2014.

Birders: Serra do Baturité, Ceará State.

PYRRHURA PICTA COMPLEX

Taxonomy

Taxonomic studies have been significant, increasing the number of recognised species. Nearly all sub-species of the Painted Conure were recognised as distinct species following a review in 2002. However, in 2006 a study based on DNA showed a much more complicated picture, that *picta* and *leucotis* were intertwined – for example, it was proposed that *emma* should become a sub-species of *picta*, not *leucotis*. The classification of these two species and all the forms formerly considered as sub-species has had taxonomists scratching their heads in bewilderment and resulted in various different proposals to the South American Classification Committee, one of which was described as the most confusing and complex ever received.

There is not universal agreement. It might be thought that the matter could be settled indisputably with DNA analysis but this is more useful at species level than with sub-species. In any case, DNA analysis can differ according to the method used to calculate the results. It might be considered as a suggestion – not a solution.

When Leo Joseph published his paper in 2002 he called it "Beginning an end to 63 years of uncertainty: The Neotropical parakeets known as *Pyrrhura picta* and *P. leucotis* comprise more than two species." This was somewhat ironic as he started a new era of debate! Also, according to Thomas Arndt, who has studied the *picta/ leucotis* complex since the mid-1990s, there are mistakes in the molecular genetic research, partly because some specimens were misidentified.

Classification of the Painted Conure
Pyrrhura picta, past and present

P. picta amazonum	now Santarem or Hellmayr's Conure *P. amazonum*
P. picta microtera	now *P. amazonum microtera* or synonymous with *amazonum*.
P. picta lucianii	now Bonaparte's Conure *P. lucianii*
P. picta roseifrons	now Rose-fronted Conure *P. roseifrons*
P. picta subandina	now *P. subandina* Sinú Conure
P. picta caeruleiceps	now *P. caeruleiceps* Perija Conure or Todd's Conure
P. picta pantchenkoi	now synonymous with *caeruleiceps* or recognised as a sub-species of *caeruleiceps* (Pantchenko's Conure)
P. picta eisenmanni	now *P. eisenmanni* Azuero Conure.

Since Leo Joseph and his colleagues published on this taxonomy, other taxonomists have added to the debate, making the situation look very complicated.

For further information refer to the article published in *Papageien* by Heinz Schnitker, in two parts: *Zur Systematik der Rotschwanzsittiche – der Neueste Stand* (Systematics of the *Pyrrhuras* – the latest knowledge), Part I, 2018 (1): 19-22 and Part II, 2018 (2): 55-59. Part II includes 25 illustrations by Thomas Arndt showing the many forms described in the *picta-leucotis* complex. These are divided into six clades (species believed to have been derived from a common ancestor). *P. pfrimeri* and *roseifrons* are the sole members of their clades. Also illustrated are forms not mentioned in this book which are arguably distinct and are unlikely to be recognised in aviculture, if they exist. Three are illustrated in the article mentioned, with photographs of live birds, *P. amazonum araguaiaensis, P. dilutissima pereneensis* and *P. lucianii orosaensis.* A distribution map is included.

Since then, Raphael Sabongi Lúcio Marcelino of the University of São Paulo (Instituto de Biociências, Departamento de Zoologia) has studied the *Pyrrhura picta-leucotis* complex. He explained: "Depending on the author, this complex can comprise between seven and 15 species, in addition to a varied number of subspecies. Many of those taxa lack well-defined diagnostic parameters, which generates a profusion of names in the literature." Due to the lack of clarity in the distinction of taxa, and to contribute to future studies of systematics and biogeography, his work seeks to describe the morphological variation present in the *Pyrrhura picta-leucotis* complex based on plumage and morphometry characteristics. He defines consistent diagnostic characters to elucidate the group's taxonomy and to determine the geographic distribution of taxa that prove to be valid. (Revisão taxonômica do complexo *Pyrrhura picta-leucotis* (Aves: Psittacidae), MSc thesis, 2022).

PERIJA CONURE (*Pyrrhura caeruleiceps*)

Synonyms: Todd's Parakeet, Magdalena Parakeet
Origin of name: *caeruleus* = blue, *ceps* = head
Local name: Periquito de Perijá
Taxonomy: First described by Todd in 1947. Formerly considered a sub-species of Painted Conure *(P. picta)*. Following the taxonomic revision of Joseph (2000), the former *picta* sub-species *pantchenkoi* is synonymous with *caeruleiceps*.
Description: It was believed that the 2007 photographs by members of the ProAves Project *Pyrrhura* team (financed by Loro Parque Fundación) were the first ever taken. They show a very beautiful bird with vivid, striking markings. Forehead and forepart of crown and **a wide area on the nape are blue. Hind crown is brown suffused with blue. Its most striking features are the brownish-red lores, cheeks and part of the ear coverts and area surrounding the eye, snowy-white rear of the ear coverts and scalloped feathers of the upper breast brown very broadly edged with white.** The bend of the wing is red. The tail is green above and maroon towards the tip, and dull greyish-maroon below. In the first photo of an adult, the iris of the eye is a striking white. That of the immature bird is yellowish-white.
Immature plumage: undescribed in the literature. A photograph of an immature bird (ProAves) shows much duller plumage, less extensive reddish-brown on the face and duller and less extensive white margins to breast feathers. A few red feathers can be seen at bend of wing.

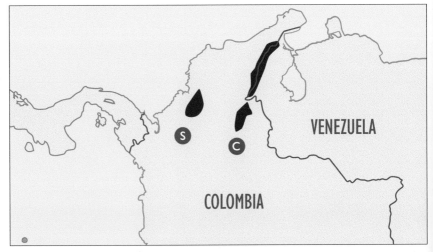

Approximate former range of *subandina* (S) and current range of *caeruleiceps* (C).

Perijá Conures feeding on the flowers of *Gliricida sepium* (local name Matarratón).
They were photographed in the Department of Cesar at La Jagua de Ibirico.

Photograph © Agnes Coenen

Range: Highly restricted, on the west slope at the northern end of the eastern Andes from south Cesar state north through Los Motilones into the Sierra de Perijá, on the border of north-western Venezuela and north-eastern Colombia. It is estimated to have lost approximately 70% of its original habitat within its Colombian distribution.

Studies carried out as part of *Projecto Pyrrhura* revealed two populations near the town of Ocaña in Norte de Santander. In 2010 ProAves researcher Fabián Guzmán discovered a third population in the foothills of the Serranía de Perijá, in patches of tropical forest – the first record in an area of 130km between historical populations and only the third population known.

Status: The Perijá Conure was recognised as a species by BirdLife International and classified as IUCN ENDANGERED in 2014. CITES Appendix II.

Habitat: mainly between 400m and 900m; up to 2,000m in dry forest in the lower zones and humid forest at higher altitudes in areas of native vegetation with canopy at a height of 10m to 20m. It has been observed where trees of the following families were well represented: Bombacaceae, Sterculiaceae, Cecropiaceae, Caesalpiniaceae and Mimosaceae. ProAves field workers watched groups of four to eight individuals and flocks of between thirty and seventy birds.

Habits: In 2008 two ProAves researchers discovered a roost site occupied by six Perijá Conures, in an avocado tree approximately 12m high. There were three cavities. Fruits, such as those of *Ochorma* were eaten. The feeding range was reported to cover 100 hectares (247 acres).

Threats: Severe loss of habitat for cattle pasture and cultivation, especially drugs. Internationally financed eradication campaigns force traffickers and growers to constantly relocate, making drug-related activities a principal cause of forest loss. Removal of chicks from nests by farmers is another source of concern.

Population: Small, not quantified, but believed to be decreasing. In 2007, searches in 22 areas revealed the presence of the conure in only two localities.

Project: The ProAves team found thirty to fifty individuals in 2007 at their study site at 1,000m, five to six hours' hike from the end of the main road. Searches were made between 500m and 1,300m, where 50% of the landscape has been converted to cultivation and cattle pasture, regenerating secondary forests and coffee cultivation. In 2008, 286 individuals were counted within an estimated area of 109 ha. They were seen flying over pastures in search of food and nest sites, near houses. The field team witnessed uncontrolled fires, the cutting of forest to create more pasture, and the presence of people in the parakeets' foraging areas. A 30-day survey during 2011 resulted in the discovery of two new populations in Los Motilones Mountains, on the north-eastern boundary of Colombia with Venezuela. Most flock sizes were of three to ten individuals but one flock of 90 birds was recorded. In 2015 ZGAP, the German conservation NGO, financed an expedition to the department of El Cesar in northern Colombia. Flocks of 18, 22 and 30 individuals were seen on the fifth day. In March 2016 eight were photographed feeding on guavas. At another farm groups of from eight to 36 appeared daily. They also fed on *Inga*, *Erythrina* and *Cecropia* trees and on typical trees of the region, *Bursea simaruba* and *Acacia tamarindifolia* (Strewe *et al*, 2017).

Conservation: In 2008 the nest-box programme was extended to the Hormigero de Torcoroma reserve even although the conures' presence there was not confirmed. An education programme to prevent trapping in various parts of Norte de Santander is ongoing.

SINÚ CONURE (*Pyrrhura subandina*)

POSSIBLY EXTINCT

Origin of name: *subandina* = below the Andes.
Known only from 17 museum specimens. Its range, isolated from other members of the *picta* complex, is considered justification for treating it as a full species. There is the suggestion that it evolved independently. It differs from *picta* in the **dull red and blue frontal band, dull brown (not whitish) ear coverts, dusky-brown breast and green (not red) bend of wing.**

Pyrrhura subandina illustrated by Thomas Arndt.

Range: Sinú watershed, Cordoba, north-western Colombia. No birds were found in searches in 2005; local people did not know it. Thomas Arndt searched for it in the 1990s when this area was already almost deforested. He believes that the species became extinct several decades ago. See map on page 170.

Status: IUCN Critically Endangered (probably extinct). A large proportion (estimated at 98.1%) of its historic distribution has been lost to deforestation through conversion to agriculture. Loss of habitat continues due to indiscriminate logging, intensive forest extraction, the expansion of illicit plantations and agricultural crops. Between 2004 and 2008 the Loro Parque Fundación (LPF) supported Fundación ProAves to conduct searches for *P. subandina*, and not one was found. Nevertheless over the ensuing years, doubt that the species is extinct has persisted. This stimulated the Sociedad Ornitológica de Córdoba (SOC) and Fundación Vida Silvestre to undertake more searches, ongoing at the time of going to press, again financed by LPF. Searches covered agricultural areas with remnants of forest habitat and more extensive forest cover, in or near Paramillo National Park, much of which remains unexplored.

Conservation: From the outset, this project has emphasised the importance of community participation, because if and when the Sinú Parakeet is rediscovered, immediate action will be needed to protect the area. This will be much easier if support from the local community has been prepared by awareness activities which explain the precarious situation of the parakeet and that it is unique to the Sinú valley. The SOC team has distributed posters and stickers in various strategic places. Endangered sub-species are seldom of conservation concern so it was unfortunate that not until 2002 was it elevated to the status of species.

AZUERO CONURE (*Pyrrhura eisenmanni*)

Origin of name: named for Eugene Eisenmann (1906-1981), American ornithologist. This conure was discovered by Francisco Delgado in 1979 (Delgado, 1985) and was originally classified as a sub-species of the Painted Conure.

Description: It differs from *caeruleiceps* in its narrow dull red frontal band and green bend of the wing.

Length: 22cm. **Weight:** not recorded.

Range: central Panama, in the south-western part of the Azuero Peninsula, including the Cerro Hoya National Park (32,557 hectares). It also occurs around Cañas, Los Santos, according to cattle herders.

Habitat: Forest (especially lowland humid forests) and margins up to 1,660m.

Status: IUCN Endangered (2014). CITES Appendix II. It is vulnerable due to its very small range, estimated at less than 700km^2 (270 square miles).

Habits: Kees Groenendijk owns two eco-tourism companies in Panama, on the west coast of the Azuero Peninsula. He states that this conure occurs only in the Cerro Hoya Mountains, on the southern tip of the peninsula. These mountains are protected in the Cerro Hoya National Park which has no roads, no facilities and no accommodation. When Kees Groenendijk and his partner were looking for a property, they went to the end of the road into the mountains, a little village called Flores on the edge of the national park. They met Juan Velásquez, a farmer who lives on the forested hills that abut the park's mountainous margins. From Juan they discovered that Azuero Conures visited his fig trees every year, to feast on the fruits. However, once the figs were consumed, the parakeets were gone, not to be seen regularly until the following April or later, when they would return every now and then to assess the stage of ripeness of the fruits.

In June 2011 Kees organised a trip to look for this species, when the birds descend the mountains to feed in the fig trees. They also eat the small fruits of

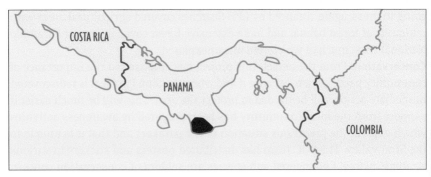

Approximate range of *eisenmanni*.

nance (*Brysonimia crassifolia*), which are rich in oil and in Vitamin C. During the two days in the locality the participants were able to watch the birds for several hours and/or on several occasions. There were two flocks, one of about 15 and another of about 25 birds. In June 2012 I visited the area with Kees but due to lack of rain, resulting in late fruiting of the fig trees, I was too early. The conures arrived about three weeks after I left!

In January 2022 Kees told me: "There is no evidence of deforestation on our side of the Cerro Hoya and, as far as I know, no deforestation in parakeet habitat on the other side either. There have been incidental observations that suggest that the Azuero Parakeet may breed and roost in tree holes quite high up in the mountains. Juan reported a cavity used for breeding at about 900m above sea level. And during my last overnight trip, we heard the parakeets pass by on two consecutive mornings and evenings. In the morning they came from higher altitudes, presumably to feed on fruiting trees lower down. I would not dare to guess if the population is stable. There are no reliable data. The Azuero Parakeet remains an enigma for the time being."

Aviculture: Probably unknown outside Panama, from where there is no legal export. The first recorded captive breeding occurred in 2017 at the Istmo Zoo in Colón, Panama. Due to the interest of the director, Jacobo Lacs, four pairs were acquired with permission from the Ministry of the Environment. One female laid four eggs, three of which hatched in May 2018 (Lacs and Silva, 2019).

Birders: Cerro Hoya National Park.

Azuero Conures at Istmo Zoo in Panama.
Photograph © René Wüst

PAINTED CONURE (*Pyrrhura picta*)

Origin of name: *picta* = painted.
Local names: Venezuela: *Perico Pechiescamado*; Brazil: *Tiriba-de-testa-azul*, *Marrequém-do-igapó*.
Description: Forepart of crown blue; narrow line of blue on nape, dividing the green of the upperparts from dark greyish-brown crown to nape. Lower part of cheeks: blue; lores, cheeks and narrow area above eye: rich brown (brownish-maroon). **Scalloping on throat and upper breast: chevroned-shaped, grey margined with white or yellowish-white. Bend of wing red.** Maroon patch on abdomen and another from lower back to upper tail coverts. Tail feathers: maroon above with green markings on outer part of upper feathers; coppery-red below. Bare skin surrounding the eye is grey.
Immature birds: bend of wing green with a few scattered red feathers. Bare skin surrounding eye is whitish or grey.
Distinguished from *Pyrrhura emma* by the chevron or pointed shape of the markings on the scalloped breast feathers which are rounded in *emma* (like those of *leucotis*).
Length: 23cm. **Weight:** about 60g.
Range: Venezuela, south of Orinoco river, Bolívar and eastern Amazonas, through Guianas to northern-most Brazil in states of Amapa, Pará and Amazonas.

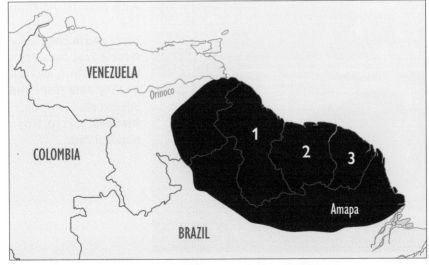

Approximate range of *picta*. See map on page 125 for range in Brazil.
Key: 1. Guyana; 2. Suriname; 3. French Guiana.

Painted Conures (*Pyrrhura picta*) feeding on *Pehria compacta*.
Photograph © Agnes Coenen.

Habitat: forest in lowlands and foothills but up to 1,000m, and up to 1,800m on Cerro Yavi, Amazonas. In Amazonas and in western and southern Bolívar most sightings are from slopes of flat-topped mountains called *tepuis* (ie, above range of *melanura*). In eastern Bolívar it occurs in lowlands and in the vicinity of Gran Sabana (south-eastern Bolívar) it is replaced on the slopes of *tepuis* by *egregia* (Hilty, 2003). According to Sigrist (2009), in Brazil it occurs in humid forests on sandy soils and in adjacent open grasslands with scattered trees. In Suriname it is found in forested coastal sand-ridges, as well as the interior.

Habits: It nests in abandoned woodpecker holes and in cavities in large trees. Although a common and widespread species, information is sparse.

Status: Least Concern (IUCN). CITES Appendix II. Common.

Aviculture: There are records of the Painted Conure being kept in France, with breeding successes by Madame Lécallier in 1918 and by the great aviculturist Jean Delacour in 1920. Presumably they came from French Guiana and were therefore what was then the nominate race. This conure was almost unknown until the 1970s when a few consignments reached the USA and Europe. Guyana was the main exporting country and has for many years been extremely active in the parrot export trade. It seems, though, that trappers do not target this species, concentrating on more profitable Amazons and macaws and to a lesser degree Black-headed Caiques. The official Customs export figures for the years 2000 to 2007 show only six Painted Conures exported – in the year 2007. In that year Guyana had an export quota of 300 for Painted Conures, 120 for Fiery-shouldered and, as comparison, 990 for the Orange-winged Amazon (*Amazona amazonica*) (Figures courtesy John Caldwell, CITES Trade Database Manager, WCMC, Cambridge).

Although it is a pretty bird, it has never gained the popularity of certain other members of the genus as it usually has a more aloof personality. The clutch size is five to eight, occasionally more, yet it cannot be considered as one of the most free-breeding members of the genus. In the USA, Howard Voren is a leading breeder of conures. He wrote of the Painted Conure on his website (www.voren.com): "This bird has been imported in sufficient quantities to allow for a domestic population boom. Most pairs, however, are very reluctant to produce. There are aviculturists who are lucky enough to have one or two very prolific pairs, but on the whole, the painted has not been established in captivity." He suggested that colony-breeding, which had failed to increase production with other conure species, might be worth trying.

Colin Scott also found that some pairs were reluctant to breed. He had three pairs in 2000. One pair hatched and reared four chicks in an indoor aviary in January 2001. In the second clutch three young were reared from four eggs. The other two pairs did not attempt to breed. Colin Scott wrote: "My experiences with this species echo other breeders' results in that if you have a pair that breeds then they can be quite prolific, but there are a lot of pairs that show no sign of breeding." The successful pair reared seven young in 2001, three in 2002, one in 2003, ten in 2005 and six in 2006 – a total of 27 young during a period of six years. The female was incubating eight eggs in May 2007 (Scott, 2007).

The Breeding Register of the Parrot Society UK, recorded the following numbers reported bred by its members: 1981 and prior, 0; 1984, 20; 1990, 22; 1991, 18; 1992, 60; 1994, 33; 1998, 92; 2000, 39, 2002, 26, 2004, 3; 2007, 15; 2008, 4; 2010, 8; 2014, 0; 2021, 4.

The first reported breeding in the USA occurred in 1982. William Wilson of Norshore Pets, Illinois, acquired three males and three females in 1981. In July 1982 one female laid seven eggs. Six hatched and five young were reared. The other two pairs made no attempt to breed. It was noticed that they often hung on the side of their flights, calling to each other. Mr Wilson thought they had paired up before he had parted them. When reunited both pairs nested in 1984 and the three pairs reared 21 young to maturity. In this case the Painted Conures just needed different partners!

During my time as curator at Loro Parque, Tenerife, the pair there reared young in 1988. They were observed mating on April 12. On May 17 there was one newly hatched chick in the nest and eight or nine eggs. Three eggs were removed. One was infertile and the other two were fostered to Maroon-bellied Conures – but did not hatch. A second chick hatched with the parents; it was judged to be about eight days old on May 30. The young left the nest on July 7 and 11, the eldest at 51 days. **Birders:** Guyana, Iwokrama Forest Reserve; Venezuela, Canaima National Park, south-eastern Bolívar .

BONAPARTE'S CONURE (*Pyrrhura lucianii*)

Synonym: Prince Lucien's Conure, Deville's Conure
Origin of name: after the French ornithologist M. Charles-Lucien Bonaparte. His works included *Iconographie des Perroquets* (1857).
Taxonomy: Formerly considered a sub-species of *P. picta*. Much confusion arose from the early 20th century when distinctive red-crowned and often yellow-eared south-western Amazonian birds (red-crowned, *parvifrons*) were thought to be adults of brown-crowned, buff-eared west-central Amazonian birds, *P. lucianii*). This is not the case.
Description: differs from *picta* in **green bend of wing and lack of (or very little) blue on forecrown; ear coverts: dark brown; breast feathers dull green scalloped with yellowish-buff.**
Range: It has a very small range in the western Amazon region, mainly around the River Purus, but the limits of its range are unknown. In 2017 *Pyrrhura lucianii* was found on private property in the municipality of Senador Guiomard in Acre State, Brazil. This was the first record of it in the state, expanding its distribution by 219km (136 miles) to the south of Pauini, the nearest location. The species was observed consuming salt, used as a cattle feed supplement. See map on page 125.
Habitat: Forests and their margins, up to 800m.
Status: IUCN Least Concern. CITES Appendix II.
Aviculture: Bred by Lloyd B.Thompson in Canada in 1960 according to a note in the *Avicultural Magazine* (vol 67, (1), 36. The editor, A. A. Prestwich, rightly pointed out: "The Prince Lucien has been described as 'common in captivity and easily reared.' But actually *Pyrrhura picta lucianii* is very rare and such records as exist almost undoubtedly refer to the Red-bellied *P. frontalis frontalis*. The breeder has sent an excellent photograph of the six young ones and there is no mistake about correct identification. This success is in all probability a world 'first'". Nevertheless, without a description or photographs, the identification remains in doubt. Lloyd Thompson reported that the female laid six eggs. "They are fantastically tame and we have really enjoyed them. American breeders say they have never been bred on this Continent."
Birders: Mamirauá Reserve, near Tefé.

Pyrrhura lucianii. painted by Eduardo Parentoni Brettas and reproduced from *Terra Papagalli* (2015) by kind permission of Edoardo Rivetti, M'Arte, São Paulo.

GARLEPP'S CONURE (*Pyrrhura parvifrons*)

Origin of name: named after Gustav Garlepp (1862-1907), a German bird collector in South America.

Taxonomy: Recent investigations by Arndt & Wink (2017) suggest that *parvifrons*, on the basis of genetic and morphological differences to *P. roseifrons*, should be classified as a stand-alone species. Their genetic investigations revealed that the second population along the Amazon river must be included in *P. lucianii*. Originally, it was believed that *P. parvifrons* consisted of two populations, one in the area west of Tarapoto and a second one along the Amazon, east of Iquitos, Peru.

Description: *P. parvifrons* differs from *P. roseifrons* in having the rose-red colour on the head restricted to a narrow band on the forehead and a few scattered feathers in the dark brown crown. The ear coverts are paler grey-brown and there is a strong scalloped pattern on the upper breast (BirdLife International (2020). Species factsheet: *Pyrrhura parvifrons* from http://www.birdlife.org). However, the eastern population is said to show more resemblance to *lucianii*, while the western birds from Tarapoto (San Martin), at the edge of the Andes, are more like *roseifrons* (del Hoyo *et al*, 2013).

Range: restricted to two separate areas in northern Peru, in northeastern San Martin and western Loreto, with an apparently unconnected population in northeastern Loreto (Arndt 2008). It appears to meet the range of *P. roseifrons* around Tarapoto in the Huallaga valley and that the two have contact in the area of the confluence of Río Cushabatay and Río Uyacali. *P. parvifrons* lives in a white river sand area, unlike the

The red areas indicate the two separate populations of *parvifrons*.

southwest Amazon moist forest occupied by *roseifrons*, also by *peruviana* and *dilutissima* (Arndt and Wink, 2017).

Status: IUCN Least Concern. CITES Appendix II.

Departments of Colombia

WAVY-BREASTED CONURE (*Pyrrhura peruviana*)

Local name: *Perico de Pecho Ondulado.*
It remained largely unrecognised in museum collections, until Peter Hocking and the late Emmet Blake examined specimens, and named it together with Leo Joseph (Joseph, 2002).
Description: Distinguished from *lucianii* by **more extensive cream or yellow margins to breast feathers and the blue in forecrown. The ear coverts are buff;** *lucianii* is darker.
Length: 20cm (Hodel, 2012a). **Weight:** about 50g (estimated).
Immature: Photographs of birds bred by Jörg Hodel show duller plumage and less well defined breast markings. The upper mandible was flecked with white, soft pads white and bare eye skin also white. The iris was dark.

Wavy-breasted Parakeets in Chikai, Peru. Photograph © Thomas Arndt

Range: south-eastern Ecuador to northern Peru; also southern Peru. Both *peruviana* populations are located at the border of the main *roseifrons* population. It has been suggested by Thomas Arndt that the proposed new sub-species *dilutissima* might even be sympatric with *roseifrons*. Its plumage is paler than that of *peruviana*. Map not included. Insufficient information on range.

Habitat: Thomas Arndt described his journey to Peru to observe and photograph *peruviana* and *dilutissima* (Arndt, 2018a, Arndt 2018b) – including excellent photographs of the birds and their habitats.

Aviculture: According to Thomas Arndt, the few birds in northern Europe thought to be *peruviana* belong to the *amazonum* complex. In June 2012 the Swiss magazine *Gefiederter Freund* published an article by Jörg Hodel relating to his breeding success with *peruviana*. The photographs show birds which agree with the description of this species. He kept his two pairs in accommodation where the temperature varied between 12°C and 25°C with humidity between 65% and 75%. Lighting included Arcadia ultra-violet daylight lamps. The nest-boxes measured 40cm x 14cm x 14cm with a 5cm entrance hole. One pair laid five eggs, three were fertile and all hatched, but the youngest chick died at two days old. The two survivors were ringed at 15 days with 4.5mm rings. The second pair produced two clutches of three infertile eggs. Jörg Hodel stated that they were not noisy (Hodel, 2012a).

In a house in Huampani on the Rio Cenepa Thomas Arndt encountered two young *peruviana* being kept as pets. Photograph © Thomas Arndt

ROSE-FRONTED CONURE (*Pyrrhura roseifrons*)

Origin of name: *rosei* = rosy, *frons* = forehead.

Local name: Brazil *Tiriba-de-cabeça-vermelha*

Formerly considered as a sub-species of the Painted Conure (*P. picta*).

Description: Distinguished from *picta* by **red forehead, lores** and (eventually) crown and a few feathers on nape; ear coverts orange-tinged buff. Bend of wing: little or no red. Lower back and part of abdomen: maroon. Tail: green near base and maroon for about half its length. Bare skin surrounding eye whitish or tinged grey and less conspicuous than in most members of the genus.

Aviculturists who know *roseifrons* only from the illustration in *Parrots of the World* (1989) would be disappointed. It was made from an exceptional bird: ear coverts are yellow and the rest of the head is scarlet. However, it can take up to three years for full adult plumage to be acquired. The red gradually extends patchily towards the crown, which is dark brown. Even mature adults show variation in coloration and some (most?) never acquire yellow on the ear coverts. Some birds have more pronounced breast markings.

Immature plumage: head mainly brown, tinged with green. Lores and forepart of the cheeks: brown; rear part of ear coverts pale brown or buff. The scalloped feathers of the upper breast are dark brown, margined with green; abdomen: only a hint of maroon. After the first moult there is some red on forehead and forepart of crown, just reaching top of lores. The maroon area on the abdomen is larger.

Length: 22cm. **Weight:** 55-60g

Range: Western Brazil (see map on page 124) in Amazonas state between the Juruá and Javari Rivers (Silveira and Brettas, 2015) and north-eastern Peru south to Junín in eastern Peru and south-eastern Peru to Teoponte, northern Bolivia. Note that Forshaw (2010) describes two separate populations, with a break in the range in central Peru. Arndt (pers. comm., 2012) disputes this.

Habitat: Forests including margins, up to 1,200m; riverine forest with large patches of bamboo.

Status: IUCN Least Concern. CITES Appendix II.

Habits: Donald Brightsmith described censusing parrots on a small lake in Manu National Park. He often heard the quiet *pic pic* calls of a group of *roseifrons*:

"...just in time to focus my binoculars and count the flock before they disappeared into the forest on the other side of the lake. Of the dozen species of parrots and macaws I recorded during these censuses, the *Pyrrhuras* were the only ones able to sneak across the lake without me knowing. As they feed, these birds continue to avoid detection by remaining extremely quiet. Once as I walked through the forest, I was surprised to find myself below a huge fig tree with chunks of unripe figs falling like rain all around me. The only sound came from the fruits as they crashed to the ground, but I had no idea what was causing this cascade of fruit.

"I peered up into the canopy, and soon spotted movement: a Painted Conure chewing intently on a 1.5in green fig. The bird held the rather large fruit with his foot wedging it between two small branches. As I watched, the bird chewed through the outer skin and through nearly a half an inch of rather hard "pulp" to consume the mass of tiny seeds in the center. When all the seeds were removed, the bird let the fruit drop and moved down the branch to haul up another one. Before the bird could finish its second helping, I heard one quiet *cheet* from the other side of the tree. This was quickly answered by similar calls emanating from everywhere in the canopy of the tree. Within seconds, the meaning of these "its time to fly" calls were revealed as the entire flock of nearly 30 conures took flight, punctuated by the loud "thump" as each dropped their final fig" (Brightsmith, 1999).

The beautiful Rose-fronted Conure.
Photograph © Karl Heinz Lambert

Aviculture: *roseifrons* was unknown until the mid or late 1980s, except in Brazil where the noted aviculturist Nelson Kawall had reared twelve young from one pair by 1983. The first recorded breeding in Europe occurred at Walsrode Bird Park in Germany. Two young birds were acquired in 1995 which did not acquire adult plumage until they were twelve months old.

Rose-fronted family bred by Jason Wright in Australia.

Photograph © Jason Wright

They were provided with a natural nest log 29cm high and 20cm wide with a 6cm entrance hole. Five eggs were laid in the summer of the following year and five chicks hatched. The youngest died after a few days. Photographs (*Papageien*, 9/97) show one adult with three young on the perches.

The Rose-fronted Conure was late to reach the USA because of the ban on the importation of wild-caught birds in 1995. When the US Fish and Wildlife Service approved a conure breeding consortium, a limited number was imported. The first breeder was Richard Cusick in California, in about 2001. In Europe, it has been bred at Loro Parque, Tenerife, since 1996, when eight young were reared.

In the UK, *roseifrons* was established from six pairs of wild-caught birds imported by Jeff Hornsby. When they came out of quarantine one pair was bought by Steve Beaver. These two men were responsible for establishing the species. Steve Beaver's female laid two weeks after he acquired the pair and produced five young. He acquired four more pairs and in five years bred about 300 young, but there was a massive gender imbalance.

He told me: "Sexing them was easy. To me it was like looking at Eclectus Parrots! I always had them sexed, because that was what buyers wanted. When I took them to the vet to be endoscoped, I would put all the males in one box, and all the females in another. I was always right." He said that *roseifrons* is the only sexually dimorphic *Pyrrhura*, that the red on the head extends beyond the eye in the female but not in the male. The plumage of his males did not change much after they left the nest. It might be dangerous to apply his sexing method to all Rose-fronted Conures in view of the small genetic base of his birds and the likelihood that the wild-caught adults all came from the same area. In South American parrots there is often a lot of variation in one species according to the locality from which they originate.

They were extraordinarily prolific, set up in cages 1.8m long, 60cm wide and 1.2m high. The nest-box was on the inside but accessible from the outside. Often the female would lay again before the young in the nest had fledged. There would be five to eight young and up to four nests in one year. The wisdom of allowing females to rear more than two or three nests in one year has already been debated. In this case, there were only two bloodlines. In such circumstances, mutations or other defects are likely to occur. In many nests, one of the youngsters produced had plumage flecked with yellow. The degree varied, with up to 50% yellow flecking. Four or five years later, the plumage of these birds was the same. It is unknown whether this plumage aberration was a mutation or caused by some other factor.

The young birds were kept in a large flight, without nest-boxes, measuring approximately 6m x 4.5m. To make the environment more interesting, Steve Beaver made a plywood base to take two or three large rotten logs about 90cm high with a diameter of about 45cm. Into these rotten logs he jammed big branches from apple trees. Eventually, due to pressure of work, he gave up all his birds. He knew there were about ninety in this flight but when he came to catch them up there were 108. Some birds had gnawed their way into the rotten logs and reared young there. This indicated how strong was their desire to reproduce! On the other hand, some breeders find them difficult. Kris Spearman told me: "Of all the species of *Pyrrhura* available, I have found these the most challenging to breed." Possibly in-breeding was the cause if the genetics of the purchased birds were unknown.

A couple of breeders told me they thought this species did not have the right temperament to make a good pet partly because they are so restless and active when young. As a general statement this might be true but at least one owner (from "Oklahoma Green-cheeks") in the USA was delighted with her bird which "calmed down" as he matured. She described him as a very "touchy-feely" bird, who would lean into the cup of her hand to be scratched all over. She described his talking ability as higher than that of a Green-cheek but less than a Crimson-bellied. By the age of ten months he spoke several words and could imitate her laugh.

Birders: Manú Biosphere Reserve, Madre de Dios, south-eastern Peru; extreme western Brazil, Reserva Natural Palmari.

P. snethlageae and *amazonum*: more taxonomy

It has been argued that until the precise distribution areas are known *snethlageae* and *amazonum* should be maintained as one species. Some authorities favour considering *amazonum* as the nominate form with *snethlageae* and *lucida* as sub-species. More recently, it has been argued that *Pyrrhura pallescens* should be used as the valid name for *Pyrrhura snethlageae* (Gaban-Lima and Raposo, 2016). Nomenclature of the similar species remains confusing. The presence of complex geographic variation among species and the absence of clear morphological breaks among populations have led to the description of many poorly defined species and sub-species.

There is some variation in the breast markings in some parts of the range. To the east of the Rio Madeira drainage is the Santarem or Hellmayr's Conure *(P. amazonum)*. Birds south of the Amazon tend to be smaller and darker-faced than those originating north of the Amazon.

MADEIRA CONURE
(*Pyrrhura snethlageae* or *P. pallescens*)

Synonym: Snethlage's Conure.
Origin of name: after Maria Emilie Snethlage, the German ornithologist (director of the Emilio Goeldi Museum in Brazil) who first described it as a distinctive form in 1914.
Native name: *Tiriba-do-Madeira*
Description: It is notable for the **distinctive brown downward pointing, almost arrow-shaped, marks on each of the whitish or buff upper breast feathers.** Lower breast feathers are margined with pale yellow with grey downward pointing marks. This is in contrast to the more scalloped pattern of throat and upper breast in most *Pyrrhuras*. There is a narrow blue line on the forehead; forepart of the cheeks is also blue. Crown to nape is brown, some feathers narrowly

Madeira Conures. See also photograph on page 190. Photograph © Bent Pedersen

Madeira Conures at Rio Cristalino, feeding on an aquatic plant of the family Podostemaceae. Photograph © Steve Brookes, www.wildparrots.up.close.com

margined with buff, with a few blue feathers between rear of crown and nape. Feathers of ear coverts are buff and brownish, lores brownish and area below the eye brown. The iris is red-brown, the skin surrounding the eye and the feet are dark grey and the beak is black.

Length: 23cm. **Weight:** 50-65g, males heavier (specimens Museum of Zoology of the University of São Paulo).

Range: South of the Amazon River, on both margins of the Madeira River, extending eastwards to the western bank of the Araguaia River; marginally in northernmost Bolivia. Its exact limits are unknown (Silveira and Brettas, 2015). See map on page 125 for range in Brazil.

Habitat and Habits: Forested areas up to 300m, with large stands of bamboo in southern part of range. The birds in the photograph were very wary. They were drinking and bathing and eating the aquatic vegetation which is exposed when the river level is low. These Podostemaceous plants are firmly attached to rocks and other solid surfaces in seasonally strong river currents. In November 2011 I observed this species not far from the Cristalino Jungle Lodge. It was nearly noon when our guide, Jorge, spotted a flock very high up in a tree near the boat landing stage. To our eyes, they were visible only as tiny black dots. Almost immediately some of the flock departed. We walked along the river bank for closer views but the remaining dozen birds took off and flew across the river. Jorge got a boat out; we crossed the river and disembarked and he soon had his scope on them. They were perched very high above us but I was able to watch them for about 15 minutes as they preened and played (one hanging by one foot from the branch), and one pair mated. This was one of the high points of my stay in the bird-rich state of Mato Grosso.

Next day, as we retuned from several hours in the nearby forest, we encountered a group (perhaps the same one): about twenty birds high up in the canopy of a large tree. Six were sitting in a row, preening each other dry after a shower.

Status: IUCN Endangered since 2014 when it was recognised as a separate species by BirdLife International. It is common in riverine forests but it could lose large areas of habitat to deforestation.

Aviculture: Uncertain due to the difficulties of identification. In the early 1980s an aviculturist (a pilot) acquired some *Pyrrhuras* in the Rio Madeira area. They were obtained by Carlos Keller who thought they were *microtera* but when the Brazilian government imposed restrictions on maintaining all but the most common parrot species, he could no longer keep them. It seems that some birds kept in Brazil and identified as *amazonum* were in fact *snethlageae*.

P. snethlageae lucida

Origin of name: *lucida* = bright
New sub-species described (Arndt, 2008).

Description: Said to differ from *P. s. snethlageae* by the dark brown markings on the breast feathers being reduced to a narrow stripe, by its overall brighter coloration and more blackish crown. It is slightly smaller.

Range: Rio Cristalino area, Amazonas, Brazil.

SANTAREM CONURE (*Pyrrhura amazonum*)

Synonym: Hellmayr's Conure
Local name: *Tiriba-de-Hellmayr*
Description: differs from *picta* in **less extensive blue on forehead** (the blue area reaching only to anterior edge of eye), and in **green bend of wing.** The ear coverts are brownish-buff. It is described as having a darker reddish-brown face and less green at base of tail.
Length: 22cm. **Weight:** not recorded.
Range: northern Brazil in Pará, east of the Tapajos River and in Tocantins; limited by the western bank of the Araguaia and Tapajos Rivers (Silveira and Brettas, 2015). See map on page 124.
Habitat: Deciduous forests, especially less densely vegetated areas up to 600m.
Status: IUCN Endangered since 2014 when it was recognised as a separate species by BirdLife International. As with *snethlageae*, it is forecast to lose large areas of habitat to deforestation. Between 2009 and 2021 scientists produced an inventory of wildlife at Fazenda Fartura, on the borders of the states of Para (to the north), Mato Grosso to the south and Tocantins to the east. Prof. Luis Fabio Silveira, who led the research, reported in 2022 of *amazonum*: "Common, we found birds every day, and in groups which varied from 8-12 birds but sometimes, at the same fruit tree, up to 20 birds."
Aviculture: A Brazilian endemic species, this conure has seldom been in aviculture outside Brazil. In 1976 Mrs J. Spenkelink van Schaik of the Netherlands reared six from a pair described as *amazonum*, acquired from a Brazilian aviculturist. However, for a long time in Brazilian aviculture *snethlageae* (not then recognised as a sub-species) was wrongly identified as *amazonum* – so the sub-species is in doubt. It seems unlikely that this species exists in Europe at the time of writing. In Brazilian aviculture there were probably fewer than five pairs (pure-bred) in 2022, according to Prof. Luis Fabio Silveira of the Museum of Zoology of the University of São Paulo.
Birders: Carajás National Forest in Parauapebas, Pará.

P. amazonum microtera

According to Thomas Arndt, who has studied the *picta* complex since 1995, it differs from *amazonum* only in the smaller size.

(*Pyrrhura amazonum microtera*)
Photograph © Thomas Arndt

BLACK-TAILED CONURE (*Pyrrhura melanura*)

Synonym: Maroon-tailed Conure (could apply to many other members of the genus).

Origin of name: *melanura* = black-tailed. (Other members of the genus have the upper side of the tail green or maroon).

Local names: Brazil *Tiriba-fura-mata*; Venezuela *Perico Cola Negra*.

Taxonomy: Confusion exists over the three races, *melanura*, *souancei* and *berlepschi*. Attempting to differentiate has baffled some of the best ornithological minds. Those interested are referred to Ridgely and Robbins (1988). Not recognised as a species by BirdLife International until 2019.

Description: head green and brown/grey. Feathers of crown and nape: brown, edged with green. Cheeks and ear coverts: green with feathers of latter brownish-red (sometimes visible) at base. Feathers of throat, upper breast and sides of neck are green narrowly edged with buff-white and tipped with dusky brown to give typical scaled appearance. Underparts green, with **no red patch on abdomen.** Under wing coverts green; alula (small, stiffened wing feathers) green but one or more feathers might be red and margined on the inner web with orange-yellow. There are yellow edges to the **red primary coverts, this colour increasing on the inner coverts; carpal edge of wing also red.** Upper surface of tail is very dark maroon, almost black in some birds, except for the green base; underside also dark maroon. The **bill is light brownish-grey;** very prominent area of bare white skin surrounding the eye. Feet are dark grey.

In 1926 Chapman established that *souancei* **differs from *melanura* in its relatively wider pale breast scaling.** Ridgely and Robbins agreed, and pointed out that "gene flow apparently occurs between these two forms" and that "these broad-scaled birds also appear to exhibit geographic variation" and that several birds from south-eastern Colombia seemed virtually identical with the type of *souancei*.

The three museum specimens of the nominate race that I examined differed from *souancei* in having a less extensive area of red on the primary coverts, the red feathers having *almost hidden yellow tips, the hidden feathers being completely yellow.* This might be irrelevant. Aviculturists should note that it seemed impossible to differentiate exported birds without knowing their origin.

Head colour: Not all examples of *melanura* conform to written descriptions of the known forms. In 1998 I photographed a family on exhibit at Loro Parque, Tenerife, which puzzled me. However, throughout the large range, it is very likely that there is variation in head colour in different localities.

Hein van Grouw (Curator, Bird Group, of the Natural History Museum at Tring, UK) kindly checked the Ecuador specimens in the museum collection. He told

Black-tailed Conures, probably the nominate race. Photograph © Rosemary Low

me: "We have six specimens from Ecuador (all identified as sub-species *souancei*) from Guilea, Santiago Samora, eastern Ecuador (four specimens) and from Rio Napo, Ecuador (two specimens). I do not see any difference between them and the *souancei* specimens from Peru. However, we have one *souancei* with remarkable lighter coloured cheeks and ear coverts but this bird was in captivity so no locality is known. It died in June 1937 and belonged to H. Whitley[2]. Besides the pale olive colour on the head this bird also has hardly any blue in its primaries and the tail is completely green without any trace of reddish brown as in the other *melanura* specimens." The possibility cannot be ruled out that this bird was a hybrid.

Immature birds: margins of upper breast feathers are fainter, greyish-white, and less extensive. Mrs Spenkelink van Schaik noted that the young from four pairs had "hardly any or no red at all on the wing coverts." According to Rosemary Cooper, the wing coverts are red and green "intermixed in variable amounts" (in *berlepschi*) but one Souancé's Conure was green under one wing and had a large red patch under the other (Cooper, 1979). The beak is light grey in newly fledged young.

Photographs of Horst Mayer's *melanura* chicks, aged 33 to 37 days, showed the bright olive head coloration, compatible with Mrs Spenkelink's observations that some of the green feathers abrade to leave a darker colour.

---

2 Herbert Whitley was a well-known aviculturist with a large collection in Paignton, Devon, UK, the forerunner of Paignton Zoo.

Length: 26cm **Weight:** 70-75g. Weights of nine wild-caught birds 64g to 77g (average 73.3g) (Ridgely and Robbins, 1988).

Range: The nominate race has a wide distribution over the western side of northern South America in south-eastern Colombia (Vaupés, Guainía, Amazonas), southern Venezuela (Amazonas, Bolívar), north-western Brazil (Rio Negro and Rio Solimôes and their tributaries) and through eastern Ecuador (Rio Napo drainage). It also has one of the broadest altitudinal ranges, from sea level to 3,000m.

Status and threats: CITES Appendix II. Least Concern – because it has a large range and the population is believed stable. Common or locally very common, it still occurs in large flocks, especially in foothills of mountains of the departments of Caquetá and Putumayo. Deforestation seems to have favoured its expansion (Rodriguez-Mahecha and

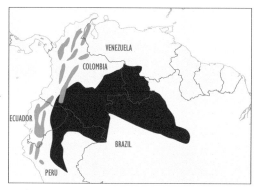

Red area: approximate range of *melanura*. It is mainly a lowland species and the blue areas indicate mountain ranges. See map on page 125 for range in Brazil.

Hernández-Camacho, 2002) but it is persecuted as a crop pest where it feeds on maize. It is not trapped for the pet trade.

Habitat: Lowland wet forest in premontane zones up to 500m, seasonally-flooded forest, borders and partially cleared areas. Also cloud forest; *P. m. soucancei* has been recorded up to 3200m and *P. m. berlepschi* up to 1500m.

Habits: My first sight of a *Pyrrhura* in the wild occurred in 1976 in this area, on Santa Sofia island, not far from Leticia (near where the first specimen of *melanura* was described by Spix in 1824.) It was the wet season so the only dry land was near the "lodge". The only sensible mode of transport was canoe. As we rounded a bend I saw a cluster of Black-tailed Conures in a smooth-trunked palm close to the water's edge. Our guide edged the canoe right under the *Euterpe* palm where the conures were engrossed in feeding on the fruits. There were about 35 in all, some clinging to the trunk of the palm where they had gnawed away two large areas of bark, too low down to be protected by the overhanging fronds. Others were sitting in small groups, mutual preening.

Aviculture: It was rarely seen until 1967 when some were imported into Europe. They did not achieve any popularity during the few years they were available. Rather few breeding successes occurred and probably included hybridisation of sub-species. It seems unlikely that breeders will ever again have the opportunity to ponder the identification problem.

The first breeder in the UK was Mrs B. Rhodes in Yorkshire who bred *souancei* in 1970 in an indoor cage 91cm long. Four eggs were laid at the beginning of February; two young were reared. The pair nested again in December of that year. Five eggs were laid and four young fledged. At the age of four weeks they were covered with

Black-tailed Conures, 26 to 30 days old.
Photograph © Horst Mayer

dark grey down with some quills just apparent. All the young birds were housed in a separate cage where they would "roll about and fight just like a bunch of puppies", she told me.

The most successful breeder was almost certainly Mrs Spenkelink van Schaik. Her observation was that "*melanura* thrives best in an open aviary. In closed aviaries breeding is slow to start or does not start" might explain why, in this age of cage-breeding, the Black-tailed Conure has almost been lost from aviculture – or perhaps its temperament does not appeal. I found it different from the more outgoing species.

However, there are always exceptions, as recorded by Rosemary J.Cooper. She acquired her birds in 1970 and believed they were *berlepschi*. Before their aviary was ready, she housed them in a secluded cage measuring 1.8m long by 38cm wide and 38cm high. After three months the female laid an egg on the floor so a nest-box was provided. Another five eggs were laid and three chicks hatched. One died after one month and the other two fledged at 54 days and were feeding themselves well three weeks later. A second clutch, of five eggs produced two more fledged young. They did not breed in 1972. In 1973, when they were housed in a 2.7m long outdoor aviary, the female again laid five eggs. Three young fledged, two at 54 days and the third at 58 days, and were left with their parents. Circumstances changed and the conures were looked after by other people (Cooper, 1979). In recent years this species has almost been lost from aviculture in Europe. It is questionable whether it will survive.

Birders: La Selva Jungle Lodge, Napo State, Ecuador.

SOUANCÉ'S CONURE and BERLEPSCH'S CONURE
(*Pyrrhura melanura souancei* and *P. m. berlepschi*)

Origin of names: named for Baron Charles de Souancé, French ornithologist who wrote *Iconographie des perroquets*, 1857. Named for Hans Karl Hermann Ludwig von Berlepsch (1850-1915), a German ornithologist who specialised in collecting neotropical birds.

Description: *souancei* – see pages 193 and 194.

Description of *berlepschi*: scalloped feathers of upper breast and sides of neck described as more conspicuous than those of nominate race, the feathers being broadly edged with buffish-white. Red on primary wing coverts is more extensive and the yellow lacking. The distinction between the two sub-species is not clear; they may prove to be synonymous. According to Count Salvadori (who described the type from Chyavetas, eastern Peru), *P. m. berlepschi* has light margins to the feathers of throat and breast much broader, approaching *rupicola* in this respect. However, there is apparently considerable variation so this distinction might not be significant. Chapman (*Bulletin of the American Museum of Natural History*, 1917) described specimens of *souancei* with wider margins than those of *berlepschi*.

Range: *souancei*: eastern base of Andes, southern Colombia in departments of Meta, Caquetá and Putumayo, probably also in extreme south of departments of Cauca and extreme south-east of Nariño (Rodríguez-Mahecha and Hernádez-Camacho, 2002), and probably also in adjacent north-eastern Ecuador. *P. m. berlepschi*: a small area on eastern slopes of Andes in north-eastern Peru and south-eastern Ecuador (Ridgely and Robbins, 1988).

Aviculture: due to its relatively small range, *berlepschi* is the least likely to have been exported. However, Mrs Spenkelink van Schaik carefully researched *melanura* and apparently kept all forms except *pacifica*. She described *berlepschi* as a rare bird that was found only in the ravine of the river Huallaga in south-east Peru, with "no grey but more brown head feathers. The green cheeks have an olive tinge. In direct sunshine this sub-species shows a bright 'golden' glow on the shoulder and back. From the young birds I bred there were some that had one or more totally red feathers in their wings or in their tails. The bill of the *berlepschi* is dark horn coloured. It is very curious that this is the only sub-species that has spotted legs."

Birders: Narupa Reserve (Fundación Jocotoco), Napo Province, northern Ecuador.

CHAPMAN'S CONURE (*Pyrrhura chapmani*)

Synonym: Upper Magdalena Parakeet

Origin of name: named for American ornithologist Frank Michler Chapman (1864-1945), author of major works on the distribution of birds in Colombia and Ecuador.

Taxonomy: formerly treated as a sub-species of *melanura*. Note these comments about the *melanura* complex: "... the correct placement of other subspecies, particularly *chapmani* ... [A] more detailed analysis including a consideration of voice, biometrics and molecular data of the whole group is needed to take this one forwards, in light of the lack of vocal differences and puzzling distributions. The proposal to split *pacifica* may well be correct as part of dealing with this group, but such a treatment may be an incomplete and overly simplified approach." (Donegan *et al*, 2016).

Description: The distinguishing features, compared with nominate *melanura*, are the whiter, more prominent and extensive white markings of the feathers of the upper breast extending to make a nuchal collar. There are varying descriptions in the literature and wrongly captioned photographs on the internet and elsewhere. I refer readers to Donegan *et al* (2016) for photographs of museum specimens compared with *pacifica* and nominate *melanura*. They state: "The Huila population, *chapmani*, emerges as an even stronger candidate for species rank from our review of specimens, based on plumage differences. It has the bluest primaries of all *melanura* group populations, a darker head than all the other populations, a more extensive buffy nuchal region and more extensive mottling on the breast." Note the horn-coloured bill, not black.

Species	Tail length (mm) average	No. of specimens	range
orcesi	98.2	11	90.0–103.1
pacifica	92.9	6	90.0–99.6
melanura	109.9	19	101.6–120.0
souancei	112.5	8	102.7–112.5
chapmani	125.2	13	118.1–132.6

Weight: not recorded.

Range and habitat: Colombia, in the Upper Magdalena Valley on the eastern slope of the Central Andes in the departments of Tolima and Huila. Known from a small number of localities including the La Riviera and Los Yalcones reserves, *chapmani* occupies different habitats to the other species in the *melanura* complex.

Left: Chapman's Conure in a small flock observed by Esteban Botero-Delgadillo. Below: Agnes Coenen's excellent photograph shows only slight variation of breast markings in individuals. It was taken in the Department of Huila, near Palestina, in a very small settlement called Jerico. The images reproduced here show larger and more intense white margins to the upper breast feathers than in the museum specimens.

Photographs © E.Botero-Delgadillo/ SELVA and Agnes Coenen

It occurs at high elevations in the less humid upper Magdalena valley, at 1600-2800m elevation (Rodriguez-Mahecha and Hernández-Camacho 2002), rather than at low elevations in humid forest and adjacent upslope regions. However, on March 4 2021 *chapmani* was found at the lowest level of the species (200m) so far. It was also an extension of the range in the east of Colombia.

Status and threats: IUCN Vulnerable (2019). The population is believed to be small and declining. Its strong dependence on cloud forest makes it vulnerable to deforestation which continues in its restricted range. In 2013 Robert Ridgely told me: "I have not seen this form since 1976, when I found it to be quite common at Finca Merenberg, Huila department. I hope it still is common, but there has been ongoing deforestation in that area, and for a long time the security situation was very bad indeed." There was little or no illegal trapping, probably due to the dangers of entering the area.

Conservation: As part of an educational project launched in 2005 by ProAves (supported by Loro Parque Fundacion), named Project *Pyrrhura*, ProAves members visited various communities, often remote ones. They used the specially fitted out LoroBus. By means of talks, workshops, games and videos in the interior, they motivated the communities to respect biodiversity and nature, especially birds. However, the most vital action for this species' survival is preventing further deforestation (Botero-Delgadillo and Paez, 2011b).

Breeding: A nest was found in a dead palm, whose trunk was armed with sharp thorns that probably deterred predators. The nest was at a height of 5.8m with a cavity 95cm deep from the entrance hole. Incubation commenced during the second week of July. It is believed that several females laid. Boxes have been erected.

Project: Local community visits by Loro Bus (an educational project launched in 2005) by ProAves.

Aviculture: Probably unknown but possibly kept in the Netherlands in the 1970s (Spenkelink van Schaik, 1980).

In 2005 ProAves launched the LoroBus to travel around the Andes, spreading conservation messages.

Photograph © ProAves/Paul Salaman

PACIFIC CONURE (*Pyrrhura pacifica*)

Synonyms: Magdalena Parakeet, Chocó Parakeet
Local name: *Periquito Coligranate del Pacífico*
Taxonomy: Following the recommendations of Ridgely & Greenfield (2001) and because of its geographical distribution, it is considered a full species. This treatment is also valuable from the conservation aspect.
Description: Features that distinguish it from *melanura* are **lack of prominent white area of bare skin surrounding eye** (this is grey and inconspicuous). There is a very narrow line of dark red feathers above the beak. Cheeks and ear coverts: dark green; crown: dark brown; scaled feathers of upper breast narrowly margined with brownish-white, and much less extensive and much reduced on nape. Underparts and wings are dark green; primary coverts red. The beak is grey.
Length: slightly smaller than *souancei*.
Immature birds: primary coverts are green and there is a red feather or two only at bend of wing. The scalloping on the breast feathers is much fainter.
Range: north-western Ecuador on Pacific slope of Andes in Pichincha; Colombia, only in department of Nariño in south-west; isolated from the range of *melanura* sub-species. It is geographically isolated from other species, separated by the Andes in one of its highest parts. It occurs only in south-western Colombia and is not found in the Cauca or Magdalena valleys. Most of the rest of the group occurs east of the Andes.
Status: IUCN Least Concern (2014).
Habitat: tropical and pre-montane rainforests between 650m and 1,700m. With a rainfall of 700mm per annum, this is an area where trees are covered in a profusion of epiphytes and mosses. It was relatively common in the Barbacoas area, Nariño, with flocks of from six to 22 birds, but the population there was estimated at no more than 140 individuals. Probably few populations exist and, overall, numbers could be decreasing (Botero-Delgadillo and Páez, 2011b).

Threats: Trapping for pets locally or for trade; habitat destruction as the result of illegal cultivation.

Aviculture: Rare – and possibly overlooked in the 1960s and early 1970s. (Colombia ceased to export parrots in 1973.) In November 1968 I bought three

Range of the Pacific Conure

birds that differed from the others in a consignment of Souancé's Conures. I did not discover their identity until several months later. They had a more nervous temperament than my other *Pyrrhuras* (*frontalis* and *coerulescens*).

One was in poor health; it was a cold time of year so I kept it indoors for a while and discovered that it loved Cheddar cheese! Later, it developed a great liking for lory nectar. On several occasions I counted it taking 60 or 70 sips without stopping. This suggests to me that it had something seriously wrong with it. Its breast plumage turned an unhealthy looking brown, perhaps indicative of a liver problem. However, six months later its health and plumage had recovered. It had another bout of ill health, again recovered but died suddenly in February 1970. It was kept in a small group of *Pyrrhuras* and had befriended a Pearly Conure. The other two nested at the end of October 1970. Two chicks hatched but died soon after (Low, 1972). Sadly the male died in the following February. I have always regretted failing to breed this bird at a time when it was otherwise unknown in aviculture.

Adult Pacific Conure in the Rio Silanche bird reserve about 130km (81 miles) west of Quito, Ecuador. It was one of a group feeding on the fruits of the African oil palm. A plantation was located next to the reserve.

Photograph © Steve Brookes
www.wildparrotsupclose.co.uk

There is very little in the avicultural literature about *pacifica*. It has been represented in the collection of Loro Parque, Tenerife since 1994. From that year until 2011, forty-seven chicks were ringed. Hopefully, those who acquire this species will realise that it is of conservation significance and under no circumstances hybridise with it.

In Switzerland Simon Boner acquired one pair in 2006 and placed them in an aviary with a 2m x 1m outside flight and an inside flight where the nest-box

Pacific Conures with one youngster bred by Simon Boner in Switzerland.
Photograph © Simon Boner

(60cm high and 16cm square) was situated. The female laid for the first time in 2009. When the two chicks were three and five days old the female parent was found on the floor with an injured foot. The chicks were moved to a brooder and hand-reared. In 2010 Simon Boner acquired a 2009-hatched male from Germany and made up a pair, with his young female. The following year they were moved to a new aviary with an outside flight 3m long, 80cm wide and 2m high. In 2011 the female laid three eggs. For two weeks after the chicks hatched it was not possible to inspect the nest because the female would not leave. Then he saw two chicks and ringed them with 5.5 rings. One chick died at four weeks and the other left the nest at about 50 days (Boner, 2012).The diet consisted of 70% fresh fruit, vegetables and berries (also defrosted berries), a seed mixture without sunflower and Orlux eggfood.

Birders: Colombia: Nariño and Rio Nambi reserve; Ecuador (north-west): Rio Canande Reserve (Jocotoco), Esmeraldas.

BLACK-CAPPED CONURE (*Pyrrhura rupicola*)

Synonym: Rock Conure
Origin of name: *rupes* = rock; *cola* = dweller.
Local name: Brazil *Tiriba-rupestre*
Description: Mainly green with scaled markings of throat and upper breast brown, each feather with grey-brown pointed area boldly margined with white. Crown is very dark brownish-black; hind-neck: feathers brown edged with green. Abdomen: only a hint of maroon. Flight feathers: black; bend of wing green; carpal edge and primary coverts red: under wing coverts green. Tail is green above, blackish-brown below.

In the literature only subtle plumage variations are suggested. Forshaw (1989 and 2006) states that *sandiae* is distinguished by narrower buff-white edges to feathers of neck and breast, particularly on hind neck where almost absent. However, there is much greater variation in the plumage and, considering wide range of species, there might be a cline, or subtle intergrade, from north to south or altitudinal differences. Some birds have green cheeks with little contrast with the ear coverts, whereas in others, more commonly seen in captivity and described as *sandiae*, ear coverts are lighter green. Some birds have feathers of lower part of upper breast strongly marked with pale yellow; in others, only a tinge of yellow.

It is not unusual for adult and immature birds to have some toes partly unpigmented (white) or even a white toenail.
Length: 25cm (10in) **Weight:** 70-75g.
Immature birds: Breast markings are less well defined, with narrower whitish margins or with brown centre of feather lighter in colour. There are fewer red feathers on carpal edge of wing and on primary coverts. Feet: darker grey; upper mandible dark ivory-coloured and lower mandible ivory-coloured.

Sub-species: *P. r. sandiae*

P. sandiae is described as having ear coverts and area above hind part of eye yellowish-green. The white margins to the breast feathers are *said to be* narrower but, as mentioned above, knowledge is incomplete.

Black-capped Conures.
Photograph © Karl Heinz Lambert

Range: nominate race from central-eastern Peru – range imprecisely known. Those from south-eastern Peru to westernmost Brazil and northern Bolivia are usually assigned to sub-species *sandiae*. In Brazil it occurs in extreme south-west Amazonia, especially around Plácido de Castro in Acre. Its large range covers approximately 546,000km^2.

Status: IUCN Least Concern; downlisted from Near Threatened in 2020 due to less habitat loss than predicted.

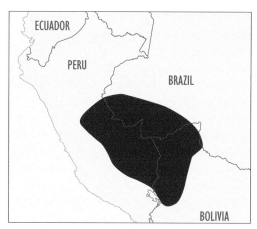

Approximate range of the Black-capped Conure. For range in Brazil see map on page 124.

Much pristine habitat apparently persists within the range. CITES Appendix II.

Habitat: Mainly humid lowland forests; along eastern base of Andes, also in foothills. In south-eastern Peru and Brazil it occurs in forests that never flood and in seasonally flooded forests *(varzea)*.

Habits: Donald Brightsmith spent many hours censusing parrots in Manu National Park, Peru. Black-capped Conures visited a small section of a clay bank. "They usually arrived in small flocks of 10 or less and landed in the canopies of the trees behind the bank. These small groups would fly quietly to the wall of vines above the bank and descend through the inside of the tangle to the clay." The section was roofed and partly covered with dense vines. The conures' behaviour was different to that of the other parrot species that waited until large groups of birds had gathered in the area and then descended as a group to take clay from wide open sections of the bank" (Brightsmith, 1999).

Aviculture: Unknown until US importer Don Wells brought in a few *sandiae* that were trapped in the state of Beni, in north-western Bolivia, in 1979. They were sold to Tom McCoy in California who gained the American Federation of Aviculture's first breeding award for this conure in 1981. In the following year Tom Ireland in Florida bred from birds which were probably from the same consignment. There were then several more importations into the US and into Europe, where the first recorded breeding occurred in Switzerland by a Mr Leumann. He had acquired five in 1980 and reared young in 1982.

In Germany Horst Mayer bred *sandiae* after unknowingly keeping two females together. In 1998 and 1999 infertile eggs were laid. When he acquired two males, chicks were hatched in 2000. They were ringed with 5.5mm rings at 14 or 15 days.

After 49 and 50 days the three young left the nest. The breast markings were less well defined than in the adults and the crown feathers were lighter brown (Mayer, 2001).

Most birds known to aviculturists are said to be *sandiae*. In 1988 a pair, sub-species not identified, was in my care at Loro Parque, Tenerife. The female had produced four eggs by January 22. They measured approximately 27mm x 20mm. By February 2 eight eggs had been laid and six days later there were ten eggs, three of which were placed in an incubator. One chick hatched on February 10 and another on February 17. On March 25 the male was seen trying to pull one out of the nest by its tail so both chicks were removed to hand-rear. A chick that had been fostered as an egg to Souance's Conures was eventually removed for hand-rearing. The three young were placed on exhibit on April 29 where they entertained the public with their playful behaviour.

Birders: Manú Biosphere Reserve and Tambopata National Park, Madre de Dios, south-eastern Peru *(sandiae)*.

Black-capped Conures *(Pyrrhura rupicola)* in the breeding centre of Loro Parque Fundacion, Tenerife in 2018. The bird on the right is probably typical of what is called *sandiae,* whereas the one on the left has yellow markings on the upper breast. If this is due to natural variation in the species is unknown.

Photograph © Rosemary Low

WHITE-NECKED CONURE (*Pyrrhura albipectus*)

Origin of name: *albipectus* = white-breasted
Synonym: White-breasted Conure
Description: This extremely handsome bird has the **ear coverts orange (exceptionally, orange-red). A broad whitish collar on hind neck joins up with feathers of throat and upper breast which are white without scalloping, or white tinged yellow, shading to yellow.** Crown feathers are brown, streaked green, with paler edges; cheeks are green, some feathers tipped white. Carpal edge of wing and primary coverts are scarlet. Tail is green, maroon towards tip. The rest of the plumage is dark green. The bill is grey and the feet are dark grey.
Length: 24cm. **Weight:** 83g.
Immature plumage: Duller than adults, especially on ear coverts, with carpal edge of wing and primary coverts green. Upper breast is white with upper part of abdomen cream and rest of abdomen and flanks lime green (adults have abdomen tinged with reddish-brown and duller green flanks). The bill is white, becoming grey at base (Toyne *et al*, 1992).
Range: South-eastern Ecuador and adjacent area of northern-most Peru: on eastern slope of Andes: Podocarpus National Park (PNP), Cordillera de Cutucú in Morona Santiago province north of PNP, Cordillera del Condor in Zamora-Chinchipe province east of PNP (Toyne, 1994). The usual altitudinal range is between 900m and 1,700m. The area of distribution is small.

The White-necked Parakeet occurs in Ecuador, just reaching into northern Peru.

The White-necked Conure occurs in the area of Morona Santiago and Zamora-Chinchipe. In 2006 the White-necked Conure was reported from the Peruvian border in the Cordillera del Cóndor. Ornithologist and artist John O'Neill informed me in January 2007: "The parakeet was fairly common in small groups of four to eight birds flying erratically just below the canopy as most *Pyrrhuras* do. It was especially exciting for me because for most of my life I had looked at the painting by Fuertes in the Chapman Ecuador book and always hoped I would find the bird. The area was the wettest and coldest in all my time in Peru – about six to eight days with some sun in two months and heavy rains for ten to fifteen hours at a time on some days, gentler rain on others."

In October 2011 Robert Ridgely informed me: "There are local populations all along the base of the Cordillera del Cóndor, mainly on the Ecuadorian (western) side, but it's curiously local; for instance it appears to be absent from the upper Río Nangaritza valley, this despite much field work there (no *Pyrrhura* is present). That the populations are separated appears likely, but it's hard to be sure. The population in the extreme upper Río Chinchipe valley is surely separate; that's where Tapichalaca is located, and it occurs there at elevations up to 2,200m, very high for the species. It continues to increase at our Tapichalaca Reserve in the southeast, but it's still scarce, most of that reserve being at too high an elevation. We just found a lot of them at Fruta del Norte in the northern Cordillera del Condor. "

Status: Vulnerable (upgraded from Near-threatened in 1994). CITES Appendix II.

Threats: loss of habitat by illegal colonists who clear the forest for cattle ranching or agriculture. Gold mining poses a serious threat as some concessions cover up to 11% of the Podocarpus National Park. After the discovery of gold, including within the conure's habitat, up to 1,000 illegal prospectors were operating at San Luis. They killed animals, including parrots, to supplement their diet and polluted the rivers with the liquid mercury used to recover the gold (Toyne, 1994). Illegal trapping has occurred and could pose a threat.

The distinctive White-necked Conure. Photograph © Nick Athanus

According to BirdLife International's Species Factsheet, there is little or no threat of deforestation in the Peruvian part of the range but there is a mining concession in the area.

Habitat: upper tropical and subtropical forest, usually between 1,000m and 2,000m. Apparently fairly adaptable regarding habitat use: found in partially degraded forest as well as pristine forest.

Habits: Flocks of up to nineteen birds, including young, were observed in PNP in early September, flying fast and just above the canopy, calling. While foraging they emitted repetitive one-note calls. Prior to leaving the feeding tree, one individual would start calling and the rest would join in: "…a clamour of accelerating foraging calls was heard and then they would suddenly fly off" (Toyne, 1994). Their food items included seeds in the pods of *Mollia gracilis*, fleshy fruits of figs, and of *Miconia punctata*, small flowers of the liana *Mikania leiostachya*, small green fruits of *Alchornea glandulosa* and the small red berries of *Tetrorchidium macrophyllum* (Toyne *et al* 1992).

Conservation: In the early 1990s the environmental group Arcoiris led an environmental awareness campaign, monitoring mining developments and other threats. The Ecuadorian NGO, Jocotoco, in collaboration with Loro Parque Fundación, erected ten nest-boxes for the parakeets in 2008. Groups numbering four to seven roosted inside. However, disadvantages are probability of theft of chicks and occupation by bees. In 2009 Mery Juiña studied breeding behaviour in the Tapichalaca Reserve (3,500 ha). Nest-boxes were erected and two were used. In one nest thirteen eggs were laid (perhaps by two or three females) by a group of six birds; eight hatched and all the young fledged.

Aviculture: Considered to be unknown in captivity except for the occasional bird reported in a village bordering Podocarpus National Park. Nothing has been published in the avicultural literature except the belief that five males were imported into Switzerland (Dupas and Garnier, 2015).

Birders: Present all year at Rio Bombuscara valley, Podocarpus National Park, south-eastern Ecuador.

Chicks in the Tapichalaca Reserve, photographed by Mery Juiña.

FLAME-WINGED CONURE (*Pyrrhura calliptera*)

Synonym: Brown-breasted Conure
Origin of name: from the Greek *kallós* = beautiful and *pteron* referring to the colourful wing feathers.
Local names: *Cotorrita pechiparda, Perico de páramo, Periquito aliamarillo.* **Description:** Forehead and crown are ashy-brown, ear-coverts dull red and cheeks and area above eye green. Feathers of nape and upper breast are margined broadly with white and faintly with ashy-brown. **Feathers of lower part of upper breast are mainly pale brown. Primary coverts and feathers at edge of wing are yellow,** spotted with orange in some birds (and, in one skin I examined, partly red). Scalloped feathers of nape are more prominent (widely margined with white) than in the few artists' illustrations; some bear little resemblance to the living bird. The beak is whitish and the feet are grey.
Length: 24cm (10in). **Weight:** 75-85g.
Immature birds: Differ from adults in green primary coverts and carpal edge of wing (Forshaw, 2006). However, a photo taken in the wild (ProAves) shows a very young bird with yellow feathers at edge of wing. Its plumage is duller throughout; ear coverts are greenish tinged red and breast markings less well defined and less extensive.
Range: Colombia in a few fragmented populations in the Eastern Andes between 1,700m and 3,400m, in the departments of Boyacá, Meta and Cundinamarca. Formerly present on both slopes, it has been recorded at only one location on the western slope (in Santander) until the 1980s. On the eastern slope it is currently known from Norte de Santander, Ferallon de Medina (Cundinamarca) and Ramiriquy and Soata (Boyacá). In 2000 it was known from fewer than ten populations. It is common in Chingaza National Park and adjacent Rio Blanco-Olivares Forest Reserve and Carpanta Biological Reserve.

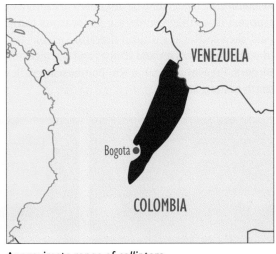

Approximate range of *calliptera*.

The Flame-winged or Brown-breasted Conure.
Photograph © ProAves/Loro Parque Fundación

Status: CITES Appendix II. Vulnerable (IUCN 2008) due to its very small range and fragmented and rapidly declining populations.

Threats: There has been severe deforestation due to logging, cattle grazing, agriculture, road building and human settlement, throughout much of its range. The area most affected is that below 2,500m on the western Andean slope. On the eastern slope some large areas of intact forest have survived, despite logging. It is persecuted by farmers when it raids their crops. Nest site availability is considered to be the factor most limiting population growth.

Population estimate: Estimated at 5,000 to 10,000 by Paul Salaman for the Parrot Action Plan (2000) but population decline continues.

Habitat: Upper subtropical and temperate forest between 1,850m and 3,000m, elfin woodland and second growth (3,000m to 3,400m) and adjacent areas of páramo and agricultural land. It is said to be known from only ten localities.

Habits: It feeds on fruits, seeds and cultivated maize, also on grass seeds and leaves in open areas where the largest flocks have been observed. Breeding occurs between September and February.

Perhaps this conure had not been photographed until ProAves Colombia field workers (funded by Loro Parque Fundación) started to study it in 2004. These included Ana Maria Gonzales, working for her PhD thesis. In January 2005 she was my guide when we drove 70km north of Bogotá into the department of Cundinamarca. At 2,400m we left the car and climbed a hillside covered in sphagnum moss and familiar-looking wild plants such as the yellow-flowering hawkweed *(Hieracium)*, until we came to a small forest patch.

Without local knowledge, one could search for months with little hope of finding this conure but we had only to wait a few minutes to hear its calls. Several Flame-winged Conures flew towards us and landed in a tree about 18m away. Gradually, we crept nearer. Four-on-a-branch, they sat together preening in the sun, the yellow patches in their wings shining like little beacons when they stretched. At last we moved too close and they took off. Then I discovered, to my surprise, that there were ten! We waited on a rock and they briefly re-appeared in the distance – but the show was over.

Ana Maria Gonzales studied the feeding and nesting habits of the Flame-winged Conure. Mating was observed most often between August and October. Observations were also made at roosting sites, often woodpecker holes in trees, with a maximum depth of 1.7m, the entrances well disguised by bromeliads. The conures leave their roosts between 5.25am and 5.50am, as soon as the first light enters the hole.

Ana Maria showed me a tree on which they feed, covered in small reddish fruits. I noticed flowering clover and asked her if they ever fed on the ground. Sometimes they did feed on the clover but they always posted a sentinel to sound the alarm. Their diet includes the pulp of ripe fruits, the seeds of green fruits (such as *Drimys granadensis*) and the seeds of opened fruits such as *Clusia multiflora*. The trees at this altitude are lavishly bedecked with bromeliads – and it is from these that they drink. Even in the dry season the early morning mist brings enough moisture to secure their drinking supply.

This conure was being studied at three sites; at two in the Chingaza National Park *(páramo)* there were flocks of thirty-eight and thirty-three. It was common in Chingaza and in the region of Guavio. At the site I visited the maximum number of individuals seen was fifty.

In 2007 David Arena-Mosquera of ProAves studied the breeding biology in Chingaza National Park. Six individuals attended one nest between November 6 and January 8, there were seven birds at a nest between September 27 and January

Female with chicks in a nest-box in Chingaza Natural National Park.
Photograph © ProAves/Loro Parque Fundación

3, nine birds at another nest from September 22 until November 7 and nine birds at the fourth nest between September 24 and January 13.

Conservation: In addition to ProAves personnel studying their biology, an education programme was carried out, in the field and at a local college, to teach people about the threats facing this endemic parakeet. Searches for it will be made in other areas. The erection of nest-boxes proved extremely successful (See Chapter 15, *Conservation and the Future*).

Aviculture: Unknown outside Colombia. In 2015, two Flame-winged Conures were confiscated and sent to the Fundación Bioparque La Reserva, close to Bogotá. The German organisations ZGAP and Strunden-Papageien-Stiftung (SPS) funded the building of an aviary and provided husbandry guidelines for this *ex situ* conservation strategy. These are the only legally owned *calliptera* in existence. Unfortunately the two birds were of the same sex. In April 2022 they were joined by four more confiscated birds. Hopefully breeding success will follow.

Birders: Chingaza Natural National Park, north-east of Bogota, Colombia.

FIERY-SHOULDERED CONURE *(Pyrrhura egregia)*

Synonym: Demerara Conure
Origin of name: from the Latin *egregious* = illustrious.
Local names: Venezuela *Perico de Pantepui*; Brazil *tiriba-de-cauda-roxa*.
Description: Forehead to nape: feathers brown, tipped with green, with flecks of red on lighter brown ear coverts. Lower neck and upper breast: feathers scalloped with grey and white; lower breast feathers grey, faintly margined with yellowish-white. Abdomen: green, faintly marked with maroon; tinge of maroon around vent. Bend of wing: fiery orange; carpal edge: yellow-orange. Its real beauty is appreciated when the wings are open: greater under wing coverts are yellow and lesser under wing coverts orange. Tail: dark reddish-brown above and blackish, tinged with red-brown, below. The beak is ivory coloured, the cere whitish and the feet grey.

In illustrations in some field guides (e.g., Helm *Parrots of the World*, 2010) the adult and juvenile illustrated are hardly recognisable: plumage is too light green, ear coverts are brown (they are partly green and partly reddish or orange-brown in adults and light green in juveniles); scalloped markings of breast feathers bear no resemblance to reality.

Length: 25cm. **Weight:** 70g to 75g. Two captive adult pairs were weighed: both males 73g, females 69g and 75g.

Approximate range of *egregia* in eastern Venezuela, western Guyana and northern Brazil. See page 125 for range in Brazil.

Breeding pair of Fiery-shouldered Conures, female on the left.
Photograph © Rosemary Low

Immature plumage: very narrow frontal band brown or reddish-brown. Breast markings indistinct, the green feathers margined with light and/or dark grey. Abdomen: only a hint of dull maroon; bend of wing and under wing coverts pale orange.

Sub-species: *P. e. obscura* is reputedly darker green above and slightly darker green below.

Range: Limited to Pantepui region of borders of south-eastern Venezuela, western Guyana and north-eastern Roraima, Brazil. In Venezuela the nominate race occurs in the *tepuis* (isolated, flat-topped mountains, called *mesas* in the USA) of south-eastern Bolívar from upper Rio Caroni east to forests on Gran Sabana (*obscura*) and on slopes of Cerro Roraima (nominate race).

Status and threats: CITES Appendix II. Least Concern. According to BirdLife International, although the population appears to be decreasing, and the range is small, the decline is not believed to be sufficiently rapid to approach the thresholds for Vulnerable. It is probably quite common in its restricted range but there is no information on population size.

Threats: It is projected to lose 3.3-10.5% of suitable habitat over three generations (given as 18 years) based on a model of Amazonian deforestation published in 2011. Its decline is projected at about 25% over three generations – surely a serious population loss, considering the short generation time which, in fact, is probably about three years. Possibly some trapping occurs.

Habitat: *Tepuis* in forested areas in the tropical and sub-tropical zone, between 700m and 1,800m. It is common above 1,000m on Sierra de Lema.

Protection: the natural landscape. It remained unknown in aviculture for such a long time because the area is difficult to invade, with its steep-sided flat-topped mountains covered in forest and ravines.

Habits: It has been observed feeding on *Cecropia catkins*.

Aviculture: virtually unknown until 1988 when a few pairs were imported into Europe – perhaps originally into Switzerland. The first time it was imported into the UK was probably in 1992. Thirteen wild-caught birds were acquired by Jeff Hornsby who sexed them by behaviour. As luck would have it, there were six males and seven females. Three of the birds were a different shade of green and had, according to him, red on the rump (possibly *obscura*). They were very prolific. One female reared 43 young – and most were females! Despite its delightful temperament, which means that it makes a wonderful pet, the Fiery-shouldered is not one of the most popular species. This is regrettable: it deserves more attention.

In 1993 I looked after two surgically sexed pairs, which had been hatched in the previous year. They were still in quarantine when the first egg was laid! On arrival, on April 1, each pair was housed in a quarantine cage measuring 102cm long, 51cm wide and 77cm high. One female laid her first egg on April 28; there were two eggs by May 1, three by May 4, four by May 6. The fifth was laid before May 10. The date of the sixth egg was unknown because the female was incubating so tightly.

A chick hatched on June 1 and the second on June 2. The third egg was opened by the parents and contained a chick which was full-term dead-in-shell.

The female was extremely protective of the small chicks. When the eldest was 16 days and had to be ringed (5.5mm) the chicks were removed and photographed. The second down was starting to erupt in little white blobs on body and wings. The upper mandible and feet were pink. Three days later the orange feathers at the bend of the wing and two or three of the orange wing coverts were starting to erupt. The development of the youngest chick was several days behind its sibling. When the eldest was 22 days its flight and tail feathers were just breaking through their sheaths.

At 28 days the crown was dull green, the cheeks brighter green and the bend of the wing quite brilliant orange. Scapulars and secondary coverts were bright green. The tail of the eldest was about one third the full length, the dark brown feathers being tipped blackish. Much dense whitish-grey down was apparent, as would be appropriate for a mountain species (denser than in lowland species). The beak was still pinkish with brown at the base of the upper mandible. The beak pads were white.

The young were fully feathered one week later, both with an extensive area of yellow and orange at the bend of the wing. In *Parrots of the World* Forshaw states that in immature birds the colour in this area is "much reduced" – but this did not apply to these birds. At 54 days the eldest differed from the parents only in the dark base of the upper mandible and in duller breast feathers lacking white margins. The eldest youngster left the nest during the last week in July. When the youngest was 57 days old it was still in the nest – but weak. It was removed for hand-feeding but sadly died the next day. The cause of its death could not be established (Low,1994). In Germany Sigrid and Gerhardt Schmidt have kept *Pyrrhura* parakeets since 1967. Initially captivated by the Maroon-bellied Conure (just as I was in the same era), they are still breeding them and now keep ten species. "… we leave the independent young ones with their parents for a year or two, in short, until they reach sexual maturity. This is how we breed, for example, Fiery-shouldered Parakeets. One year the parrots reared five chicks that we left with their parents. The following year, the adult pair nested again, and reared four young ones. Interestingly, all seven parrots spend the night in the nest-box together, even during the breeding season. We even observed that the young birds participated in rearing the new chicks." When the young ones fledged, all 11 roosted in the box together (Schmidt, 2022).

Birders: Canaima National Park (La Escalera area), Bolívar, Venezuela.

Fiery-shouldered Conures and chicks in Australia bred by Jason Wright.

Photographs © Jason Wright

BLOOD-EARED CONURE (*Pyrrhura hoematotis*)

Synonym: Red-eared Conure
Origin of name: *hoema* = blood, *otis* = ear
Local names: *Perico cola roja, Perico de cuello rojo*
Description: Feathers of forehead and front half of crown are brown, with bluish margins; back of head olive green, cheeks green and ear coverts brown-red. Feathers of sides of neck are edged with brown-grey and throat and upper breast are green with a slight olive tinge. Feathers of centre of abdomen, maroon, nearly hidden by the green edges. Carpal edge of wing bluish, primary coverts and primaries are blue and under wing coverts green and blackish. Tail is maroon, tipped with olive-green, underside coppery-red. Bare skin surrounding eyes is inconspicuous and dull grey; iris brown and beak pearly grey.
Length: 24cm. **Weight:** 70g.
Immature plumage: duller throughout. The beak is dull grey – slightly darker than adults'.
Sub-species: *P. h. immarginata*
Said to differ from the nominate race in lacking the brownish-grey margins to feathers of sides of neck, and breast feathers in lacking the dusky grey barring. Hilty (2003) states: "greener below". Ridgely (in Pasquier, 1980) noted that the Lara population, described as a separate sub-species, was described only from skins.
Range: Venezuela, the coastal range of the north-central area, from Aragua eastwards to Miranda (nominate) and south-eastern Lara *(immarginata)*. It reaches its northern-most limit in the mountain ranges of Lara and Yaracuy, which reach 2,000m (Boesman, 1998). In Lara State it is found only in a very limited area of Cubiro. The total range of the Blood-eared Parakeet is very small, believed to cover only 2,712km^2 – greatly reduced from its original range.

Habitat: Forests from 600m to 2,400m, also forest edges and adjacent clearings and second-growth woodland; occasionally in higher cloud forest.

Habits: Mainly occurs in the lower subtropical zone but seasonal movements (local and elevational) occur. It travels in tight, fast-flying flocks of about six to twenty-five birds, or

Left area indicates approximate range of *immarginata*, right area nominate race.

more, "that swoop through forest canopy then alight suddenly and disappear. Just as abruptly may burst into flight with a volley of screeching and fly off swerving through canopy." Its flight call is "a grating squeal, lacking harshness of some in genus" (Hilty, 2003).

Doug Kelson encountered *immarginata* several times over a couple of days while on a birding trip in the Yacumbú National Park in Lara State in the vicinity of El Blanquito lagoon. It was usually fairly high in the canopy of mountain forests so steep that on occasion he was able to look horizontally from track or road and see these conures in the tree tops. The leaf-veining and berries of the tree in which they were feeding suggested a kind of dogwood *(Cornus)*. He wrote: "The Blood-eareds had been (seemingly) investigating a hole in a

Immature Blood-eared Conures with a private breeder.

horizontal bough of the flowering tree about 25-30 metres from the ground. A pair of Red-billed Parrots [*Pionus sordidus*] arrived and threatened the parakeets with gape-billed displays of aggression. The Blood-eared Parakeets left and perched in the far fringes of the tree while the Red-billed Parrots stayed at the hole. One of them entered then emerged after about 30 seconds. My notes record that a 'noisy family party' of Blood-eared Parakeets arrived to feed on berries, close to this spot."

Cecilia Herrera told me: "I have seen them feeding on the seeds of a *Heliocarpus* species (could be *Heliocarpus americanus* from the Tiliaceae family) in February and March in Henri Pittier National Park located in the Cordillera de La Costa. I also have seen them feeding on guava fruits, and on some type of Lauraceae trees (wild avocados) in the same national park."

Hilty (2003) recorded that they breed in August and that: "When foraging climb about quietly and slyly among branches and foliage; eat a variety of fruit and seeds, especially *Heliocarpus* seeds".

Status: IUCN Least Concern. Little information is available but a decline is suspected due to deforestation. CITES Appendix II.

Blood-eared Conures bred at Loro Parque, Tenerife, in 2020 and 2021.

Photographs © Loro Parque Fundacion/Rafael Zamora and Marcia Weinzettl

Aviculture: Probably unknown to aviculture outside Venezuela until the early 1990s and still very rare. The first time I saw it was in a private collection in the Canary Islands in 1995. The last member of the genus to be added to the collection at Loro Parque, Tenerife, it was reared for the first time in 2020 after some birds were acquired in 2019. One female laid six eggs and produced five young. By 2022, 15 chicks had been hatched.

Birders: Rancho Grande Biological Station, Henri Pittier National Park, Aragua; Avila National Park and El Blanquito, Yacambú National Park. Ridgely noted that in 1980 it was "particularly numerous within the large and well protected Henri Pittier National Park."

HOFFMANN'S CONURE (*Pyrrhura hoffmanni*)

Synonym: Sulphur-winged Conure
Origin of name: In memory of Carl Hoffmann (1823-1859), German explorer and naturalist, who discovered this conure in Costa Rica.
Local name: *Perico Aliazufrado.*
Description: The only *Pyrrhura* with conspicuous yellow in wings and a strange mottled appearance; some green feathers of head and throat are margined with yellow. Ear coverts red, chin pink. Primary coverts, upper side of inner primary feathers and outer secondaries are bright sulphur-yellow and green towards the tips. The tail is olive-green above and dull red below. The beak is whitish.
George Smith described Hoffmann's Conure as "like a lysine-deficient Red-eared *[hoematotis]*. Some inherent 'metabolic disorder' causes the yellow streaks in the feathers" (Smith, 1982) – an interesting description.
Length: 24cm. **Weight:** 75g wild; six *gaudens* weighed at Loro Parque: 79g and 91g.
Immature birds: plumage duller; area of red on ear coverts and yellow in wing less extensive.
Sub-species: *P. h. gaudens* (Chiriquí Conure)
Said to differ in having feathers of crown and back of head shaft-streaked with greenish-yellow and orange-red, and faintly tipped with dull red. Underparts are said to be slightly darker green.
Range: southern Costa Rica (nominate race); western Panama, mainly in western Chiriquí and on Caribbean slope in Bocas del Toro *(gaudens)*.

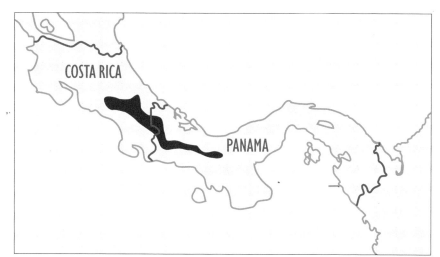

Approximate range of *hoffmanni*.

Status: Least Concern. CITES Appendix II. Generally common.

Habitat: woodlands (including logged forest) and pasture. This is a montane species although in Costa Rica it occurs at altitudes as low as 700m, but as high as 3,000m in the dry season. Seasonal altitudinal movements occur. According to Wolf (1976) these conures were seen almost daily in the Cerro de la Muerte region of the Cordillera de Talamanca between February and early July and occasionally in December and January. They frequented closed forest and secondary growth, also primary and disturbed *Quercus* forest.

In Panama it was common (according to Robert Ridgely, *Birds of Panama*, 1976) although somewhat erratic in its distribution in the highlands of western Chiriquí. It also occurs in the highlands of Bocas del Toro, occasionally being found in the lowlands, also in Veraguas.

Habits: In Panama these conures have been observed feeding on the fruits of the shrub *Leandra subseriata*. In *A Guide to the Birds of Costa Rica*, F. Gary Stiles and Alexander Skutch noted that they foraged in the canopy or in smaller trees, in shrubs along forest edges, or in second growth, feeding on seeds, fruits of *Ficus*, *Croton*, *Myrtis* and *Miconia*. The authors commented that mutual preening took place among groups, not just among pairs. Nests were found in old woodpecker holes, in hollow broken stubs and other tree cavities at from 8m to 20m.

In Costa Rica it is found in small flocks which were described as hard to locate. "The birds chatter without screeching and the unparrot-like cries of a flock can sound like a weak whirring or bring to mind a noisy group of songbirds" (Slud, 1964).

Beth Kinsey observed and photographed Hoffmann's Conures in the Cordillera de Talamanca in Costa Rica. She told me that they were feeding on ripe apples in an orchard in San Gerardo de Dota at about 2,100m. Apples grow well in the cloud forest climate. The conures would bite a piece out of the apple, nibble at the sweet flesh and then discard the skin. Tanagers then moved in to eat the exposed flesh of the apples. They were common there and usually seen flying overhead or perched in the tops of towering trees at the edge of the cloud forest.

I was supremely optimistic when I included Santa Fé on my itinerary during a short stay in Panama in June 2012. This small town is in the central northern region, province of Veraguas. The Santa Fé National Park is one of the few locations in Panama where one might expect to see the conure. The park exists on paper only; boundaries should extend down to 400m on the Pacific slope near Santa Fé and to 80m on the Caribbean slope.

At frequent intervals on a drive through the mountains we met huge items of road-building gear. The trees had been torn down to put in roads and bridges. Most were not yet passable so we had a bumpy ride in a seriously over-heating car. At Alto de Piedra there was a national parks office where we enquired about the conure with the park officials. Fortunately, *Aves de Panama* was on their table so it was certain that we were talking about the same species. "They are common!" we were told.

We were close to the break in the Tabasará cordillera within the park, west of Santa Fé, where the continental divide drops to 800m. We stopped to chat to a local man and to ask about the conure. "They are no good! I caught one but it was too noisy. I had to let it go." He thought we wanted to catch them. We saw

Hoffmann's Conures in Costa Rica. Note slight variation in the plumage of individuals.
Photograph © Steve Brookes www.wildparrotsupclose.com

several Amazons, also a group of seven Blue-headed Pionus *(Pionus menstruus)* feeding in a tree. Finally, a flock of Hoffmann's Conures flew over, about a dozen birds, giving us just a fleeting glimpse.

Deforestation is perhaps potentially a threat as serious to Hoffmann's Conure as it is currently to the *Pyrrhuras* of the Andes. The topography of the area beyond the divide is rugged, and access is difficult. The birdlife there has hardly been studied. Apparently the only information on the avifauna of the higher peaks to the east are collections made in the 1860s by Osbert Salvin, an English ornithologist, and other collections made in 1925-26.

Aviculture: uncommon. The first recorded breeding occurred in 1982 by Chris Rowley in Texas. His birds were imported into the US by veterinarian Nathan Gale who was living in Panama (see Ch. 14. *Aviculture and Conservation Potential*). According to Susie Christian and Dale Thompson, who established this species in aviculture, in the fifth year of breeding a few young birds showed intense colour – "not only just in the red but the dramatic intensity of having full yellow wings... the sub-species was showing up. After about the sixth year we felt we had enough genetic diversity in our group that we could isolate and reproduce the *gaudens* subspecies by themselves. It was a very nice bird with good intensity of both reds and yellows and even some of the greenish-yellow on the wings. On some there was a full yellow slash..." (The Hoffmann's Conure, Christian and Thompson, *Pyrrhura* Breeders Association website https://www.birdcompanions.com/pyrrhurabreedersassociation.html

This website is no longer active but is of historical interest for the articles in the newsletters).

In February 1997 Loro Parque, Tenerife, acquired six young birds (described as *gaudens*) from the consortium that had been formed in the USA. They were so rare, and then totally unknown in European aviculture, that the price of US$2,750 was paid for each pair. The pair on exhibit nested in July 1997. Four eggs were laid. Only one was fertile and the chick hatched on August 10. It was ringed at the age of 15 days and fledged on September 30.

Pairs were housed in the breeding centre in all-wire cages 3m long, 1m wide and 1m high, and 1.5m above the ground. Each cage has two nest-boxes, both 22cm square, but one 45cm high and the other 65cm high. They preferred the larger boxes. They were fed between 8am and 9am with at least four or five types of fruits and vegetables and a small amount of seed. Between 2pm and 3pm they were given a parakeet mixture. When breeding they also received corn on the cob, and eggfood before and during breeding. Clutch size was four to six. In one clutch laid in 2001 egg measurements were 28.95 x 20.92mm, 27.63 x 20.00mm, 27.95 x 21.29mm, 28.91 x 20.51mm, 28.52 x 20.85mm and 28.94 x 20.41mm (Anon, 2002).

On occasions infertile eggs were laid, especially in the first clutch of recently formed pairs. The incubation period was 24 days and young spent about 50 days in the nest. In most cases, a second clutch was laid after the young were removed from their parents (Reinschmidt and Zamora Padrón, 2007). By 2011 this species had been bred to several generations and 226 chicks had been ringed.

In Germany Plantaria bird park in Germany (sadly, closed in 2009) was very successful in breeding Hoffmann's Conures (and Emma's). Natural logs were used with machine-turned centres. The first Hoffmann's breeding there occurred in 1998 when three young were reared. On June 26 there were four eggs in the nest and one more was laid.

As recounted in Chapter 12, Hoffmann's Conure is established in aviculture in Europe and the USA although it is not numerous.

Birders: Savegre Lodge, near San Gerardo, Costa Rica; Santa Fé National Park, Veraguas, Panama.

EL ORO CONURE (*Pyrrhura orcesi*)

Origin of name: named for Gustavo Orces, Ecuadorian ornithologist.

Taxonomy: This species was unknown to science until 1980 but not formally identified as a new species until 1985.

Description: except for bright red forewing and primary coverts, it is more reminiscent of a *Psittacara*, being dark green with a red forehead. One of the few *Pyrrhuras* that lacks contrasting ear coverts, it has only a tinge of lighter green in that area. Crown feathers are green without dusky-brown centres. Hinting that it is indeed a *Pyrrhura*, the feathers of upper breast and part of nape are faintly margined with white and there is a tinge of maroon on the abdomen. Bend of wing, carpal edge and primary coverts are red. Tail feathers are green and dark maroon above and dark grey below, tinged with maroon on inner webs. Iris is dark brown and bill is light brown. An interesting feature is the bare skin surrounding the eye which is red.

Length: 22cm. **Weight:** 71g average of 14 birds, range 65g to 73.5g (Ridgely and Robbins, 1988).

Immature birds: duller in colour with less red on forehead and on bend of wing. The naked area of skin surrounding the eye is white, gradually taking on a red tinge. A photograph published in *Cyanopsitta* (June 2008) of two young in nest, one with outstretched wings, shows one or two primary coverts on each wing that were yellow and pale red. In the April 2010 issue a chick about six weeks old with wing outstretched shows four bright red primary coverts and red forewing.

Sexual dimorphism: According to Forshaw (2006), the female has green lores (and the male's are red) and only a narrow area of red on the forehead. If this was correct, it would be the only obviously sexually dimorphic member of the genus. Martin Schaefer of the University of Freiburg, Germany carried out DNA research on this species. He informed me: "The species is not sexually dimorphic. It has a red front patch that is variable in size. **Individuals with large patches are always males, but individuals with small patches can be either male or female."**

Range of the El Oro Parakeet

Range: south-western Ecuador on western Andean slopes mainly at 600m to 1,300m. It occurs in the provinces of Cañar, Azuay, El Oro and Loja and its range covers about 3,800 km² including large areas of deforestation. See page 117.

Status and threats: ENDANGERED. CITES Appendix I. It is threatened by forest clearance

El Oro Conures investigate a nest-box in the Buenaventura reserve.
Photograph © Mery Juiña/Jocotoco

and fragmentation, logging; open-cast mining, cattle-ranching and agriculture. Only 4% of the original forest remains, restricted to the most inaccessible slopes. By August 2010 ten sites had been surveyed, with details recorded of the forest and the extent to which it had been affected by human activities. Active nests located in cavities in isolated trees in open pasture and on the forest edge suggested that suitable nest sites were scarce. These nests were more exposed to predation, especially by Crimson-rumped Toucanets (*Aulacorhynchus haematopygus*). Nest-boxes were therefore installed by Fundación Jocotoco. According to Martin Schaefer, sub-populations may be isolated due to forest fragmentation, and the communal breeding system of the species might further increase its vulnerability to habitat loss. As a keen parrot photographer, Agnes Coenen observed the activity for several hours at one nest. Suddenly there was some commotion inside the box and sixteen *orcesi* came popping out – one after the other in an endless stream of green and red.

Population: In 2001 the population was estimated at only 160 individuals. By 2007, the estimate was 160 to 180. By 2011 there had been a significant increase to 225-250 individuals, approximately half of which were found in the Buenaventura Reserve. By 2019 the estimate was loosely amended to 350 -1,500 individuals.

Habitat: humid, tropical forest, mainly between 800m and 1,200m but known to descend to 300m. Researchers state that this species is particularly threatened because it does not occur above about 1,300m. It inhabits primary and secondary cloud forest and can tolerate some habitat fragmentation.

Habits: The usual group size is between four and fifteen individuals. Items eaten include figs and other fruit, also the flowers of *Cecropia*. Nests are found in tree cavities, especially *Dacryodes peruviana*, a tree which is highly sought for human use. The main breeding season is from November to March. Seasonal movements to lower altitudinal forests have been reported in the Buenaventura Reserve.

Protection: In the Buenaventura Reserve (5,520ha – 8,700 acres) near Piñas in El Oro Province (3° S, 7° W, elevation 450m to 1,200m). It belongs to the Ecuadorian NGO Fundación Jocotoco, formed in 1998. In 1999 approximately 187 hectares of forest (70%) and abandoned pasture (30%) were purchased to protect this conure. The reserve consists of lower montane tropical forest with reforestation of native trees in previously cleared areas. The El Oro Conure might also occur in the extensive Cordillera de Molleturo Protection Forest, but logging and mining occurs within and around this reserve.

Conservation: Fundacion Jocotoco is restoring the habitat and teaching environmental education (see pages 117 and 120).

Habitat corridors linking reserves are essential for the long-term survival of the species. Increased infertility and disease would occur in birds confined to small reserves. Only extended protection zones in adjoining agricultural areas can prevent the parakeet's extinction. Loro Parque Fundación (who started to support the species' conservation in 2001) is funding a collaborative effort between the University of Freiburg, Germany and the Ecuadorian Museum of Natural Sciences. DNA analysis is used to determine gene flow and potential loss of genetic diversity due to habitat fragmentation.

In 2009 seventy individuals (adults and chicks) were marked and blood samples of sixty-seven were taken for analysis. This indicated a bottleneck in the genes of the Buenaventura reserve birds, probably due to the immense forest clearance in this region between 1950 and 1990 (Anon, 2010). Only one female in this population was found to be genetically distinct.

In 2016 Jocotoco acquired 94ha (233 acres) of critically important cloud-forest habitat, with the financial support of the American Bird Conservancy and the UK-based international conservation group World Land Trust, supported by more than 200 donors. The acquisition expanded the Buenaventura Reserve from 2,259ha (5,583 acres) to 2,354ha (5,816 acres). It created an ecological corridor between Buenaventura and three proposed government reserves, encompassing an area 90km (56 miles) long. The Buenaventura reserve was becoming isolated in a landscape of cattle ranches, so this acquisition (including one of the last forests) was very important and an enormous step forward in the survival of the El Oro Parakeet. Another important aspect is the environmental education provided for the local communities in the area of the reserve.

Breeding: Co-operative breeding has been recorded. Field observations combined with genetic analysis indicated that males and females incubated. Nest-box cameras were used in nests in twelve different flocks. In 2007 thirteen out of fifty-four nest-boxes were occupied and nineteen young fledged. Fifteen out of fifty-two nest-boxes were occupied during the 2009 breeding season. Ten of the groups bred successfully and twenty-six young were believed to have survived. The breeding attempts of the other two flocks failed, possibly due to high humidity in the nest-boxes – but inbreeding might also be implicated. In six years, from 2008 to 2014, due to the provision of nest sites, the population had increased from 170-180 individuals to 300 to 400 within the reserve. In 2015 the first recorded fledging of young from some of the 60 nest-boxes outside the reserve took place Another 60 boxes had been erected within the reserve. In the 2017 breeding season 67 young birds fledged from nest-boxes – the highest number since the project commenced. In the Buenaventura Reserve, 2020 was an excellent breeding year, with 114 parakeets fledged. From the start of the nest-box programme to 2020, a total of 559 El Oro Parakeets successfully fledged from the artificial nests, most notably between 2018 and 2020 (Waugh, 2022).

Aviculture: non-existent. No legal export has occurred.

Birders: Buenaventura Reserve, El Oro Province.

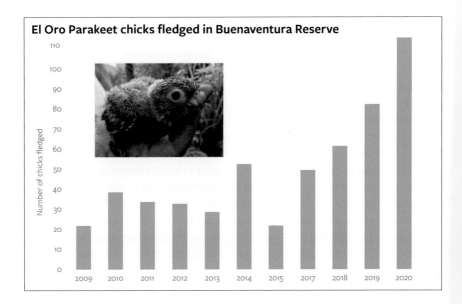

El Oro Parakeet chicks fledged in Buenaventura Reserve

ROSE-CROWNED CONURE (*Pyrrhura rhodocephala*)

Synonym: Rose-headed Conure
Origin of name: *rhodo* = red, *cephala* = head
Native names: *Perico Cabecirrojo, Cotorra Coronirroja*
Description: distinctive, with its almost white beak, white cere, red forehead and crown and almost imperceptible barring. There are dusky margins to the feathers of the neck and upper breast. Shade of red is softer than scarlet, paler on forehead and denser on crown. Chin is maroon, ear coverts are red and throat and upper breast have a golden-brown tinge in some birds. A prominent maroon patch decorates the abdomen. Tail is pink-red above and pale maroon on underside. Uniquely, primary wing coverts are white, also some flight feathers, with an odd yellow feather in some birds. Carpal edge of the wing is orange tinged white. Iris is brown and legs are grey.
Length: 24-25cm **Weight:** 75-80g.
Immature birds: Coloration varies; most bred in captivity have red on forehead and crown, extending almost to the nape in some individuals but shade less intense than in adults. UK breeder Les Waring had young leave the nest with "full head colour and a full set of white feathers in the wings" but normally with less red on head than adults. He can visually sex young in nest; cocks have more red on the head than hens. Once moulted into adult plumage, they can lose this distinction: both sexes can have the same amount of red or hens can be more colourful. DNA sexing is the only way to confirm the sex of adults. Adult plumage is usually acquired within 12 months, but the full set of white flight feathers can take up to three years to appear (Waring, pers.comm, 2011).

According to Forshaw (1989 and 2006), head colour of immature birds is green, usually with some faint bluish colouring, or even cream colour on the forehead or with scattered red feathers. The primary coverts are blue. This description is not borne out by breeders.

Approximate range of
rhodocephala.

Range: north-western Venezuela, from northern Tachira, Mérida and north-western Barinas, Trujillo, north to southern Lara.

Habitat: wet montane forests, principally at 1,500m to 2,500m in sub-tropical zone but also as low as 800m and as high as 3,000m in cloud forest, páramo and shrubland at high altitudes. It has one of the broadest altitudinal ranges of any member of the genus.

Habits: Often seen in noisy flocks, it flies low over mountain forests; unlike most other *Pyrrhuras*, it also ventures into open areas, perching in isolated trees, on fence posts and even on wires along pasture borders. It wanders widely, especially to lower elevations during the rainy months of May to November. Food consists of small seeds including *Heliocarpus* (Malvaceae) and especially on the seeds of *Chusquea* bamboo (Hilty, 2003).

Status: IUCN Least Concern (2000). CITES Appendix II. Least Concern.

Population: not quantified but believed to be stable. There is a lack of information: little field work has been carried out in Venezuela in recent years due to various human hazards.

Aviculture: Established and gaining in popularity due to its likeable temperament and pet potential. It was not until the 1990s when a few Rose-crowned Conures were privately imported into Europe, that this species became known in aviculture. By the middle of that decade breeders in the Netherlands and Germany were able to acquire them and gradually they spread throughout European aviculture.

In Germany Horst Mayer acquired his two females in September 1998. Eventually two males were acquired and young were reared: four by one pair and two by the other pair. One female laid twice, nine eggs in both clutches, and the other female laid seven in the first nest and eight in the second. Egg sizes ranged from 28.1mm x 19.5mm to 25.3mm x 20.8mm. After 24 or 25 days chicks hatched. They were ringed between 12 and 14 days with 5.5 rings. The young left the nest aged between 48 and 51 days (Mayer, 2001, Mayer 2006). Chicks have white down (Low, 2020a and Low, 2020b).

UK breeder Les Waring told me: "I have kept the Rose crowned Conure since 2003 and found it to be the most prolific breeder of all the *Pyrrhura* conures I have kept. My birds parent rear the chicks without problems and clutch size is usually four to six eggs. On a couple of occasions, seven eggs were laid.

Pet potential is good due to their delightful temperament, and the voice is not loud. UK breeder Kris Spearman told me: "I have found *rhodocephala* to have the most amazingly friendly temperament. My adult parent-reared pairs would often land on my head in the aviary. Many of the Dutch breeders say there is no need to hand-rear them."

Ian Price from Wales told me that his Rose-crowned were among the most confiding and inquisitive of the *Pyrrhuras* he keeps. When they are not breeding

A pair of Rose-crowned Conures and their four young, bred by Claus Nielsen in Denmark. The female is on the left and the male is third from the left on the perch.
Photograph © Claus Nielsen

he keeps several species together and the Rose-crowns "rule the roost", housed with Black-capped, Fiery-shouldered, Fallow Maroon-bellied and Crimson-bellied. They are slightly larger (leg ring size P). He wrote: "Both parents are quite tame. Two 2010 males will both eat from my hand. I have a 2009 male I bred who wolf whistles and blows kisses. He has picked this up from hearing a pet Senegal in our conservatory, and he is 50m away at the top of the garden.

"We house our birds in aviaries when not breeding, then place pairs into 90cm x 60cm x 60cm breeding cages with nest-boxes that measure 47cm high by 25cm square. I usually pair up Christmas week. One pair normally lays eggs by February while the other pair holds off until it is a bit warmer in April. Both my pairs are very good parents, probably because they are fairly tame".

Birders: Yacambú National Park, southern Lara; Sierra Nevada National Park (Mérida and Barinas).

SANTA MARTA CONURE (*Pyrrhura viridicata*)

Origin of name: *viridicata* = greenish
Local name: *Lorito de Santa Marta*
Description: Mainly dark green with **no pronounced barring,** although feathers of hind neck and breast are very faintly tipped with brown. Narrow frontal band is red, throat is tinged red and ear coverts are pale reddish-brown. On the **abdomen is an uneven line of yellow-tipped scarlet feathers,** below are scattered maroon ones – or in very mature birds, the scarlet extends further down abdomen. Feathers at bend of wing are yellow and orange and under wing coverts are scarlet, or orange towards edge of wing where there are several yellow feathers. Tail is brownish red, green at base.
Length: 25cm. **Weight:** 80-85g.
Immature birds: The orange pectoral band is absent in juveniles, incomplete in immature birds and heavily marked in adults (Olaciregui *et al*, 2020). A photograph in *The Latin American Bird Reserve Network* (American Bird Conservancy publication) shows an all dark green *viridicata* with a hint of brown on ear coverts and a couple of orange feathers on upper part of abdomen – presumably an immature bird. Underside of tail was pale maroon.
Range: Santa Marta mountains, Magdalena, northern Colombia (10°N, 73°W), covering only about 500km². Usual altitudinal range: 1,800m to 2,800m.
Status: IUCN ENDANGERED (2000). CITES Appendix II.
Threats: Encroachment on natural habitat, due to human immigration dating from the 1950s, especially during the 1970s and 1980s. Much illegal cultivation occurred, including marijuana, and an increase in shade-coffee growing. (*Aratinga* conures eat coffee berries – it is not reported if *Pyrrhuras* do so.) Only 15% of the original vegetation remains unaltered following decades of uncontrolled colonisation and agricultural expansion. Only about 7% (150,000ha) occurs within the altitudinal range of the species between 1,200m and 1,800m, mainly on the northern mountain slopes. In the Action Plan for the threatened parrots of Colombia 2010-2020, deforestation, cattle-ranching, illegal cultivation and lack of nest sites were considered to be the greatest threats. In 2013 it was predicted

The Santa Marta Conure occurs only in the Santa Marta mountains in Magdalena, northern Colombia.

In the El Dorado Reserve Fundacion ProAves has removed thousands of non-native pine trees and planted suitable native trees on which Santa Marta Conures feed.

Photographs © left Agnes Coenen, right ProAves

that climate change could have a serious impact on this parakeet, resulting in substantial loss of habitat.

Population: The largest single population of about 120 individuals is in the north-western part of the Santa Marta mountains. The total population was estimated at 4,000 to 4,500 and decreasing in 2009 (BirdLife International). ProAves believe that the population is lower than this.

Habitat: a privately-owned area covering 700ha (1,729 acres) of subtropical and montane forest from 900m to 2,545m. Some seasonal altitudinal movements have been recorded. A study carried out between July and December 2006 found that six habitat types were utilised. Of those, secondary forest was the most visited; also used were scrub, early secondary growth, non-native forest, open areas and some cultivated zones.

Habits: The 2006 study usually recorded flock sizes of fewer than twenty birds. The highest numbers ever recorded, at the end of the year, were flocks of twenty-eight and sixty-eight. Flocks of variable sizes fed together and a sentinel was posted during feeding bouts. The conures roosted and nested in pairs or trios in cavities in the wax palm *Ceroxylon ceriferum*. The breeding season started in December and finished in June. Low breeding success rate was attributed to disturbance by Wagler's Conures *(Psittacara wagleri)* or predation by Emerald Toucanets *(Aulacorhynchus prassinus)*.

Studies of the dietary preferences of the Santa Marta Conure were made during 2006 on the very humid San Lorenzo ridge. The four species previously unrecorded as food sources were *Cupressus sempervirens* (Cupressaceae), *Eucalyptus globulus* (Myrtaceae), *Miconia* (Melastomataceae) and *Sapium* (Euphorbiaceae). Of eleven species eaten, *Sapium*, *Croton bogotanus* (Euphorbiaceae) and *Lepechinia bullata* (Lamiaceae) were predominantly consumed. Of 86 observations, flowers represented 43.2% of the total consumed, seeds 31.8% and fruits 31.8% (Botero Delgadillo *et al*, 2010).

Conservation: In 2006 the El Dorado reserve, covering 640ha, was established – only 8km from the rapidly-growing coastal city of Santa Marta. Christian Olaciegui and Rafael Borja studied the breeding biology of the Santa Marta Conure from April to November 2006 and from February to July 2007. In May 2006, forty-eight artificial nests were installed by ProAves personnel in four sites in three altitudinal zones on the San Lorenzo ridge. Natural nest observations were conducted in Vistahermosa Farm, near Kennedy Peak. Nine nesting attempts were recorded: two in 2006 and seven in 2007. Six occurred in artificial nests and three in natural nests. Another five bird species made use of the artificial nests. The average conure clutch was four to six eggs. In October 2006 five young fledged from one of the nest-boxes. In December, the next breeding season (2006-2007) started and again nest-boxes were used. Funding for the nest-box programme was provided by Loro Parque Fundación and the American Bird Conservancy.

In 2008 ecological restoration commenced, the aim being to remove 20,000 plants of non-native, invasive *Pinus patula* from El Dorado Reserve and to reforest with native trees of key food plants. Local community members provided information on the presence of the conure. The peak nesting period was December to April in complex wooded habitats; nesting also occurred from July to October in open vegetation with trees and scattered palms. Wagler's Conures were breeding in nest-boxes in the open zones but at this time Coral-billed Parrots *(Pionus sordidus)* and Scaly-naped Amazons *(Amazona mercenaria)* had finished breeding. This suggests that the more aggressive species nested in palms in the open zones and when they vacated the palm nests *viridicata* took over.

Protection: La Cumbre reserve, the experimental station of San Lorenzo and El Dorado, are the only protected areas within the range of this conure. The El Dorado Reserve is owned by Fundación ProAves which identified the key area in which most breeding birds occur, in the reserve and in its buffer zone. Despite the fact that the Sierra Nevada de Santa Marta is an international Biosphere Reserve, little was done to protect its biodiversity until the birth of ProAves.

Aviculture: unknown.

Birders: El Dorado Reserve, northern Colombia. This is the only accessible subtropical forest reserve in the Santa Marta mountains.

BLUE-THROATED CONURE (*Pyrrhura cruentata*)

Synonyms: Ochre-marked Parakeet, Blue-chested Parakeet
Origin of name: from the Latin *cruentatus* = bloodstained.
Local names: *Fura-mato, Tiriba Cara-suja, Tiriba grande.*
Description: Head coloration: most unusual (for any neotropical parrot). **Feathers of forehead, crown and nape dark brown, edged with dull orange to give a streaky appearance. Patch of orange behind reddish-brown ear coverts; upper cheeks and lores and very narrow line above eye also reddish-brown.** Lower cheeks: green. **Blue throat merges into extensive blue area on breast (not scalloped).** Abdomen: dark red, also lower back and rump. Bend of wing crimson. Tail: golden-olive above, brownish-red below. The iris is yellow; skin surrounding the eye dark grey. The beak is black.
Length: 28cm-30cm. **Weight:** about 90g but some variation.
Immature plumage: slightly duller with less red on bend of wing. Bare skin around eye lighter grey. Beak is light coloured, marked with grey, gradually becoming darker over a period of months.
Range: Brazil – Atlantic forest of the south-east in Bahia and Espirito Santo. Smaller numbers survive in the states of Rio de Janeiro and Minas Gerais. Although its range covers 10,000km², its habitat has been destroyed throughout most of the area. See map on page 124.
Status and threats: Vulnerable (declining). CITES Appendix I. Article 10 Exemption Certificate required to sell young. It is threatened by extensive forest clearance and some trapping.
Habitat: Highly fragmented forested areas, mostly in reserves; in lowland forest and forest edges, occasionally ranging up to 900m. In some selectively logged forests now used for agriculture, where large trees have been spared to shade plantations such as cocoa, it has persisted longer. It needs tall forest where it lives in the canopy.
Habits: Parrot population sizes and habitat use in the large reserve of Sooretama/Linhares (24,250 hectares) in the lowland Atlantic forest were examined from July to October 1998 – prior to the breeding season (Marsden *et al*, 2000). The Blue-throated Conure was associated with non-pristine forest and was never recorded away from the reserve. The researchers concluded that for more effective conservation management areas immediately outside the reserve should be extended, as most parrot populations there were likely to be small. *P. cruentata* was associated with areas containing *Cecropia* (on whose fruits and seeds it feeds) and with full vegetation cover at canopy and mid-level. Its association with *Cecropia* suggested it is a bird of regenerating forest. (This project was funded by Blackpool Zoo, UK.)

Protection: protected under Brazilian law. It occurs in some national parks: Sooretama Biological Reserve in northern Espirito Santo and adjacent Linhares Biological Reserve. Probably few have survived in the Monte Pascoal National Park, Bahia, due to conflict regarding the rights of local communities (BirdLife International, 2000) but it apparently still exists in the Vera Cruz Reserve. It also occurred (Marsden *et al*, 2000) in the Chapada Diamantina National Park, in the State Parks of Rio Doce and Desengano and in several federal reserves and private reserves. There is no knowledge regarding how much of the population occurs within "protected" areas.

Reportedly, it was introduced into Tijuca National Park in 1969-70, using illegally trapped specimens (Sick, 1993.) According to Nigel Collar, author of several papers on the reintroduction of parrot species, there is no evidence to support this claim.

Aviculture: In personality, appearance, size and behaviour, the Blue-throated Conure differs from other members of the genus, in its plumage pattern, larger size and yellow iris (most species brown or orange). Bare eye skin is very dark, almost black (although in captive birds this varies). These latter two features and the large size distinguish it from other members of the genus. It is destructive to wood, the other species less so. Atypical in appearance and behaviour, it might be the relict of a different genus that once occurred in the Atlantic forest.

In February 2012 Povl Jorgensen in Denmark told me: "Our *cruentata* were always quite shy, with a character different from other *Pyrrhuras*. I felt that they were not real *Pyrrhuras* and that they had a similarity with the Nanday Conure *(Nandayus nenday)*. We have bred from two pairs since the mid-nineties. Many people said that they had to be two to three years old to breed but this is not the case – 12 months is sufficient. Our experiences in nearly 20 years is that unlike most other *Pyrrhuras* they never double clutch. Only if things go wrong will they lay again – but not always. At this moment they are the most difficult CITES Appendix I species to sell – and the price is not high."

Breeding

Although it was first bred in England as long ago as 1937, by Herbert Whitley of Paignton, it was not generally available in Europe until the late 1970s. One of the first breeders was Mrs Spenkelink van Schaik of the Netherlands. She recommended a nest-box of very thick wood as nesting birds were very destructive. Since the late 1970s the Blue-throated Conure has been bred consistently in the UK, Netherlands, Germany and Denmark and by the 1980s was well established in aviculture world-wide, although not common in the USA. Some pairs are very prolific, with clutches of up to nine eggs. However, egg-breaking is a common problem with this species (see *Chapter 9, Breeding Problems*, under *Egg-breaking*).

The Blue-throated Conure occurs only in Brazil's Atlantic Forest, where much of its habitat has been destroyed. Photograph © Agnes Coenen

Canary Islands: In my experience, this species differs from other members of the genus in that females tend to be dominant over males and may be larger and weigh slightly more. When I was in charge of the breeding centre of Palmitos Park, Gran Canaria, we had several pairs and their offspring, housed in cages made of welded mesh, on a metal framework 90cm off the ground.

Two years after they were paired up they started to breed. Large clutches were common. They were seasonal layers. Chicks usually hatched between the first week in April and the first week in June. On two occasions a chick hatched during the first week in July. This species was never double-brooded. The female of one pair had only one leg but she was a very successful breeder and hatched six chicks in her first nest. Chicks hatched over a period of sixteen days, on May 5, 8, 13, 16, 19 and 21. The incubation period appeared to be about 25 days.

The weights I recorded of parent-reared chicks, from four different pairs, varied a great deal. Chicks weighed 5g or 6g at hatching. The skin surrounding the eye started to darken at 11 days and the first feathers erupted at 17 to 19 days. Chicks were ringed between 12 and 17 days with 6mm rings. Peak weight was achieved at about 34 days. The highest weight recorded was a chick that had been fostered

Blue-throated Conures aged 32, 34 and 43 days, hatched at Palmitos Park, Gran Canaria in 1992. Photograph © Rosemary Low

to Maroon-bellied Conures at 25 days (after being starved at 22 days). It achieved 135g (with full crop) at 34 days.

In 1995 one young Blue-throated Conure suffered an accident just after it left the nest, resulting in the loss of most of its upper mandible. I hand-reared it, then weaned it on to a liquid food, until it began to take solid foods. The future for this bird might have been uncertain but for Carlos Simon Rodriguez on Tenerife who was a most caring and competent breeder of neotropical parrots. He took the bird and fed it on soft foods, such as pasta and fruit. When I saw it four years later the upper mandible was less than one third the normal length – its tongue was clearly visible. The good news was that it had produced its first youngster that year!

In the **UK** the Blue-throated Conure has been bred by aviculturists since the mid-1970s when Harry Sissen produced many young. A pair that laid for the first time for veterinarian George A.Smith in 1982 laid eight eggs, all of which hatched. The smallest chick died at an early age, three were left with their parents and I hand-reared the other four.

At Paradise Park, Cornwall, UK, *cruentata* bred for the first time in 2011. A pair produced six eggs and hatched them all. One chick died soon after. The three smallest had to be removed for hand-rearing because their growth was poor. The smallest died and four were reared. Curator David Woolcock commented: "In our original pair I would have said that the hen was the dominant bird. With our current pair it is not so marked, but that could be due to the male being a hand-reared bird and always 'in your face', so to speak!"

In **Denmark** Povl Jorgensen imported two pairs from Loro Parque, Tenerife, in March 1998. Both pairs bred every year until one female died in 2009. This bird invariably laid clutches of four eggs whereas the other female always laid six to eight eggs – more usually eight. The other pair reared six young in one clutch in 2010. Many of the young ones bred when they were only one year old.

In **South Africa,** with its warmer climate, Terry Irwin had one pair that reared *two nests of young* every year. In his experience, 6mm rings were too tight for some *cruentata*: he used 7mm rings. Egg-breaking and egg-eating are very common problems (especially with inexperienced birds), also the laying of large numbers of eggs, most of which are infertile. One of Terry Irwin's females laid 32 eggs in one year, only four of which were fertile. Successful females laid up to ten eggs and could rear up to eight young in one nest. Nest-boxes used were L-shaped with a 20cm x 30cm base and 35cm high, or upright boxes 20cm square and 60cm high. Many young were exported, with CITES documents. This presented no problems, if an import permit from the importing country was submitted with the export application.

In **Australia,** Paul Stuart's pairs were housed in aviaries measuring 3.6m long, 1.2m wide and 2.1m high, only one quarter of which was open to the elements.

These double-wired aviaries were mainly covered due to the low temperatures in winter. The pairs spent much time hanging on the wire interacting with their neighbours until a solid partition was put in, then they started to breed within one month. Other pairs were kept in cages with welded mesh bases, 3m long, 91cm wide and 1.2m high, suspended 1.2m off the ground. He believed that young birds felt more secure in suspended cages. Nest-boxes measured 45cm high and 25cm square; but the measurements were not deemed important.

In Australia they bred most of the year, including the coldest winters but not in the hottest months. During the summer, all eggs were removed for artificial incubation, due to the loss of newly hatched chicks in very hot weather. At other times, the young were parent-reared. Most of his young started to breed at the age of two years but those of one particular bloodline matured earlier, with one male breeding at the age of ten months and three pairs breeding when only one year old. Recently laid eggs weighed 7g to 7.9g and hatched in the incubator after 24 or 25 days (Stuart, 2003).

In India the Blue Bird Avian Breeding and Research Centre had reared more than 200 Blue-throated Conures in a period of just over one decade by 2020. The females were described as dominant and larger than the males. Fifteen or so young birds were flocked in an aviary measuring 7m (23ft) x 2.5m (8ft) x 2.5m for one year. When two birds bonded they were moved to outdoor breeding aviaries. Several nest-box designs were used, including vertical ones measuring 67cm (26in) high and 20cm(8in) square with two 6cm entrances (for the safety of the female). Deep boxes were preferred. The clutch sizes were very large – eight to 13 eggs; egg-breaking did not occur. This species was double-brooded in this facility.

The breeding set-up consisted of pairs or trios. With two males the female chose one male and the second male also helped to feed the chicks. In a few cases the female rejected both males but due to the large number available she was then free to chose another male. Keeping one male with two females was not successful because only the dominant female laid and incubated and there might be aggressive behaviour between the two females. All the eggs hatched but the chicks were not well cared for by the female 'because she is worried about losing the male to the other female and tries to leave the nest as soon as possible' (Maruthamuthu and Maruthamuthu, 2020 and 2022).

Birders: Linhares Biological Reserve, Espirito Santo, south-eastern Brazil.

EPILOGUE FOR AVICULTURISTS

Bird keepers need to consider this: every bird in our care is an individual, deserving of the best conditions and the most thoughtful concern of which we are capable. Just because *Pyrrhuras* are small parrots, it does not mean that they are any less sentient or less intelligent than large parrots like macaws. In fact, they are highly intelligent. If you live closely with them and come to know an individual, its likes, its fears, and its need to fly, you will be amazed that such a small bird can have such a strong personality. Most conures are extremely responsive creatures with a need that is more intense and urgent than in many parrots to be physically close to other members of their species.

Breeders who have many birds might cease to see them as individuals but treat them all as part of a project. The most enjoyment comes from keeping only a few and knowing each one as an individual. Bird-keeping has little meaning, except for those who view it as a commercial undertaking, unless there is a relationship between birds and humans in which they respond to each other. This is easily achieved with these wonderful small parrots if you spend enough time with them.

In *The Human Nature of Birds*, Theodore Xenophon Barber wrote that humans "...need a fundamental change in consciousness, a new understanding, a realization that they are not the only intelligent beings on earth – that birds, as a prime example, are as aware and sensitive and have as much practical intelligence as they."

Whatever our relationship with birds might be, let us not forget these words.

REFERENCES CITED

Anon, 2000, Painted Conure appearance of a striking mutation, *Magazine of the Parrot Society*, 34 (1): 16.

Anon, 2002, The keeping and breeding of the Chiriqui conure, *Cyanopsitta*, (66): 6-7.

Anon, 2007, *Pyrrhura griseipectus*. The eleventh hour for the Grey-breasted Parakeet, *Cyanopsitta*, (87): 17-19.

Anon, 2010, Latest discoveries about the El Oro Parakeet, *Cyanopsitta*, (95): 18-19.

Arenas-Mosquera, D., 2011, Aspectos de la biología reproductiva del Periquito Aliamarillo *(Pyrrhura calliptera)* en los bosques altoandinos de La Calera, Colombia, *Conservación Colombiana*, 14 (Marzo), 58-70.

Arndt, T., 2008, Anmerkungen zu einigen Pyrrhura-Formen mit der Beschreibung einer neuen Art and zweier neuer Unterarten, *Papageien*, 8: 278-86.

Arndt, T., 2018a, Auf der Suche nach dem Peru-Blaustirn- und dem Blassen Peru-Rotschwanzsittich, Teil I, *Papageien* (3): 100-105,

--- 2018b, Auf der Suche nach dem Peru-Blaustirn- und dem Blassen Peru-Rotschwanzsittich, Teil 2, *Papageien* (4): 136-141.

Arndt, T. and M. Wink, 2017, Molecular Systematics, Taxonomy and Distribution of the *Pyrrhura Picta–Leucotis* Complex, *Open Ornithology Journal* 10: 53-91.

Benavidez, A., E.Tallei, E.A.Lilian and L.Rivera, 2021, Feeding ecology of the Green-cheeked Parakeet *Pyrrhura molinae* in a subtropical forest of Argentina, *Neotropical Biology and Conservation*, 16 (1) 205-219.

BirdLife International, 2000, *Threatened birds of the world*. Barcelona and Cambridge, UK: Lynx Edicions and BirdLife International.

Boesman, P., 1998, Some new information on the distribution of Venezuelan birds, *Cotinga*, 9: 27-39.

Boner, S., 2012, Die Haltung und Zucht des Pazifik Schwarz-schwanzsittichs *(Pyrrhura melanura pacifica)*, *Gefiederter Freund*, 3-12: 4-5.

Botero-Delgadillo, E., J. C.Verhelst. and C. A. Páez, 2010, Ecologia de forrajeo del Periquito de Santa Marta *(Pyrrhura viridicata)* en la cuchilla de San

Lorenzo, Sierra Nevada de Santa Marta, *Ornitologia Neotropical*, 21: 463-477.

Botero–Delgadillo, E. and C.A.Pàez, 2011a, Colombian Threatened Parrot Conservation Action Plan 2010-2020: Progress, Achievements & Prospects, *Conservación Colombiana*, 14: 7-16.

--- 2011b, Estado actual del conocimiento y conservación de los loros amenazados de Colombia. (Current knowledge and conservation of Colombia's threatened parrots), *Conservación Colombiana*, 14: 86-151.

Brightsmith, Donald, 1999, Stealth Conures of the genus *Pyrrhura*, *Bird Talk*, October.

Broad, S.,1987, Imports of Psittacines into the UK (1981-1984). *Magazine of the Parrot Society*, XXI (3): 77-94 (reprinted from TRAFFIC Bulletin).

Buitron-Jurado G. and V. Sanz, 2016, Notes on the diet of the endemic red-eared parakeet *Pyrrhura hoematotis* and other Venezuelan montane parrots, Yacambú National Park, *Ardeola*, 63 (2), 2016, 357-367 DOI: 10.13157/arla.63.2.2016.sc2

Clayton, G., 2006, Mutation Green-cheeked Conures, *Magazine of the Parrot Society UK*, 40 (3): 100-107.

Cooper, R.J., 1979, Maroon-tailed Conures, *Magazine of the Parrot Society*, XIII (5): 109-117.

Delgado, B.F.S., 1985, A new sub-species of Painted Conure *(Pyrrhura picta)* from Panama, *Ornithol. Monogr*, 36:16-20.

Donegan. T., J. C.Verhelst, T. Ellery, O.Cortes-Herrera and P. Salaman, 2016, Revision of the status of bird species occurring or reported in Colombia 2016 and assessment of BirdLife International's new parrot Taxonomy, *Conservacion Colombiana* (34): 12-26. https://www.researchgate.net/publication/309618184

Dornas T., 2016, Pfrimer's parakeet *(Pyrrhura pfrimeri)*, a critically threatened and endemic parakeet of dry forests in central Brazil, *Ornitología Neotropical*, 27: 247-251.

Drew, P., 1998, Pleasures of the Painted, *Bird Keeper*, July: 43.

Duncan, S., 2007, New mutation of the Green-Cheeked Conure, *ASA Bulletin*, Sept/Oct: 16-19.

Dupas, G. and J.M.Garnier, 2015, *Monographie du Genre* Pyrrhura, Editions A.C.V. Lyon.

Forshaw, J. M., 1989, *Parrots of the World*, Third (revised) edition, Blandford, London.

--- 2006, *Parrots of the World*, an identification guide, Princeton University Press, Princeton and Oxford.

Gaban-Lima, R., 2016, The status of three little known names proposed by Miranda-Ribeiro (1926) and the synonymization of *Pyrrhura snethlageae* Joseph & Bates, 2002 (Psittaciformes: Psittacidae: Arinae), Zootaxa, Nov 27; doi: 10.11646 4200(1): zootaxa.4200.1.10.

Hilty, S.L., 2003, *Birds of Venezuela*, Princeton University Press.

Hodel, J., 2012a, Meine erstern Erfahrungen mit der Haltung und Zucht von Peru-Blaustirn-Rotschwanzsittichen, *Gefiederter Freund* 6-12: 12-13.

--- 2012b, Meine erstern Erfahrungen mit der Haltung und Zucht von Pfrimers- Sittichen *(Pyrrhura pfrimeri)*, *Gefiederter Freund* 7-12: 8-9.

Hoyo, del J., A. Elliott, J.Sargatal and D.A.Christie (eds), 2013, *Handbook of the Birds of the World (HBW)*, special volume, *New Species*, Lynx Edicions.

Irwin, T., 2007/08, The Yellow-sided Conure, *Avizandum* 19 (11): 38-40.

--- 2008/09, Blue-throated Conure, *Avizandum* 20 (11): 22-26.

Joseph, L., 2000, Beginning an end to 63 years of uncertainty: the Neotropical parakeets known as *Pyrrhura picta* and *P. leucotis* comprise more than two species, *Proceedings of the Academy of Natural Sciences*, Philadelphia, 150: 279-292.

--- 2002, Geographical variation, taxonomy and distribution of some Amazonian *Pyrrhura parakeets*, *Ornitologia Neotropical*, 13: 337-364.

Lacs, J. and T. Silva, 2019, Welterstzucht des Azuero-Sittichs, *Papageien* (1): 10-13.

Lee, A.T.K., 2010, Parrot Claylicks: distribution, patterns of use and Ecological correlates from a parrot assemblage in southeastern Peru, PhD dissertation, Manchester Metropolitan University.

Low, R., 1967, The Pearly Conure, *Avicultural Magazine*, 73 (1): 4-7.

--- 1968, The *Pyrrhura* Conures, *Magazine of the Parrot Society*, II (9): 173-179.

--- 1972, *The Parrots of South America*, John Gifford Ltd, London.

--- 1991, The White-eared Conure, *Avicultural Magazine*, 97 (3): 113-117.

--- 1994, Breeding the Fiery-shouldered Conure, *Avicultural Magazine*, 100 (3): 144-147.

--- 2009, *Go West for Parrots*, Insignis Publications, UK.

--- 2020a, Rose-headed Conure: Breeding and Fostering, *Magazine of the Parrot Society*, 54 (4): 18-21.

--- 2020b, Die Zucht des Rotkopfsittichs (Teil 2), *Papageien*, 33 (2): 52-54.

Maijer, S., S.K.Herzog, M.Kessler, M.T.Friggens and J.Fjeldså, 1998, A distinctive new sub-species of the Green-cheeked Parakeet (*Pyrrhura molinae*, Psittacidae) from Bolivia. *Ornitologia Neotropical*, 9: 185-191.

Marsden, S.J. *et al*, 2000, Parrot populations and habitat use in and around two lowland Atlantic forest reserves, Brazil, *Biological Conservation*, 96, 209-217.

Mayer, H., 2001, Von meinem Rotschwanzsittichen, *Gefiederte Welt*, 125 (1): 6-10.

--- 2006, Von meinem Rotkopfsittichen, *Gefiederter Freund*, 15 März: 12-13.

--- 2011, Pfrimers Weissohrsittiche, *Gefiederte Welt* (8): 16-18.

Maruthamuthu, M. and G. Maruthamuthu, 2020, The fascinating Blue-throated Conure, *Parrot News*, Nov-Dec: 22-25.

--- 2022, Haltung und Zucht des Blaulatzsittichs, *Papageien* (3): 92-95.

Olaciregui, C., H. Oliveros-Salas and E.Botero-Delgadillo, 2020, Breeding Biology of the Endangered Santa Marta Parakeet *Pyrrhura viridicata*, *Ardea*, 108 (1): 49-54.

Olmos, F., 1997, Auf der Suche nach Pfrimers Weissohrsittich, *WP Magazin*: 3 (5): 24-28.

Olmos, F., P. Martuscelli and R. Silva e Silva, 1997, Distribution and dry-season ecology of Pfrimer's Conure *Pyrrhura pfrimeri*, with a reappraisal of Brazilian Pyrrhura "*leucotis*", *Ornitologia Neotropical*, 8: 121-132.

Olmos, F., W.A.G. Silva and C.Albano, 2005, Grey-breasted Conure, *Pyrrhura griseipectus*: an overlooked endangered species, *Cotinga* 24: 77-83.

Pasquier, R.F. (ed), 1980, *Conservation of New World Parrots*, Smithsonian Institution Press/ICBP.

Ragusa-Netto, J., 2007, Feeding ecology of the Green-cheeked parakeet in dry forests in western Brazil, *Braz. J.Biol*, 67 (2) 243-249.

Reinschmidt, M., and R. Zamora Padrón, 2007, Mantenimiento y la cría de la Cotorra catana (*Pyrrhura hoffmani gaudens*), *Aviornis Internacional*, no. 93: 34-42.

Ridgely, R.S. and M.B.Robbins, 1988, *Pyrrhura orcesi*, a new parakeet from southwestern Ecuador, with systematic notes on the *P. melanura* complex. *The Wilson Bulletin*, 100 (2): 173-182.

Ridgely, R. S. and P. J. Greenfield, 2001, *The Birds of Ecuador*, Vol. 2: Status, Distribution and Taxonomy. Cornell University Press, New York.

Robbins, M.B., R.S. Ridgely, T. Schulenberg and F. Gill, 1987, The avifauna of the Cordillera de Cutucú, Ecuador, with comparisons to other Andean localities, *Proc. Acad. Nat. Sci Philadelphia*, 139: 243-259.

Rodríguez-Mahecha, J.V. and J.I. Hernández-Camacho, 2002, *Loros de Colombia*, Conservación Internacional, Colombia.

Schmidt, S. and G., 2022, Our passion for breeding the *Pyrrhura* genus Parakeets, *AWI Parrots* (2): 72-77.

Scott, C., 2007, My experiences with the Painted Conure *Pyrrhura picta* in Captivity, *Magazine of the Parrot Society UK*, 41 (July): 294-295.

Sick, H., 1993, *Birds in Brazil*, Princeton University Press, New Jersey.

Sigrist, T., 2009, *Guia de Campo Avis Brasilis/Avis Brasilis Field Guide to the Birds of Brazil* (species accounts), Avisbrasilis, Sâo Paulo.

Silveira, L.F. and Brettas, E.P., 2015, *Terra Papagalli*, M'Arte, Sâo Paulo.

Slud, P., 1964, The Birds of Costa Rica: distribution and ecology, *Bulletin American Museum of Natural History*, 128: 1-430.

Smith, G.A., 1982, *Pyrrhura Conures, Magazine of the Parrot Society*, XVI (12): 365-372.

Somenzari, M. and L.F. Silveira, 2015, Taxonomy of the *perlata-coerulescens* complex (Psittaciformes: Psittacidae), with description of a hybrid zone, *J. J Ornithol* 156 (4).1049–1060. https://doi.org/10.1007/s10336-015-1216-3

Spenkelink-van-Schaik, J.L., 1980, The Maroon-tailed Conure (Pyrrhura Melanura), *Magazine of the Parrot Society*, XIV (8): 181-183.

Stanford, M., 2006, Provision of Ultraviolet Light in Captivity and Calcium Metabolism and Diet in *A Guide to Grey Parrots* by Rosemary Low, ABK Publications.

Strewe, R., C. Navarro and N.Sanchez, 2017, Der Magdalenasittich in Nordost-Kolumbian, *Papageien* (2): 58-64.

Stuart P., 2003, The Blue-throated Conure, *Australian Birdkeeper*, 16 (6).

Toyne, E.P. 1994, The Plight of Parrots in Southern Ecuador, *PsittaScene* 6 (3): 10.

Toyne, E.P., M. Jeffcote and J. Flanagan, 1992, Status, distribution and ecology of the White-breasted Parakeet *Pyrrhura albipectus* in Podocarpus National Park, southern Ecuador, *Bird Conservation International*, 2: 327-338.

Valentine, M., 1987, Chromosome Analysis of Maroon-bellied and Green Cheeked Conures, *Watchbird*, XIV (3):19.

Vannieuwenhuyse, G., 1997, New challenge for enterprising Conure lovers, *Cage & Aviary Birds*, May 24: 17.

Waugh, D., 2022, Conserving the El Oro Parakeet and other psittacines in southern Ecuador, *AWI Parrots* (1): 40-47.

Welch, J., 2020, *Pyrrhura* Conures, An Australian Experience, part I, *Australian BirdKeeper*, (33), 4: 214-217.

Wolf, L., 1976, Avifauna of the Cerro de la Muerte region, Costa Rica. *American Museum Novit*. No 2606: 1-37.

Zgurski, J., 2013, Living with *Pyrrhura* Conures and tracking them in the wild, *Parrots*, March: 20-23.

INDICES

Index of common names
relating to *Pyrrhura* conure/parakeet. Please check both indices as the common or scientific name might be used.

Bold type indicates an illustration.

Azara's 137.
Azuero 9, 109, 168, 174-175, **175**.

Berlepsch's 193, 194, 195,196-197.
Black-capped 6, 7, 13, 91-92, **92**, 99, 101, 107, 108-109, 120, 124, 204-206, **204**, **206**.
Black-tailed vii, 6, 7, 12, 13, 47, 66, 101, 104, 109, 114, 123, 125, 177, 193-196, **194**, **196**, 198, 201.
Blaze-winged 7, 101, 109, 114, 115, 124, 138-139, **138**, **139**.
Blood-eared 13, 98-99, 101, 109, 158, 218-220, **219**, **220**, 221.
Blue-chested – see Blue-throated
Blue-throated 1, 3, **5**, 12, 15, 17, 18, 29, 61, 64, 69, 72, 73, 78, 84, 101, 109, 114, 115, 121, 124, 235-240, **237**, **238**.
Bonaparte's 7, 12, 95, 101, 109, 125, 168, 179, **179**, 180, 182.
Brown-breasted – see Flame-winged

Chapman's 101, 109, 198-200, **199**.
Chiriqui 221.
Choco – see Pacific
Crimson-bellied 1, 7, 11, 15, 23, 29, 30, 31-33, **32**, 36, 40, **44**, **49**, **51**, 58, 60, **67**, 69, 71, 76, 81, **84**, 85-87, **86**, 93, 97, 99, 101, 109, 114, 115, 116, 124,145-149, **145**, **147**, **149**.

Demerara – see Fiery-shouldered
Deville's –see Bonaparte's

Eisenmann's – see Azuero
El Oro 3, 4, 5, 9, 13, 73, 100, 101, 106, 108, 109, 114, 115, 116-117, 120, 198, 225-228, **226**, **228**.
Emma's 29, 72, 101, 109, 158-160, **159**, 224.

Fiery-shouldered 13, 72, 79, 93, 101, 104, 109, 125, 214-217, **215**, **217**.
Flame-winged 7, 13, 46, 67-69, 96, 101, 103, 109, 114, 115, 119, 120, 210-213,
 211, **213**.

Garlepp's 180.
Goias – see Pfrimer's
Green-cheeked vii, 9, 11, 12, 14, 15, 28, 31, 33, 41, 52, 59, 60, 61, 62, 69, 72, 73,
 77, 79, 82, 88-90, **89**, **90**, 92, 95, 98, 100, 101, 108, 109, 112, 113, 123, 124,
 126-129, **128**, **133**.
Grey-breasted 7, 9, 73, 89, **97**, 101, 103-104, **107**, 109, 114, **119**, 121, 125, 150,
 159, 161-167, **166**.

Hellmayr's – see Santarem
Hoffmann's 7, 9, 13, 23, **23**, 29, 101, 109, 111-112, 221-224, **223**.

Madeira **96**, 99, 101, 105, 109, 114, 115, 125, 188, 189-191, **189**, **190**, 192.
Magdalena – see Perija
Maroon-bellied 10, 14, 37, 59, 67, 71, 72, 77, 91, 93, 95, **96**, 98, 101, 105, 109,
 112, 125, 133-137, **133**, **136**, 138, 178.
Maroon-faced – see Pfrimer's
Maroon-tailed – see Black-tailed

Ochre-marked see Blue-throated

Pacific 101, 109, 118, 198, 201-203, **202**, **203**.
Painted vii, 12, 13, 14, 91, 95, 97, **98**, 101, 105, 109, 116, 123, 125, 168, 169,
 170,176-178, **177**, 179.
Pantchenko's – see Perija
Pearly 10-11, **11**, 12, 101, 109, 110, 114, 115, 116, 122, 125, 140-143, **142**, **143**, 145,
 202.
Perija 95, 96, 101, 109, 110, 114, 118, 168, 170-172, **171**.
Pfrimer's 15, 52, 73, 96-97, 98, 99, 101, 103, 109, 114, 121, 125, 154-157, **155**,
 159, 161, 169.
Prince Lucien's – see Deville's

Red-eared – see Blood-eared
Red-bellied, Reddish-bellied – see Maroon-bellied
Rock – see Black-capped
Rose-crowned 3, 7, 8, 13, 29, 47, 56, 59, 63, **67**, 69, 75-76, 79, 92, 101, 109,
 229-231, **231**.

Index of scientific names

Pyrrhura species and sub-species

Bold type indicates an illustration.

ALSO BY ROSEMARY LOW

Available from the author rosemaryhlow@gmail.com
For further information visit www.rosemarylow.co.uk

Go West for Parrots!
An inspiring travel book for lovers of parrots and nature.
320 pages, 100 mono illustrations.
ISBN 978-0-9531337-6-5

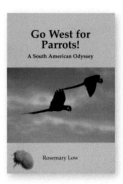

This book will appeal to a wide audience, not only aviculturists and twitchers, but to those who enjoy tales of exploration and wish to know a little of the environment of the countries visited. Rosemary vividly sets the scene, recalling all sensory experiences so that the reader can imagine themselves with her. Her sheer enthusiasm for the jungle forests, flora and fauna is infectious and makes you want to read on further. She writes: "The lure of parrots in the wild draws me back to the tropics over and over again. It provides me with a satisfaction that is unlike any other and strengthens my desire to aid their conservation."

— **DAVID WOOLCOCK**, Curator Paradise Park, Cornwall.

Female Heroes of Bird Conservation
The stories of amazing women, past and present, who have dedicated their lives to conserving birds.
254 pages, 100 illustrations – most in colour.
ISBN 978-1-7399130-0-7

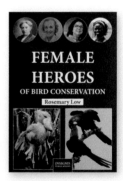

This remarkable volume is well-written and easily read, illuminating and educational, and should be on every bird-lover's bookshelf. It gives a great insight into the lives and input of some of the major female characters involved in the conservation of birds since the middle of the 19th century until the present day. The author's passion and enthusiasm for her subjects shines through, but she also manages to display the passion and tenacity of these remarkable women.

— **ALAN K JONES**, BVetMed, MRCVS, January 2022.

The author profiles 30 women whose stories will amaze you!